TALL buildings + URBAN habitat

Volume I

Editors:
Steven Henry & Antony Wood

Bibliographic Reference:
Henry, S. & Wood, A. (2018) *Tall Buildings + Urban Habitat, Volume I.* Chicago: Council on Tall Buildings and Urban Habitat.

Editors: Steven Henry & Antony Wood
Writers: Jason Gabel & Daniel Safarik
Design: Annan Shehadi
Layout: Liwen Kang

© 2018 Council on Tall Buildings and Urban Habitat

Printed in the USA

The right of the Council on Tall Buildings and Urban Habitat to be identified as author of this work has been asserted by them in accordance with sections 77 and 78 of the Copyright, Designs and Patents Act 1988.

All rights reserved. No part of this book may be reprinted or reproduced or utilized in any form or by any electronic, mechanical, or other means, now known or hereafter invented, including photocopying and recording, or in any information storage or retrieval system, without permission in writing from the publishers.

Trademark notice: Product or corporate names may be trademarks or registered trademarks, and are used only for identification and explanation without intent to infringe.

Library of Congress Cataloging-in-Publication Data
A catalog record has been requested for this book

ISBN: 978-0-939493-62-3

CTBUH Headquarters
The Monroe Building
104 South Michigan Avenue, Suite 620
Chicago, IL 60603, USA
Phone: +1 312 283 5599
Email: info@ctbuh.org
www.ctbuh.org
www.skyscrapercenter.com

CTBUH Asia Headquarters
College of Architecture and Urban Planning (CAUP)
Tongji University
1239 Si Ping Road, Yangpu District
Shanghai 200092, China
Phone: +86 21 65982972
Email: china@ctbuh.org

CTBUH Research Office
Iuav University of Venice
Dorsoduro 2006
30123 Venice, Italy
Phone: +39 041 257 1276
Email: research@ctbuh.org

Università Iuav
di Venezia

CTBUH Academic Office
S. R. Crown Hall
Illinois Institute of Technology
3360 South State Street
Chicago, IL 60616
Phone: +1 (312) 283-5646
Email: academic@ctbuh.org

The projects profiled in this book are those submitted to the Council on Tall Buildings and Urban Habitat's 2018 Global Awards program (see page 274).

Contents

6 Introduction

AMERICAS
16 35XV, *New York City*
20 150 North Riverside, *Chicago*
24 American Copper Buildings, *New York City*
28 City Hyde Park, *Chicago*
30 Enbridge Center, *Edmonton*
32 Gaia Building, *Quito*
36 Grove at Grand Bay, *Miami*
38 Hotel EMC2, *Chicago*
40 Jersey City Urby, *Jersey City*
42 Madison Square Park Tower, *New York City*
44 Metropolitan, *Quito*
46 Porsche Design Tower, *Sunny Isles Beach*
48 River Point, *Chicago*
50 Shirley Ryan AbilityLab, *Chicago*
52 The Globe and Mail Centre, *Toronto*
54 Three Alliance Center, *Atlanta*
56 Torre KOI, *San Pedro Garza García*
58 University of Chicago Campus North Residential Commons, *Chicago*
60 Wilshire Grand Center, *Los Angeles*
62 30 Park Place, *New York City*
609 Main at Texas, *Houston*
615 South College, *Charlotte*
88 Scott, *Toronto*
AQWA Corporate, *Rio de Janeiro*
64 Biscayne Beach, *Miami*
BRIC Phase 1, *San Diego*
CF Calgary City Centre Phase I, *Calgary*
Cielo, *Seattle*
Equus 333, *San Pedro Garza García*
66 Hotel Las Americas Golden Tower, *Panama City*
INDX Condominiums, *Toronto*
Jade Signature, *Sunny Isles Beach*
L'Avenue, *Montreal*
Level BK, *New York City*
68 Northwestern Mutual Tower and Commons, *Milwaukee*
Optima Signature, *Chicago*
Park Avenue West, *Portland*
Ten Thousand, *Los Angeles*
The Collection, Tower, *Honolulu*
70 The Encore, *New York City*
The Hub, *New York City*

ASIA & AUSTRALASIA
72 1 William Street, *Brisbane*
74 35 Spring Street, *Melbourne*
76 161 Sussex Street, *Sydney*
78 Chaoyang Park Plaza, *Beijing*
82 City Center Tower, *Taguig City*
84 Eq. Tower, *Melbourne*
86 FV, *Brisbane*
88 Guangzhou CTF Finance Centre, *Guangzhou*
90 Hangzhou Gateway, *Hangzhou*
92 Huangshan Mountain Village, *Huangshan*
96 Light House, *Melbourne*
98 Lotte World Tower, *Seoul*
102 Marina One, *Singapore*
106 Namdaemun Office Building, *Seoul*
108 Ping An Finance Center, *Shenzhen*
112 Poly International Plaza, *Beijing*
116 Raffles City Hangzhou, *Hangzhou*
118 Tencent Seafront Towers, *Shenzhen*
122 The Tembusu, *Singapore*
124 Tsinghua Ocean Center, *Shenzhen*
126 Zhengzhou Greenland Central Plaza, *Zhengzhou*
128 1 Parramatta Square, *Parramatta*
177 Pacific Highway, *Sydney*
Aquaria Grande Tower, *Mumbai*
Chinachem Central, *Hong Kong*
Golden Eagle International Shopping Center, *Nanjing*
130 Gravity Tower, *Melbourne*
Green Residences, *Hangzhou*
IM tower, *Tokyo*
Kyobashi EDOGRAND, *Tokyo*
Nakanoshima Festival Tower West, *Osaka*
132 Ningbo Bank of China, *Ningbo*
One Avighna Park, *Mumbai*
Parnas Tower, *Seoul*
Rosewood Sanya and Sanya Forum, *Sanya*
Shenyang K11, *Shenyang*
134 Talan Towers, *Astana*
Telkom Landmark Tower 2, *Jakarta*
The Summit - Plot 554, *Suzhou*
The Suzhou Modern Media Plaza, *Suzhou*
136 Upper West Side, *Melbourne*
Urbana Tower 2, *Kolkata*
Zhongzhou E-CIASS, *Shenzhen*

EUROPE
- 138 A'DAM Toren, *Amsterdam*
- 140 Angel Court, *London*
- 144 Axis, *Frankfurt*
- 146 Canaletto, *London*
- 150 Dollar Bay, *London*
- 152 New'R, *Nantes*
- 154 The Silo, *Copenhagen*
- 158 Tribunal de Paris, *Paris*
- 162 Upper West, *Berlin*
- 164 White Collar Factory, *London*
- 166 Arena Tower, *London*
     De Verkenner, *Utrecht*
     Federation Tower, *Moscow*
     Millennium Center 1, *Sofia*
     Q22 Tower, *Warsaw*

MIDDLE EAST & AFRICA
- 170 Azrieli Sarona, *Tel Aviv*
- 174 Beirut Terraces, *Beirut*
- 178 Rothschild Tower, *Tel Aviv*
- 182 Zeitz MOCAA, *Cape Town*
- 186 Britam Tower, *Nairobi*
     Iran Telecom Research Center, *Tehran*
     Landmark Group Headquarters, *Dubai*
     The 118, *Dubai*
     The Shahar Tower, *Givatayim*

URBAN HABITAT
- 190 Barangaroo South/International Towers, *Sydney*
- 194 City Tower Musashikosugi, *Kawasaki*
- 196 Dua Menjalara, *Kuala Lumpur*
- 198 Greatwall Complex, *Wuhan*
- 202 National September 11 Memorial, *New York City*
- 206 Oasia Hotel Downtown, *Singapore*
- 210 SKYPARK, *Hong Kong*
- 214 SOHO Fuxing Plaza, *Shanghai*
- 218 The Pavilia Hill, *Hong Kong*
- 220 Univ360 Place, *Seri Kembangan*
- 222 Wolf Point West, *Chicago*

CONSTRUCTION
- 226 56 Leonard, *New York City*
- 228 111 Main, *Salt Lake City*
- 230 461 Dean Street, *New York City*
- 232 The EY Centre, *Sydney*
- 234 Warsaw Spire, *Warsaw*

A LOOK FORWARD

INNOVATION
- 238 3D-Printed Building
- 240 CAST CONNEX High Integrity Blocks
- 242 Hickory Building Systems
- 244 High-Resolution CFD for Wind Loading Tall Buildings
- 246 Hummingbird Tuned Liquid Column Gas Damper
- 248 Lean Core + Prefab Blade Wall System
- 250 MULTI
- 252 Timber Construction at Tallwood House

A LOOK BACK

TEN YEARS ON
- 256 Bahrain World Trade Center, *Manama*
     Manitoba Hydro Place, *Winnipeg*
     San Francisco Federal Building, *San Francisco*
- 258 Comcast Center, *Philadelphia*
- 259 Hong Kong Polytechnic University Community College, *Hong Kong*
     Mode Gakuen Cocoon Tower, *Tokyo*
- 261 The Red Apple, *Rotterdam*
     Boutique Monaco, *Seoul*
- 262 Poly Real Estate Headquarters Towers, *Guangzhou*
     Tornado Tower, *Doha*
     Torre Cepsa, *Madrid*
- 264 New York Times Tower, *New York City*
     Hegau Tower, *Singen*
- 266 Lumiere Residences, *Sydney*
- 267 Newton Suites, *Singapore*
- 268 Shanghai World Financial Center, *Shanghai*

LIFETIME ACHIEVEMENT
- 270 Larry Silverstein
- 272 Aine Brazil

- 274 About the CTBUH & its Tall Building Awards Program
- 276 Index of Buildings
- 277 Index of Companies
- 281 Image Credits
- 283 CTBUH Organizational Structure & Members

Introduction

A survey of the best in the design and implementation of tall buildings and urban habitat in the past year, the projects represented in this book span the entire globe and acknowledge the wide scope of disciplines involved in bringing skyscrapers from concept to reality. They address the approaches and built examples that can help guide us through the challenges we face, not only in the sense of the built environment, but where climate change and urbanization collide; humanity itself. The expertise and inventiveness demonstrated by these projects provide inspiration and show the great potential offered by "city shapers" to solve the problems of today and tomorrow. If these projects and solutions are any indication, we can anticipate cities that are both more exciting and more humane in the future, as a number of trends, some summarized below, become evident across these pages.

Nature and Height Intertwine
For more than a century, the assumed trade-off between urban living and nature was a binary one — one could either live in the city or live in nature. But innovative tall buildings, particularly in Asia, where the greatest wave of urbanization in history is taking place, have proven this not to be true.

In Singapore, decades of urban policy driving the theme of "city in a garden," combined with a proliferous tropical climate, have delivered one of the greenest and densest cities in the world. There, greenery has become an essential part of the architecture and marketing of tall buildings.

At Marina One (see page 102), a complex occupying a square block in the city center, comprises three high-rise buildings, which accommodate office, residential and retail functions. Most strikingly, they contain an abundance of communal green space, with the multitude of functional spaces strategically paired to promote connectivity and community within the green areas. The usable area of the green space represents 125 percent of the original site surface area.

The Oasia Hotel Downtown (see page 206) literally wears its green heart on its sleeve, with a green plot ratio of 1,000% — that is, the amount of greenery on the site is now 10 times what it was before the building was constructed.

The perforated metal façade, painted bright red, is festooned with creeper vines, revealing itself in a dynamic dance with the changing growth, attracting animals and insects. Offices, hotel and club rooms are located on different strata, each with its own sky garden. These additional "ground" levels allow generous public areas for recreation and social interaction throughout the high-rise. They are open-sided for formal and visual transparency, allowing breezes to pass through the building, making them functional, comfortable tropical spaces with greenery, natural light and fresh air.

In Hong Kong, a combination of mountainous topography and similarly forward-thinking planning has meant that much of the surface area of the densely populated city is in fact vegetated. However, there are precious few green spaces within the built-up areas. SKYPARK (see page 210), a mixed-use development located at Mongkok, one of the densest urban districts in the city, uses several strategies to alleviate this condition. At the ground level, a plaza, internal street, plantings, grand staircase, outdoor furniture, openable windows and skylights create an outdoor atmosphere throughout the shopping mall, called "the Forest." Most notably, on its roof, vegetation and public gathering space cover every available square meter, providing an escape from the urban hardscape with its openness, spectacular city views, greenery, fresh air and sunlight.

In mainland China, one featured project's condition is entirely the opposite. At Huangshan, a UNESCO World Heritage Site, known for its dramatically sculpted mountain peaks and traditional architecture embedded within, the challenge was not to disturb the essence of the Taiping Lake site. With this in mind, the design team organized the buildings of this residential project in a linked configuration across the southern slope of the lake, so that they form a dynamic relationship with the site and each other. The residential units within Huangshan Mountain Village (see page 92) are efficiently stacked, but also provide private views and appear to "grow" organically out of the sloping terrain.

Another variation on the theme occurs at Chaoyang Park Plaza in Beijing (see page 78), where a natural landscape is translated to the city, with greenery, ponds and paths

Nature and Height Intertwine: Marina One, Singapore (top), encloses a lushly planted green space within its central courtyard, flanked by undulating, planted walls. Oasia Hotel Downtown, also in Singapore (left) features an intensely vegetated external screen and large voids along its height to provide new areas for public recreation and contact with nature. SKYPARK in Hong Kong (right) offers vegetation and public gathering space across all available space on its rooftop.

threading among towers, which have been abstractly smoothed into shapes resembling historic paintings and garden representations of mountains. This has the effect of thematically connecting the development to the city's largest park, as well as drawing park strollers across the street into its serene enclosure.

Reuse, Recycle, Inspire

In cities all around the world, the skyscrapers of the Postwar "Jet Age" period, built for a workplace typology that today is disappearing, are beginning to show their age, and many face demolition. But some owners have sought innovative ways to avoid this wasteful, environmentally damaging outcome. The team behind A'DAM Toren (see page 138) saw potential in the former Shell office building across the River IJ from central Amsterdam. The project now consists of an observation deck with a thrill-ride swing, multiple bars and restaurants (including a revolving restaurant), several meeting rooms, a boutique hotel, an underground dance club and public parking. The "Amsterdam Dance and Music Tower" is now, appropriately enough, the home of several leading companies in the music industry.

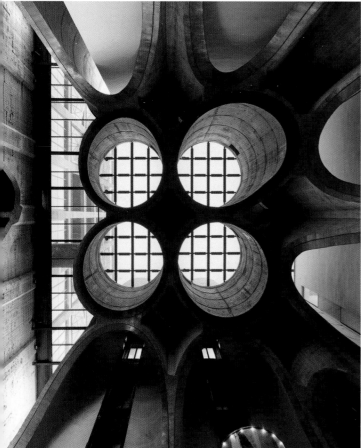

It has now become common for old industrial buildings to become repurposed for commercial or residential use, but these are usually low-slung, if massive, structures. But in Denmark and South Africa, two tall grain silos have found new life in different ways, and in the process become striking new features in their context. Copenhagen's The Silo (see page 154), was transformed into a residential building that has apartments with floor heights up to seven meters. The interior has been preserved as raw and as untouched as possible, while a façade made of galvanized steel has been installed on the exterior of the former concrete silo to serve as a climate shield. The Zeitz MOCAA (see page 182) in Cape Town is an incredibly creative reinvention of a grain elevator and storage complex into a luxury hotel and Africa's first international art museum dedicated to contemporary art from the continent. The two major parts of the complex are connected by a central atrium carved from the silo's cellular structure. Main circulation routes are housed within the atrium, via cylindrical lifts that run inside two bisected concrete tubes.

Forming Connected Communities

It's undeniable that much of the motivation for, and praise of, skyscrapers comes from the impression they make on the skyline. But in recent years, as more people urbanize and spend time in city centers for reasons beyond work, the importance of connectivity — both internally and between the building and the ground plane — and comprehensiveness — in terms of functional and urbanistic offerings — has increased.

In Chicago, for example, 150 North Riverside (see page 20) takes advantage of its constrained available footprint by returning much of the site to public use. The passage of the public walkway along the Chicago River on one side is complemented by a new public park and see-through, glassed-in lobby on the other. That same public walkway passes beneath and around Wolf Point West (see page 222), another slim, tall building, whose design and development team saw value in returning as much of the building site as possible to the public realm.

In Sydney, the central business district's interface with Darling Harbour had been limited, partially blocked by an elevated highway and a disused industrial port. The incentive to develop tall buildings along this waterfront is strong, but a forward-looking project resisted the temptation to "wall off" the city from this amenity. At Barangaroo, a massive redevelopment of a former shipyard, the International Towers (see page 190) were angled and sited to preserve the street grid, connect to the water, and provide new pedestrian-first areas for dining and strolling.

Connectivity is also the emphasis at Tencent Seafront Towers in Shenzhen (see page 118). Here, however, the connections are internal, in the form of skybridge "links" between the development's two towers. The objective is to provide community amenities for the 11,000-strong workforce,

Reuse, Recycle, Inspire: Copenhagen's The Silo (opposite top), shown here during renovation, was transformed into a residential building that has apartments with floor heights up to 7 meters. Similarly, the Zeitz MOCAA in Cape Town (opposite bottom), made its former use as a grain silo a central design aspect of its regeneration into a hotel and museum.

Forming Connected Communities: 150 North Riverside, Chicago (above), uses its thin profile to "step aside" and open up new public space on its site along the Chicago River.

facilitating chance encounters and generating new ideas for the high-flying tech company that commissioned this audacious project.

Likewise, the American Copper Buildings in New York (see page 24) emphasize connection at height, in this case between two towers that seem to lean into each other. In addition to providing amazing views outward and from each tower to the other, the skybridge connecting the towers contains common amenities that are meant to encourage residents to interact.

Connectivity and community alike are forged in another sense at the Shirley Ryan AbilityLab in Chicago (see page 50). Here, the central mission of physical rehabilitation is augmented by placing therapy spaces in multi-story, outside-

facing rooms, painted in bright colors and filled with light. This facilitates the healing process by connecting inhabitants closely with urban life outside — and similarly, dissolving the narrative that healing must take place somewhere isolated or insular. The place of prominence given to the therapy spaces also means that the internal community is drawn to the places where healing happens, reinforcing the mission among employees and patients.

On an equally humanistic note, the National September 11 Memorial in New York (see page 202) stitches together a gaping wound in the psyche of the city and nation. The site of the towers destroyed in a terrorist attack has been converted into a public square in the heart of the city, surrounded by new towers that rose from a scene of devastation. It connects the community in many senses of the word. It provides new pedestrian access from the riverfront to the Financial District that had once been blocked by the World Trade Center podium, and then its remains; it delivers new and improved public transit facilities below the plaza; and it provides a place where community can be forged through the sharing of collective memory.

Forging New Paths in Tall Building Construction
Several of the tall buildings prove innovative in their construction techniques. At 461 Dean Street (see page 230), part of New York's Pacific Park development, delivering an affordable project was a pre-eminent goal. The use of modularization and prefabrication was critical to the success

of the project. Modules were constructed off-site — and completely outfitted with structural, architectural and MEP components — at the Brooklyn Navy Yard and transported to the site. Though factory production techniques were used, the project still was able to have variation — among its 930 modules, there are 225 unique types.

Though uncrowded in comparison to New York, Salt Lake City's downtown does have some problematic building sites, such as at 111 Main (see page 228), where a Class-A office tower was constructed next to, and partially over, a theater. The design solution, a "hat truss," suspends the southern portion of the office tower over a section of the four-story theater, avoiding perimeter tower columns puncturing its space.

Pushing the Envelope
There are few elements as character-defining for a tall building as its façade. It is a building's first line of defense against the elements and the last word on its relationship with its surroundings. The Poly International Plaza in Beijing (see page 112) is the first tall building to incorporate a four-story diagrid frame without perimeter columns, making for an expressive exterior façade that resembles a Chinese paper lantern. This allows both long spans on the office floors and the installation of a double-skin façade and atria. These semi-climatized interstitial spaces mediate exterior temperature extremes, reducing the overall building energy consumption by 23 percent and carbon emissions by 18 percent.

Canaletto (see page 146), a new residential tower in London, manipulates the horizontal panels of its façade into two- and three-floor groups, bookended by forward and reverse "letter-C"-shaped extrusions, breaking down the scale of the tall tower to units comparable to that of the neighboring buildings while also creating dynamic outdoor spaces for the individual units. Also in the high-density City of London, Angel Court (see page 140) is a repurposed 1970s office building that replaced a dated, opaque façade with a light opal-fritted glass, wrapping around the walls of the original, irregular octagonal form. Set in a preservation district, the lower floors were treated differently, with deep-set windows, faced in rough-hewn Carlow Blue limestone, so as to better fit in with the surroundings than the original building ever did.

Forming Connected Communities: The National September 11 Memorial in New York (opposite top) restores a sense of collective belonging to a devastated area of downtown Manhattan.

Forging New Paths in Tall Building Construction: The construction process for 461 Dean Street (opposite bottom), New York City, involved pre-assembling modules at the Brooklyn Navy Yard.

Pushing the Envelope: Poly International Plaza, Beijing (top left), uses its unique diagrid frame to create generous internal spaces that also help reduce energy consumption and carbon emissions. Canaletto, London (top right), breaks down its scale by using facade extrusions, which also offer shading and privacy to units.

Not far away, the White Collar Factory (see page 164) is a research-driven return to first principles of natural ventilation, as demonstrated through its glazing, which is interspersed with metal panels punched with "portholes" and banded with anodized aluminum panels. Operable windows are provided throughout the building, allowing 70 percent of the floor plate to be naturally ventilated.

At an entirely different scale and in a different context, the world's fourth and seventh-tallest buildings, both in the Pearl River Delta of China, also make a statement with their façades. The Ping An Finance Center (see page 108) in Shenzhen features the largest stainless-steel façade in the world to date, to preserve its appearance in the salty coastal atmospheric conditions of Shenzhen. Jet mist granite, hand-selected from Virginia for its beauty and durability, complements the steel and glass portions of the façade. Upriver at the Guangzhou CTF Finance Centre (see page 88), terracotta panels mask operable vents that allow building users access to fresh air, even at considerable heights where the daily use of operable windows would otherwise be impossible. This smart skin lowers the building's energy use by allowing access to fresh, unconditioned air and limiting the use of glass.

Innovation: A Look Forward…
The enormous financial and time investment in tall building design, construction and operation are accompanied by a robust culture of research and development by architects, engineers, academic research institutes, and construction firms, among others. In the very near future, a steady march of innovations will continue to allow the industry to build not only taller, but faster, safer, more efficiently, and more responsibly. One of the biggest constraints on tall building height has been the need to have multiple shafts and banks of elevators within a system of sky lobbies to reach high floors. The higher the building, the less floor space is available for occupants and rent. A new elevator technology has the potential to fundamentally alter this calculus. MULTI (see page 250), the world's first and only rope-less, sideways-moving elevator, ushers in the end of the 160-year reign of rope-dependent elevators, harnessing the power of linear motor technology to move multiple cars in a single shaft vertically and horizontally. MULTI requires fewer and smaller shafts than conventional elevators and can increase a building's usable area by up to 25 percent, adding rentable/leasable space. Instead of one cabin per shaft moving up and down, MULTI offers multiple cabins operating in a loop, much like a metro system inside a building. Though not yet implemented in a built project, MULTI has been thoroughly tested and possibilities for future implementations abound.

Progress has recently been seen in the testing and implementation of new materials. The world's first fully functional and permanently occupied 3D-printed building (see page 238) has been completed in Dubai, UAE. The structure of the building was manufactured using an additive concrete "printing" technique using a 3D printer 6 meters high, 36.5 meters long and 12 meters wide. Electronic monitoring of the building provides continuous feedback on its structural performance and can offer designers of future 3D-printed high-rise buildings valuable information to inform their own designs.

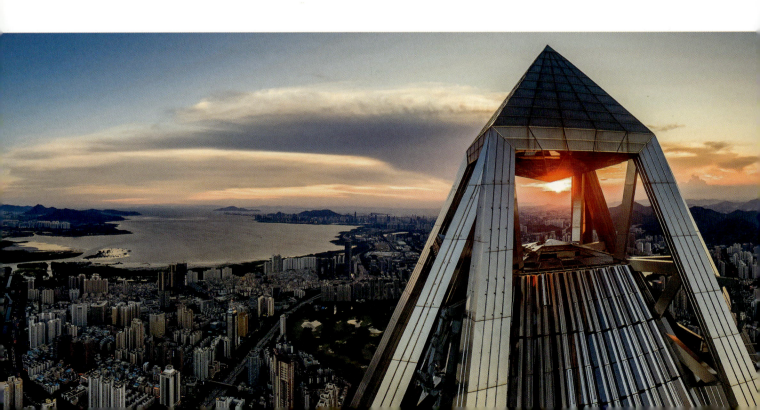

Although it is by no means a "new" building material, the use of wood in general, and engineered timber in particular, is new in the world of high-rises. A great example of this is the timber structural system used at Tallwood House at Brock Commons (see page 252), an 18-story, 400-bed student residence on the campus of the University of British Columbia, Vancouver, Canada. By utilizing the two-way spanning capabilities of CLT, both cost and the fabrication and erection times were dramatically reduced. This floor system also significantly reduced the structural depth and created a clean, flat surface for unobstructed service distribution.

A Look Back...

To chart a course and realize the promises of the future, we must also remember to reflect on the past — so that we might learn from the challenges already solved, and to see where the paths already walked are now leading us today. By looking back at projects completed 10 years ago (see pages 256–269), we can develop an informed understanding of true "innovation." Buildings that have recently entered their decennial year provide a convenient time frame for such reflections — mature enough for their lasting influence to be apparent, but contemporary enough for their solutions to remain relevant today.

Some of the most memorable skyscrapers reflect the growing consciousness about sustainability at the time, resulting in pioneering attempts to open up skyscrapers to natural ventilation and vegetation. Experimentation with programs beyond the traditional office/hotel/residential functions is evident through the example of several high-rise schools and the integration of significant retail, cultural, and public spaces. This was prominently reflected in the overall morphology of these projects, as well as the detailing of their envelopes and street interfaces. Structural expression and daring forms were also on the rise, as well as a deeper consideration of the treatment of the facade and implementation of solar shading. Many of the themes seen emerging a decade ago — most exciting when they converged in a single project — are now reflected in the forefront of tall building design.

There is also immense value in recognizing the people who have made large impacts on our urban environments, that we might glean and replicate the personal approaches leading to their success. The persistence, tenacity, and commitment to pass on knowledge to the next generation has defined the industry as much as the built legacy of their work. We therefore recognize both the projects and people that have been foundational to the course of the tall building industry up to the present day.

Next

As you explore these pages in more detail, bear in mind that innovation is and must always be the watchword of tall building development. What follows is representative of tall and urban innovation in all its forms. We hope that it will inspire you to seek out and drive innovation in your own communities, so that the highest aspirations in tall and urban continue to be met for future generations.

Pushing the Envelope: The Ping An Finance Center (opposite), Shenzhen, features the largest stainless-steel façade in the world, shown here at its termination at the tower's crown.

Innovation: A Look Forward...: A diagram depicts how the MULTI ropeless, multi-directional elevator system (top left) could be deployed in a group of tall buildings. The Office of the Future, Dubai (top right), the world's first fully functional and permanently occupied 3D-printed building, shows a potential path to the future of tall.

AMERICAS

With North America as the birthplace of the modern skyscraper and many areas already densely developed, space is at a premium and the default model of an extruded box at the maximum lot line still prevails. But a handful of recent projects are challenging this norm — buildings that dance, tilt, "kiss," overhang, skew, and step lightly on their sites have made way for generous public space and enticing silhouettes on the skyline. Likewise, renewed interest in urban living has meant that the distinctive charm of older cities is considered worth preserving, so values like neighborliness and historic preservation are also finding their ways into increasingly intriguing tall building solutions.

35XV

New York City, United States

35XV is a unique, hybrid residential-academic building located in New York's vibrant Chelsea neighborhood in Manhattan. Rising above a mid-block site, the tower utilizes excess development rights from the historic Xavier High School to resolve two important local imperatives: a demand for increased housing in the area, and a need for the high school to expand its tight, urban campus. The building's six-story base incorporates classrooms, a STEM lab, rehearsal space and a commons for Xavier. The top 18 floors house a mix of one-, two-, three-, and four-bedroom residential units, while a seventh-floor amenity space includes a gym, lounge, children's play room, shared wine cellar, and communal terrace.

Offering space to Xavier grew from an awareness of the school's predicament: the institution was losing potential students to suburban schools with more expansive facilities, but was not in a position to expand its own facilities upwards. Thus, a deal was made with the project team that allowed Xavier to expand outwards, on its site, while maintaining its historic campus with no interruptions to school-year operations. This inventive financial structure underwrote the cost of the school's expansion to allow additional classrooms and multi-purpose spaces, vastly improving the student experience.

The building design establishes distinct identities across two conditions, one addressing the street realm and one addressing the vertical realm. Anchoring the building, a stone-clad monolithic base responds to, and continues the scale of the block's street wall, which is institutional in character. Careful modulation of fenestration — the arrangement of windows and doorways on the elevations of the building — and a "chiseled" design vocabulary accommodate the school's day-to-day functions, while creating a well-defined visual expression for the residential function. The public sidewalk is amplified at the building entrance, which is carved back from the street wall. Poised above, the tower's sloped, crystalline form and staggered "fish-scale" glass cladding reflect the sky, appearing to de-materialize the building. Along its height, the tower leans away from its base, adhering perfectly

Completion Date: September 2016
Height: 102 m (334 ft)
Stories: 25
Area: 11,463 sq m (123,387 sq ft)
Primary Functions: Residential / Education
Owner: 35XV Condominiums
Developers: Alchemy Properties; Angelo, Gordon & Co.; Xavier High School
Architect: FXCollaborative (formerly FXFOWLE) (design)
Structural Engineer: Severud Associates Consulting Engineers (design)
MEP Engineer: Dagher Engineeringm, PLLC (design)
Main Contractor: NOHO Construction LLC
Other CTBUH Member Consultants: Cerami & Associates (acoustics); Gilsanz Murray Steficek (façade); Langan Engineering (civil); Van Deusen & Associates (vertical transportation)
Other CTBUH Member Supplier: thyssenkrupp (elevator)

to local setback requirements, while offering residents desirable views of the surrounding cityscape and dramatic, bright and airy interior living spaces. From a distance, its light and floating form can be fully appreciated. The tower's distinctive silhouette makes it easily recognizable from afar, while the articulation of glass and metal on its façade responds to different atmospheric conditions, emphasizing its presence in the skyline.

Given the project's zoning requirements and formal restrictions, 35XV utilizes a hybrid structural system with a steel frame at the base housing the school's extension. This allows the tower to cantilever 5 meters over the existing school and, with struts, 11 meters over the rear yard. As a result, 40 percent of the tower's residential footprint does not sit on its base. The tower itself is constructed with flat-plate concrete, allowing for maximum floor-to-ceiling height within the height-restricted envelope.

In an effort to promote a healthy living environment for residents, the project used low-emitting, wet-applied products low in volatile organic compounds (VOCs) and free of added urea-formaldehyde. In addition, 93 percent of all construction waste was diverted from the project and 38 percent of all architectural building materials were extracted or manufactured within 500 miles (805 kilometers) of the project site.

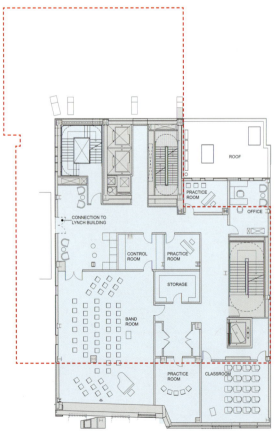

A hybrid structural system with a steel frame and struts at the base allows 40 percent of the tower's residential footprint to cantilever 11 meters beyond the base.

Opposite Left: 18 residential levels (typical floor plan, top) sit above a six floor high school extension (5th floor plan, bottom).

Opposite Right: The tower's sloped, crystalline form is broken up by its staggered "fish-scale" cladding.

Left: The stone-clad monolithic base continues the scale of the existing street wall.

Bottom: The tower massing fits perfectly within zoning limits, creating dynamic interior spaces.

150 North Riverside

Chicago, United States

The 150 North Riverside site is located prominently at the confluence of the three branches of the Chicago River and less than one block away from one of Chicago's busiest commuter train stations. With exposed railroad tracks on the west side of the site and the city requirement for a public right-of-way on the east side, the remaining area on which to build was considered impossibly narrow, and the site sat undeveloped for decades.

Utilizing a unique core-supported structure with a very small footprint at grade, the design resolves the site challenges and provides a Class A office tower with efficient, column-free floor plates. The building's unusual core-supported design results in a 221-meter tower resting atop a base that is merely 12 meters wide. The building's narrow height-to-base ratio of 20:1 is among the world's thinnest. In consideration of this, the building also contains the first-ever application of a 12-tank tuned liquid mass damper (TLMD) at the tower's top to manage both building drift and acceleration. With a total of 605,665 liters of water, the TLMD also provides city-approved fire protection storage tanks to supply the building's sprinkler system, a creative dual purpose that is a Chicago first. The 16 sloping columns at the cantilevers feature the largest rolled-steel shapes ever used in a high-rise building in the US. The shapes are 1,092 millimeters deep and weigh 1,377 kilograms per meter.

This narrow building footprint accomplishes several strategic goals, in addition to facilitating column-free office space. It also creates a dramatic interior space in the lobby, while allowing for more than 75 percent of the property to be unenclosed outdoor space. The tower's limited footprint and the angled sweep of its underside appear to usher the river past the site, breaking down the tower's considerable mass and presenting a balanced composition.

Tenants and visitors enter through a dramatic, 27-meter-high lobby enclosed by a glass-fin wall hung from the structure above. The lobby features the "150 Media Stream," a one-of-a-kind curated multimedia wall that showcases the work of local and other digital artists. The

Completion Date: January 2017
Height: 221 m (724 ft)
Stories: 51
Area: 136,010 sq m (1,463,999 sq ft)
Primary Function: Office
Owner/Developer: Riverside Investment & Development
Architect: Goettsch Partners (design)
Structural Engineer: Magnusson Klemencic Associates (design)
MEP Engineer: Cosentini Associates (design)
Main Contractor: Clark Construction Group
Other CTBUH Member Consultants: CBRE (property management); Permasteelisa Group (façade)
Other CTBUH Member Suppliers: ArcelorMittal (steel); Schindler (elevator)

46-meter-long, site-specific installation provides a lobby focal point while also addressing the transition between the opaque wall over the parking deck and the glass-fin wall above, using 89 LED blades, carefully choreographed in varying lengths and widths.

Building amenity spaces include a restaurant, bar, fitness center and conference center — all with water views. The condensed lobby and elevator cores open the majority of the 8,093-square-meter site as a landscaped public park, plaza and riverfront promenade.

Outside, the park and plaza provide more than 300 linear meters of seating, multiple assembly/event spaces and 110 meters of at-grade Riverwalk frontage, which has already become one of the most populated walkways for downtown commuters. Those who negotiate the grade change of the landscaped plaza on the west side of the tower find themselves in the unique position of being outdoors and at eye level with Chicago's famous elevated train, without being in a station.

The structural acrobatics performance has paid off commercially as well as urbanistically, taking what was once deemed an unbuildable site and creating an optimal mix of leasable floor space, public outdoor space, and semi-public indoor space.

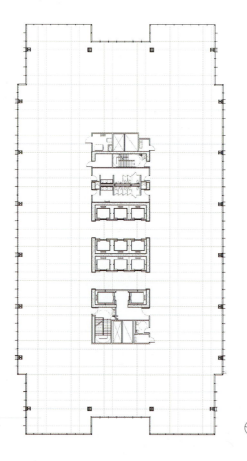

The building's unusual core-supported design results in a 221-meter tower resting atop a base that is merely 12 meters wide.

Above: At its base, the tower narrows to only 12 meters wide to fit between existing train tracks and the river walk.

Left: Typical office floor plan.

Opposite Top: The glass-enclosed lobby features a 46-meter-long multimedia wall.

Opposite Bottom: The narrow base allows for 75 percent of the property to remain open space.

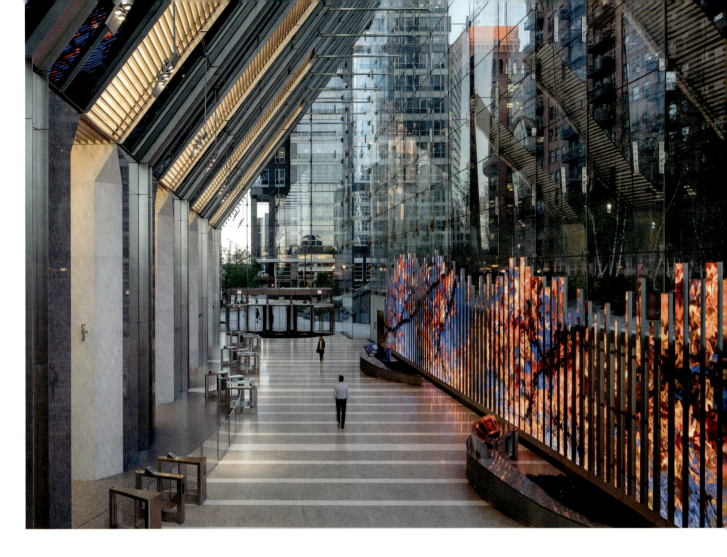

American Copper Buildings

New York City, United States

Comprising two bold and dynamic residential towers, the American Copper Buildings represent a venturesome and highly visible architectural statement along the edge of New York City's East River. Clad in copper on the north and south façades, the color and refractive qualities of the towers will patina gracefully over time, shifting from a russet brown to a signature blue-green throughout the years, much like the iconic Statue of Liberty. Previously the location of a razed power plant, the development brings an inspirational tone to an area that has been historically underutilized, particularly in terms of residential offerings.

The pivoting shape of the American Copper Buildings, with their slightly askew angles — one bending east/west, the other north/south — creates a unique profile on the skyline. The formal approach also allowed for hundreds of unique unit layouts in the building, a departure from the "copy and paste" floor layouts of older residential towers in the city. In total, the building has 761 units — all of which are rental apartments, and 20 percent of which are designated as affordable.

Perhaps the most conspicuous structural element is the three-story skybridge connecting the East and West towers. The skybridge not only serves as an amenity space, complete with a pool spanning the entire length, but also as an important connection for the towers' MEP systems. As a result of this connection, the space normally reserved for mechanical systems at the top of the East Tower was repurposed for a rooftop deck and infinity pool. Additional building amenities include a lounge, a fitness center with a climbing wall, a spa, and a screening room. Set at an angle between the corners of the two towers, the skybridge not only provides views outward, but also towards the towers, creating some intriguing corner spaces and providing residents a unique way to appreciate their special home.

The buildings' exteriors consist of 15 different façade panel "types," due to the leaning and bending of the two towers' dynamic shapes, yet only four different glass sizes were installed on all the standard floors. The punched windows on the copper faces create a moiré pattern that gestures toward the skybridge. Collectively, the façades span approximately 40,900 square meters, with nearly 23,900 square meters of glass and more than 17,000 square meters of copper panels used in the project.

Occupying a site that flooded during Hurricane Sandy in 2012, resiliency strategies were of central importance to the project's design and execution. In advance of legal mandates that require mechanical systems to be installed above the floodplain elevation, the project team committed to creating a set of structures that will not just survive future disasters, but allow residents to live in comfort through them. One strategy employed was to install emergency generators in the top floor of the West Tower — replacing a penthouse — to ensure that each apartment would have enough energy from an emergency generator to power the refrigerator and one outlet in every apartment for a week.

The site is highly advantageous for its transportation options, offering residents immediate proximity to the nearby ferry and its expanded service, the Queens-Midtown Tunnel, bike-share facilities, bus services, train stations, and even a local helicopter service, in addition to private valet parking.

Completion Date: 2017
Height: West Tower: 165 m (540 ft); East Tower: 143 m (470 ft)
Stories: West Tower: 47; East Tower: 40
Primary Function: Residential
Owner/Developer: JDS Development Group
Architects: SHoP Architects (design)
Structural Engineer: WSP (design)
MEP Engineer: Buro Happold (design)
Main Contractor: JDS Construction Group
Other CTBUH Member Consultants: Cerami & Associates (acoustics); West Tower: Buro Happold (façade, lighting)

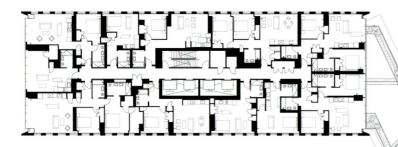

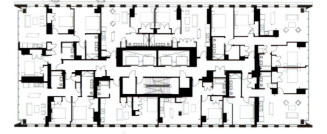

The pivoting shape of the two towers allowed for hundreds of unique unit layouts, a departure from the "copy and paste" floor plans of older residential towers in the city.

Opposite Top: The two slender towers look out to the river with narrow all-glass façades.

Opposite Bottom: Typical residential floor plan with skybridge in elevation below.

Right: The two-story skybridge houses a swimming pool spanning its entire length on its lower level.

Below: The glass-clad skybridge connects the two copper-clad towers, which will patina to a blue-green color with time.

City Hyde Park

Chicago, United States

Completion Date: January 2016
Height: 52 m (172 ft)
Stories: 14
Area: 18,541 sq m (199,574 sq ft)
Primary Functions: Residential / Retail
Owner: Silliman Group
Developer: Antheus Capital, LLC
Architect: Studio Gang (design, architect of record)
Structural Engineer: Magnusson Klemencic Associates (engineer of record)
MEP Engineer: WMA Consulting Engineers (design)
Main Contractor: James McHugh Construction Co.

Located at a busy commercial intersection and adjacent to a commuter rail station, City Hyde Park, one of the neighborhood's first new residential high-rise developments in decades, aims to positively impact the evolution of Chicago's South Side.

The building responds to its distinctly different north and south environs, with both sides of the tower utilizing structure for architectural identity. On the north, where solar infiltration is less of an issue, a faceted façade of bay windows overlooks the city skyline. On the south, where more solar protection is required, the geometric façade is defined by a playful array of stacked and alternating concrete panels that form columns, bays, sunshades, and balconies. This provides both privacy and social space that connects residents to the surrounding neighborhood and the city. The balconies offer oblique views to neighbors above, below, and on each side, creating a vertical community that encourages social connectivity.

The balconies are supported by an innovative structural system that functions like an exoskeleton, with balcony "stems" acting as columns that carry the entire gravity load directly to the ground. This innovation allows the balconies to be thermally separated from the building mass — the first in Chicago to employ this method. Embedded slab sensors are included to measure heat loss and effectiveness toward interior comfort. Complementing the effectiveness of the balcony strategy, a green roof provides storm water retention on-site, reduces heat island effects, and increases thermal insulation.

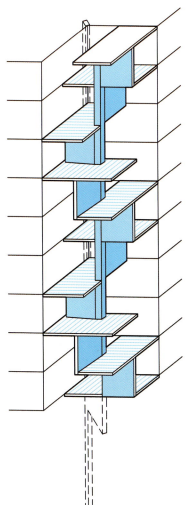

Opposite: The north façade features bay windows to capture the northern city views.

Top: The south façade comprises serrated balconies to provide solar shading.

Bottom left: An array of stacked and alternating concrete panels form columns, bays, sunshades, and balconies, acting as "stems" that carry the entire gravity load to the ground.

Bottom right: Balconies project in dynamic angles outward from the residential units.

Enbridge Centre
Edmonton, Canada

Completion Date: July 2016
Height: 111 m (363 ft)
Stories: 26
Area: 51,190 sq m (551,005 sq ft)
Primary Function: Office
Owners/Developers: John Day Developments; Pangman Development Corporation
Architect: DIALOG (design)
Structural Engineer: DIALOG (design)
MEP Engineer: MCW Consultants Ltd. (design)
Main Contractor: Ledcor Construction Limited

Enbridge Centre evokes a dramatic statement from the ground up. Offering an eclectic mix of old and new, the tower provides the latest in modern conveniences while retaining the historic charm of the old Kelly and Ramsey buildings that originally stood on its site. The new building was designed to retain the historic charm and integrity of the original buildings, which were heavily damaged by fire and rendered inhabitable. The intent was to unite the existing hand-crafted, historic façades of these buildings with an ultra-modern glass tower and provide an urban motif that contributes to the sustainable goals of the city. Incorporating the historic facades pays homage to the past influence of the site, while the new state-of-the-art features address current and future demands of its tenants.

The façades from these two buildings were carefully dismantled, stored off site, and then re-applied to the new four-story base podium. As the tower rises, it transitions from its original heritage façades to a sleek contemporary curtain wall, topped with a mechanical penthouse accentuated by translucent glass and LED lighting. Building Information Modeling (BIM) technology was utilized throughout the entire project, and was of particular use in recreating intricate limestone elements from the original façades that had been damaged beyond repair. Using BIM, the masonry contractor was able to "model" each damaged limestone piece and then input the model into a specialized Computer Numerical Control (CNC) saw, which then cut exact replicas of the model resulting in a seamless blend of old and new.

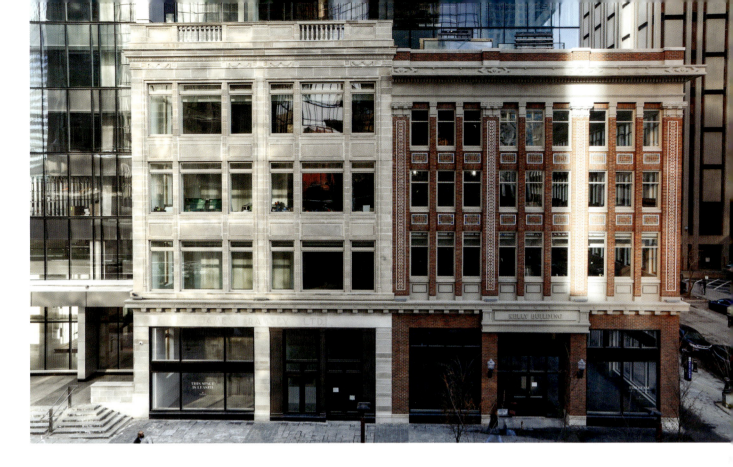

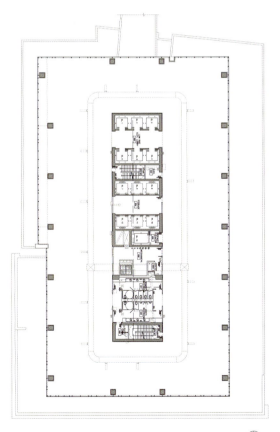

Opposite: The modern tower rises from a base of carefully reconstructed facades of heritage commercial buildings.

Top: Limestone and brick elements from the original façades that had been damaged beyond repair were reconstructed using Building Information Modeling (BIM) technology.

Bottom Left: The standard open-plan floors of the modern office tower are fully ensconced within the legacy buildings' footprint.

Bottom Right: A view through the lobby of the building reveals the provisions made for admitting light into the space.

Gaia Building

Quito, Ecuador

Located in the Ecuadorian capital of Quito, the Gaia Building is sited at an important intersection in the city. Its immediate surroundings include a future station on Quito's first metro line, a newly proposed government building, a shopping center, and Parque la Carolina, which contains the city's botanic gardens and Dinosaur Museum. The name "Gaia" is a reference to the Greek mythological deity that was believed to have created the world.

In this bustling location, the Gaia Building merges commercial opportunities on the ground floor with offices on the next four levels, and residential units the rest of the way to the top. A large roof garden visually connects occupants to the distant Andes Mountains.

Inspired by the area's dynamism, the main concept of the design was to impart a sense of movement through manipulation of the façade, from which portions are strategically "excavated," such that the building has no exterior right-angled corners. Instead, corners are cut away from the smooth, deep perimeter balconies, to emphasize those orientations that face highly trafficked intersections or are in need of greater solar shading. As a result, double- and triple-height gaps in the banded rhythm of the façade are generated, taking the shape of arches and rounded cowls.

Exterior areas take advantage of the equatorial climate. The deep balconies allow for the extensive use of glass in the façade, without sacrificing passive climatic design. On the roof deck, a green lawn dotted with bench-encircled trees facilitates recreation, while a light-dappled trellis and perimeter canopy provide relief from the sun, creating a prospect from which to comfortably scan the Quito skyline.

On the interior, the design varies with use. In one office space, light-colored wood paneling and exposed decking, beams and services on the ceilings, give the space a bright and airy feel. In some spaces, the angled and curved solid pieces cross in front of the vision glass, sometimes at oblique angles in more than one dimension, creating interesting shadow patterns and interstitial spaces between inner and outer façade. In the lobby, visitors and residents are greeted with a sculpted wooden wall, with extrusions pulled into the room spelling out "Gaia," and a delicate, cable-hung staircase, offering a quiet moment as one transitions from street to accommodation.

The concrete-frame building is easily recognized due to the undulating white bands around its perimeter, rendered in glass-fiber-reinforced concrete (GFRC) panels up to 4 meters wide by 2 meters tall. After a series of material mock-ups, GFRC panels were chosen, primarily to reduce weight on the overall structure. The close relationship between analog mold-making and parametric digital modeling proved key to the façade's efficiency. The use of a repeating pattern system allowed for reduced fabrication costs and production time, due in particular to the reduced number of required molds, as compared to traditional cast concrete methods.

A system of adjustable metallic connections allows the complex forms to align easily. In all, 31 unique panel types were designed to create the façade, which consists of 364 total panel units. At the time of construction, this was the first time GFRC panels had been used in Ecuador, representing a giant step in the advancement of construction possibilities for a country where concrete blocks and stucco are the norm.

Completion Date: October 2016
Height: 59 m (194 ft)
Stories: 15
Area: 15,000 sq m (161,459 sq ft)
Primary Function: Residential / Office
Owner/Developer: Uribe & Schwarzkopf
Architects: Uribe & Schwarzkopf (design); Leppanen + Anker Arquitectos (design)
Structural Engineer: Ingeniero Patricio Ramos (design)
MEP Engineer: Constructura Naranjo Vela SA (design)
Main Contractor: Uribe & Schwarzkopf

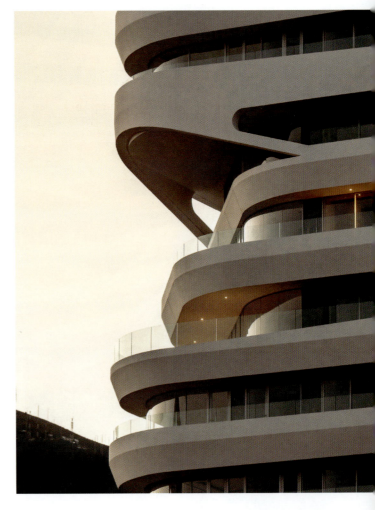

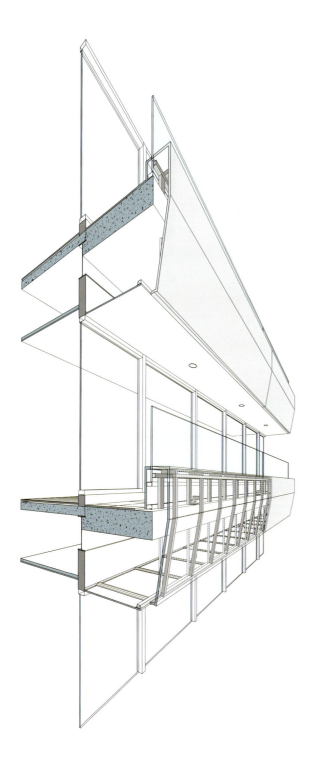

The main concept of the design was to impart a sense of movement through manipulation of the façade, from which portions are strategically "excavated."

Opposite Top: In addition to providing outdoor space, the deep inset balconies represent a passive climatic solution that minimizes solar heat gain.

Opposite Bottom Left: At some points, the façade panels peel away from the windows, resulting in large sculptural overhangs.

Opposite Bottom Right: An exterior view of the overhang condition shows how this distortion fits into the overall rhythm of the envelope.

Above: A perspective section drawing shows the configuration of the exterior glass-fiber-reinforced concrete (GFRC) panels.

Right: From below, the angled façade elements take on an almost aeronautical character.

Grove at Grand Bay

Miami, United States

Completion Date: September 2016
Height: 94 m (308 ft)
Stories: 21
Primary Function: Residential
Owner/Developer: Terra Group
Architects: Bjarke Ingels Group (design); Nichols, Brosch, Wurst, Wolfe & Associates (architect of record)
Structural Engineer: DeSimone Consulting Engineers (design)
MEP Engineer: HNGS Engineers (design)
Other CTBUH Member Consultants: Langan Engineering (geotechnical); Lerch Bates (vertical transportation)

Grove at Grand Bay is a residential project located in Miami's Coconut Grove district. The project features two towers rising above a lushly landscaped, two-story podium, containing 98 spacious custom homes featuring 3.6-meter-high ceilings and 4.3-meter-deep balconies. The site, on Biscayne Bay, is on an oddly-shaped lot. Typical rectilinear towers set side-by-side would have blocked views from many units. As the buildings rise above neighbors, the optimum views change to favor a panorama that incorporates the nearby marina and the Miami skyline to the north.

To capture the full panoramic views of Biscayne Bay and the Miami skyline, the towers are rotated incrementally by 38 degrees along the height, so that neither tower is in the "back" or "front" of the property, and more of the ground plane is freed up. This way, the roof of the parking and amenities podium could be covered in the lush greenery for which Coconut Grove is famous, but which it has steadily been losing to development.

The design concept posed numerous structural challenges that demanded a fresh, innovative approach. With slanted columns, gravity loads are partially horizontal. These are transmitted partially via the floor slabs to the vertical core, and partially by a hat truss — a rigid horizontal cap at the roof. The hat truss converts multi-directional forces to vertical forces, reducing torsion in the core by approximately 30 percent, and in turn significantly reducing shear-wall thickness. This allowed the developer to regain considerable sellable space within the buildings, and to offer column-free interiors.

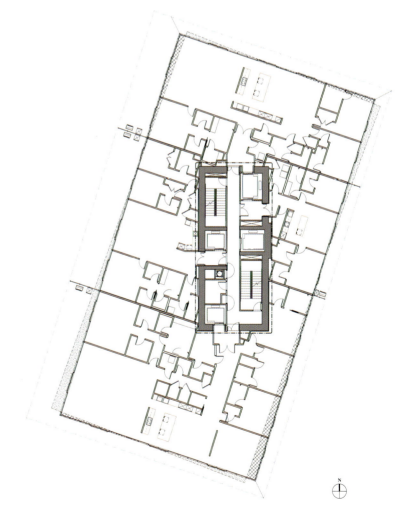

Opposite: The towers rotate a total of 38 degrees along their height.

Top: The podium of parking is covered with extensive landscaping and amenities.

Bottom Left: The twist of the design captures optimum views as the towers rise above their neighbors.

Bottom Right: Floor plan of the seventh level of the North Tower show the rotation of the floor plate against the stationary core.

Hotel EMC2

Chicago, United States

Completion Date: June 2017
Height: 75 m (246 ft)
Stories: 21
Area: 10,760 sq m (115,820 sq ft)
Primary Function: Hotel
Owner/Developer: SMASHotels Chicago LLC
Architect: KOO (design and architect of record)
Structural Engineer: WSP (engineers of record)
MEP Engineers: M.A. Engineering (design); FE Moran (engineer of record); Gibson Electric (engineer of record); O`Sullivan Plumbing Inc. (engineer of record); State Mechanical (engineer of record)
Main Contractor: Pepper Construction Company
Other CTBUH Member Consultants: Arup (acoustics); GEI Consultants (geotechnical)

At height, Hotel EMC2 blends into its neighborhood high-rise setting, while the ground plane activates the streetscape with vibrant colors and a shaded outdoor dining area. The entry façade consists of three color-coated stainless-steel panels in a pattern of two-dimensional cubes, while the tower façade consists of painted aluminum rainscreen panels in shades of gray that create a larger-scale diagonal pattern as the tower rises. A lofty terrace framed by exposed concrete diagonal columns separates these two contrasting elements, communicating a "third place" of public repose between the vibrancy of the lobby and the private space of the hotel rooms above, whose exteriors are rendered in more muted two-tone gray panels. The graphical nature of the façade enlivens the mid-block location and dilutes the effect of the repeated hotel room modules.

On the ground floor of the tower is a soaring, double-height space that belies the small footprint of the building. The height is further broadcast by the two-story window wall facing the street, unifying the outdoor seating along the street with the bustle of activity within.

The building envelope exceeds International Energy Conservation Code requirements, featuring continuous thermal insulation, glazing with low-e coatings, and rainscreen detailing. A green roof promotes a reduction in the urban heat island effect and increases the thermal resistance. Hotel guestrooms are served by variable-refrigerant units, which offer increased efficiency and acoustics when compared to heat pumps.

Opposite: The front elevation consists of large scale diagonal cladding patterns to break up the repetitive hotel room modules.

Top: An outdoor terrace sits two floors above street level.

Bottom left: Typical floor plan

Bottom right: A double-height restaurant anchors the ground floor.

Jersey City Urby

Jersey City, United States

Completion Date: 2016
Height: 213 m (700 ft)
Stories: 70
Area: 63,890 sq m (687,706 sq ft)
Primary Function: Residential
Owners: Ironstate Development; Mack-Cali Realty Corporation
Developers: Roseland Residential Trust; Ironstate Development
Architects: Concrete (design); HLW International (architect of record)
Structural Engineer: DeSimone Consulting Engineers (design)
MEP Engineer: AMA Consulting Engineers, P.C. (design)
Main Contractor: AJD Construction
Other CTBUH Member Consultants: Gradient Wind Engineering Inc. (wind)

Situated one block from the Hudson River in the heart of Jersey City, New Jersey, Urby provides panoramic views of downtown Manhattan and easy access to New York City. Situated in an area dominated by office buildings, this residential tower adds liveliness to its neighborhood by adding an element of 24-hour activity through increased residential density. The apartments remain compact, as the tower aims to provide comparatively affordable urban living in a high-value metropolitan area.

The tower's design features a series of incongruous blocks stacked atop one another, clad in glass framed by sheen black aluminum. Each section is offset slightly from the adjoining block, creating a tapered effect as the tower rises. Eschewing the traditional lobby with a doorman, the tower features a publicly accessible entrance café complete with its own barista and modern seating area. Together with a large sun deck, these communal spaces allow Urby to host events such as book clubs, outdoor dinners, and musical performances.

Through technological upgrades such as the keyless entry system, residents can unlock their doors with their phones or give friends and delivery services temporary access to their apartments. The upcoming Urby app will let residents receive notifications when a package has arrived, as well as an access code for the locker in which the package is stored. Additionally, the tower offers at least one bicycle parking spot per apartment, and residents can use one of the building's communal bikes at any time.

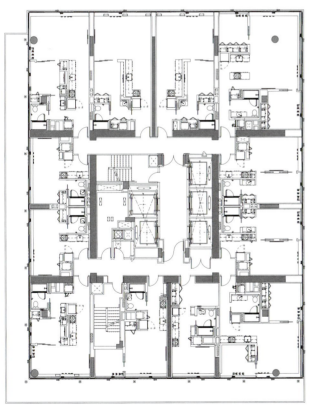

Opposite: The building's height is broken up by the visual appearance of boxes stacked atop one another.

Top: Residential units were designed compact, but efficient, to provide affordable an urban living option.

Bottom left: Typical floor plan.

Bottom right: In place of a traditional lobby, the tower features a publicly accessible entrance café.

Madison Square Park Tower

New York City, United States

Completion Date: June 2017
Height: 237 m (777 ft)
Stories: 61
Area: 23,929 sq m (257,570 sq ft)
Primary Function: Residential
Owner: Continuum Company, LLC
Developers: Continuum Company, LLC; Eichner Properties, Inc.
Architects: Kohn Pedersen Fox Associates (design); Hill West Architects (design)
Structural Engineer: DeSimone Consulting Engineers (design)
MEP Engineer: MG Engineering DPC (design)
Main Contractor: Plaza Construction Corporation
Other CTBUH Member Consultants: GERB Vibration Control Systems, Inc (damping); Permasteelisa Group (façade); Vidaris, Inc. (façade, roofing, sustainability)

Located in the historic Flatiron district of Manhattan, the 61-story Madison Square Park Tower soars above the historic, low-rise buildings that surround it. To compliment the neighborhood's 1900's-era Chicago School masonry architecture, the design team incorporated a five-story, granite-clad podium, rather than a top-to-bottom glass façade. The mirrored glass façade that encases the tower above the fifth floor reflects the New York skyline while providing floor-to-ceiling windows that allow natural light deep into the tower's residential units.

The building features an angular design that grows progressively wider as it rises from its lowest floors, with the resulting structure reaching a slenderness ratio of about 13 to 1. Due to the tower's complex geometry, every plate above the sixth floor has a distinct shape and increases in size with each rising floor. Special structural solutions were provided to overcome the challenge of the tower's top-heavy geometry and high slenderness, which created significant gravitational strain in addition to already powerful wind forces and accelerations. The solutions include high-strength concrete vertical elements, mid-height outriggers and band wall, and a 1.2 million-pound tuned mass damper at the roof to limit wind accelerations to acceptable levels.

From podium to pinnacle, the structure's external form and internal organization were impacted by the historical significance of the neighborhood and restrictive proportions of the build site. In a nod to its setting, Madison Square Park Tower seeks to blend contemporary design with mid-century architecture.

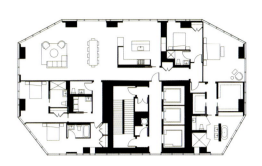

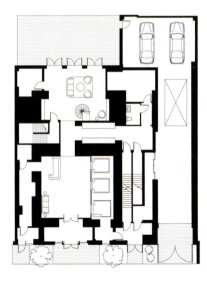

Opposite: Madison Square Park Tower rises from a five-story granite-clad podium that compliments the Flatiron district's historic masonry architecture.

Left: An upward series of floor plans — from the ground floor (bottom), to floor 30 (middle), to floor 54 (top) — emphasizes the cantilever and changing form along its height.

Top Right: Unlike its base condition, the tower contrasts greatly with some of its neighbors, such as the 1909-built Metropolitan Life Tower (center-left).

Middle Right: The tower's height relative to its context allows for sweeping views of the Flatiron district, and Midtown beyond.

Bottom Right: A double-height corner residence takes full advantage of available sunlight.

Metropolitan
Quito, Ecuador

Completion Date: July 2016
Height: 83 m (274 ft)
Stories: 19
Area: 2,129 sq m (22,916 sq ft)
Primary Function: Office
Owner: Fideicomiso Mercantil Metropolitan
Developer: Uribe & Schwarzkopf
Architects: TOMMY SCHWARZKOPF (design); Christian Wiese Architects (design)
Structural Engineer: Ingeniero Patricio Ramos (design)
Project Manager: Uribe & Schwarzkopf
Main Contractors: Coheco; Fairis

The Metropolitan, located at the center of Quito, Ecuador, plays off the expectations created by surrounding buildings and the local rectilinear grid by subtly warping its horizontal planes, just enough to cause a second look.

The building's exterior evokes perpetual motion through its asymmetric, undulating façade. Each exterior balcony is offset slightly from its neighbors, creating a fluctuating profile with a unique shape when viewed at each angle. The façade also acts as a brise-soleil, shading the interior of the building from the sun. Straight, black concrete columns rise intermittently between each balcony, contrasting with the abstract white façade. The roof is crowned with a waved awning that emulates the aquatic nature of the building's exterior while also providing shade for the rooftop terrace.

The wide central atrium features clean lines and pearl-white balconies connected by bridges that alternate over one another as they span the courtyard. The tower's lush rooftop garden provides panoramic views of the urban landscape and the peaks of the Andes Mountains beyond.

The urban space surrounding the building is complemented with gardens, courtyards, and materials that are arranged for high traffic purposes to protect pedestrians. The tower itself was conceived with inspiration from the Pichincha Volcano outside the city — an important national symbol of Ecuador's independence — and acts as a reminder of the importance of incorporating natural elements into urban design.

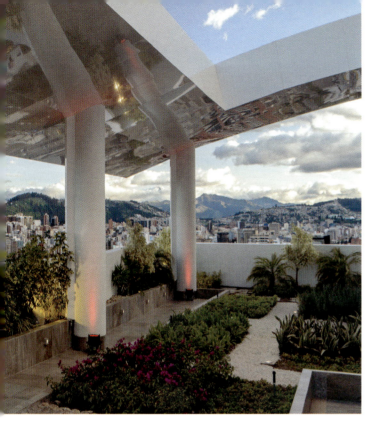

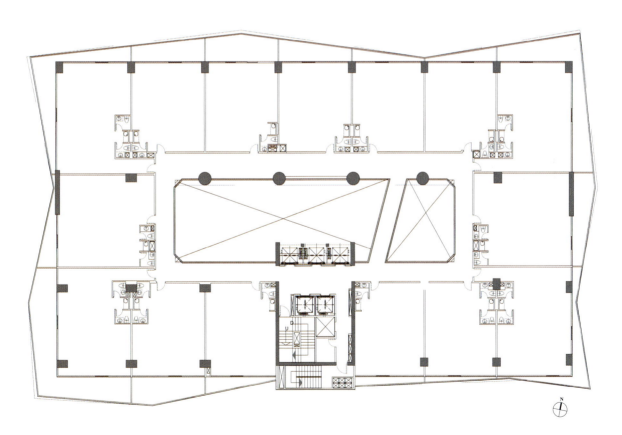

Opposite: The Metropolitan appears as a mildly-distorted rectilinear block.

Top Left: The tower's lush rooftop garden provides views of the city and Andes Mountains beyond.

Top Right: The central atrium is a sleek, skylit chasm criss-crossed by walkways.

Bottom: A plan view of the tower shows the atrium space in the center and variations in the crenellated envelope along the perimeter.

Porsche Design Tower

Sunny Isles Beach, United States

Completion Date: November 2016
Height: 195 m (641 ft)
Stories: 57
Area: 76,966 sq m (828,458 sq ft)
Primary Functions: Residential
Owner/Developer: Dezer Development
Architect: The Sieger Suarez Architectural Partnership (design)
Structural Engineer: CHM Structural Engineers, LLC. (design)
MEP Engineer: Steven Feller P.E. (design)
Main Contractor: Coastal Construction; Fortin, Leavy, Skiles, Inc.; EGS2 Corp.

Representing Porsche Design Group's first foray into residential real estate, Porsche Design Tower is notable for its first-of-its-kind automobile elevator lift system that whisks both residents and their vehicles up to their units, throughout the height of the building.

The cylindrical design of the tower was a function of the requirement to not only maximize views and privacy for each of the 132 luxury residences, but to efficiently distribute vehicles and their occupants from the lift core. The vehicle lift system consists of three elevators, each capable of lifting a total weight of 18,143 kilograms at a speed of 4 meters per second. The technology works by first scanning vehicles at ground level as they enter the building, identifying both the car and unit number. The car then enters a turntable, which is one of three circular platforms located at the building's center. After shutting off the engine, the turntable will align the vehicle with a car lift. As the car lift opens, a robotic arm pulls the vehicle into one of three glass-enclosed lifts, and takes the vehicle and its owner directly to their residence.

The tower's three-story lobby contains a glass-enclosed "car observatory," which acts as its centerpiece and distinctively showcases vehicles as they soar to their respective residences. The tower's sky garage and parking technology celebrates vehicles as literal works of art. In most units, a glass window between the living quarters and the garage allows residents to enjoy viewing their vehicles from their homes.

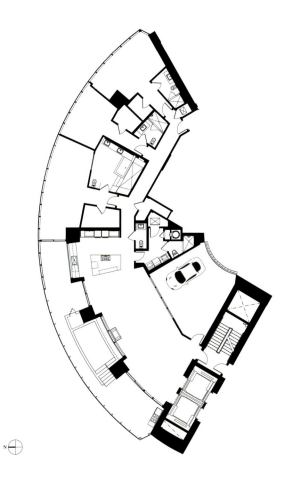

Opposite: The Porsche Design Tower's cylindrical form is driven both by the desire to maximize privacy and views, and the need to accommodate its unusual auto lift.

Top Left: A typical luxury unit plan shows the integration of the garage as part of each unit at height.

Top Right: The auto lift delivers tenants, in their cars, directly to their units.

Bottom: The central design conceit of the project is that cars are works of art and worthy of specialized display.

47

River Point
Chicago, United States

Completion Date: March 2017
Height: 223 m (732 ft)
Stories: 52
Area: 123,720 sq m (1,331,711 sq ft)
Primary Function: Office
Owners: Hines; Ivanhoé Cambridge; The Levy Organization; River Point Holdings LLC
Developer: Hines
Architects: Pickard Chilton (design); Kendall/Heaton Associates (architect of record)
Structural Engineer: Magnusson Klemencic Associates (engineer of record)
MEP Engineer: Alvine Engineering (engineer of record)
Main Contractors: Lend Lease; Clark Construction Group
Other CTBUH Member Consultants: Aon Fire Protection Engineering (fire); Cerami & Associates (acoustics); OJB Landscape Architecture (landscape); Permasteelisa Group (façade); RWDI (wind)
Other CTBUH Member Supplier: ArcelorMittal (steel)

Located on a triangular plot, the tower is designed to enhance the character of this prominent riverfront site while concealing the existing rail lines below. Set back from the edge of the river a 0.6-hectare publicly-accessible park provides the largest riverfront green space in downtown Chicago. The development also establishes 170 meters of new promenade space along the river, replacing a crumbling, inaccessible stretch of riverbank that complements and connects to new sections of a wider promenade system.

Special care taken in the design of mechanical systems, energy efficiency, and water management, as well as conscientious material selection, support the tower's sustainability goals. Selected interior strategies include light switches with motion detectors to save energy and reduce costs. Site and water management strategies include the use of native landscaping and a 50 percent green roof; a bio-infiltration system within landscaped areas that filters storm water prior to discharge; and, tower and plaza runoff that is collected and re-used to irrigate the green roof and landscape.

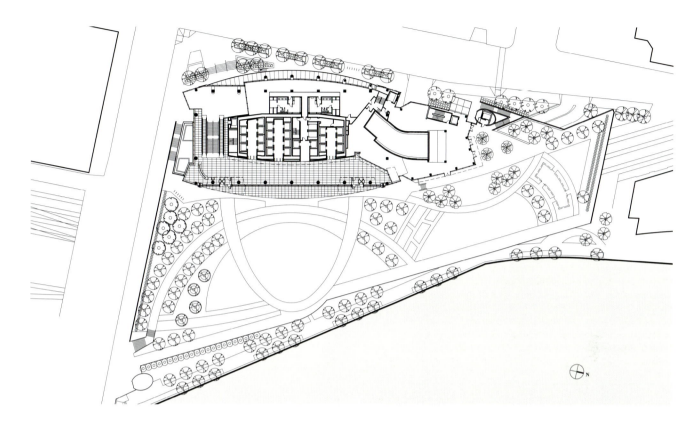

Opposite: River Point rises at the junction of two river branches just outside the Chicago Loop, with an active rail line curving through the site.

Top: The site plan demonstrates the efficiencies gained from placing the core of the tower behind the rail line and building tall, affording a riverfront park over the tracks.

Bottom Left: The riverfront park transforms rail lines into valuable public space.

Bottom Right: The building's entry arch is mirrored in the arcing pathway through the new park at its base.

Shirley Ryan AbilityLab

Chicago, United States

Completion Date: November 2016
Height: 131 m (431 ft)
Stories: 27
Area: 111,483 sq m (1,199,993 sq ft)
Primary Function: Hospital
Owner/Developer: Shirley Ryan AbilityLab
Architects: Gensler (design); HDR Architecture Inc. (design)
Structural Engineer: Thornton Tomasetti (design)
MEP Engineer: Environmental Systems Design, Inc. (design)
Main Contractor: James McHugh Construction Co.; Power Construction Company
Other CTBUH Member Consultants: GEI Consultants (building monitoring, geotechnical); Jensen Hughes (fire); Permasteelisa Group (façade)
Other CTBUH Member Suppliers: AMSYSCO (post-tensioning); thyssenkrupp (elevator)

The Shirley Ryan AbilityLab is a rehabilitation facility for people with the most severe, complex conditions — from traumatic brain injuries to cancer-related functional impairment. It was designed as a "translational" research hospital, in which clinicians, scientists, innovators and technologists work together in the same space — surrounding patients, discovering new approaches and applying (translating) research in real time. The five ability labs combine research and clinical care in a shared space to shorten the feedback loop between clinicians, patients and researchers — driving innovation of fresh solutions. The five labs are: "Think+Speak," "Legs+Walking," "Arms+Hands," "Strength+Endurance," and "Pediatrics."

The myriad windows and soaring ceilings are meant to inspire patients. Each of the five ability labs, through applied research and therapeutic spaces, provide for active, visible patient work by clinicians and researchers. They fuse sophisticated equipment and personal therapy with uplifting views and daylight, complemented by bright and cheerful colors and smooth, contemporary fittings.

A major component of healing and wellness is green space. The design complements that research with large landscaping at both the street level and throughout the upper spaces, with three immersive and accessible outdoor sky gardens, as well as extensive green roofs over the building's mechanical functions.

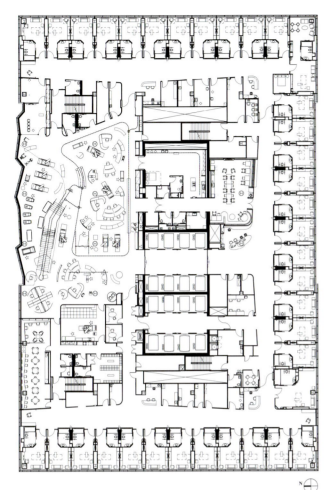

Opposite: A notch of bright color breaking up the shimmering glass façade indicates the location of the sky lobby and conference center.

Top Left: The floor plan shows the prominence given to the "lab" spaces, where the façade warps and therapy equipment is arrayed asymmetrically.

Top Right: A patient receives treatment in one of the open-plan, double-height rehabilitation labs.

Bottom: Consultation and patient rooms are arranged along the perimeter and allow controlled penetration of daylight.

The Globe and Mail Centre
Toronto, Canada

Completion Date: December 2016
Height: 83 m (273 ft)
Stories: 17
Area: 53,000 sq m (570,487 sq ft)
Primary Function: Office
Owner/Developer: First Gulf
Architects: Diamond Schmitt Architects (architect of record)
Structural Engineer: RJC Engineers (engineer of record)
MEP Engineer: Hidi Rae Consulting Engineers Inc. (engineer of record)
Main Contractor: First Gulf

Comprising 10 vertically stacked blocks of varying heights, the Globe and Mail Centre is home to the nation's eponymous newspaper of record. The stacked boxes feature alternating footprints that allow for a rhythmic sequence of cantilevered viewing terraces on all sides of the building, providing the structure with a unique and contemporary profile. Three-meter-plus windows maximize views and an advanced glazing system allows daylight deep into the tower's core. An efficient floor plate and core design support a flexible workplace for tenants and allow for maximum space utilization.

The building activates the surrounding streetscape by providing retail along all three street frontages, as well as a 24-hour public arcade that connects King Street to the north with Front Street to the south. As much as the stacked, glazed volumes are the building's calling card, care has been taken to ensure the datum lines and storefront proportions of neighboring buildings have been maintained. The building wraps around existing buildings on the corner of King and Berkeley Streets without overwhelming them.

A fully integrated and comprehensive approach to sustainable design and innovation informed this project from the start. To achieve LEED CS Gold certification, a high-performance building envelope provides exceptional thermal performance without compromising access to daylight. Lower energy costs are derived from underfloor air distribution (UFAD), high efficiency condensing gas boilers, energy recovery from exhaust air, variable speed drives for all variable loads, and demand-controlled ventilation.

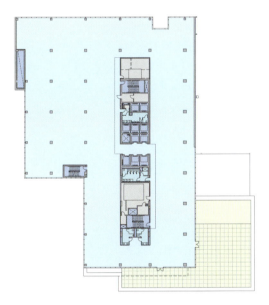

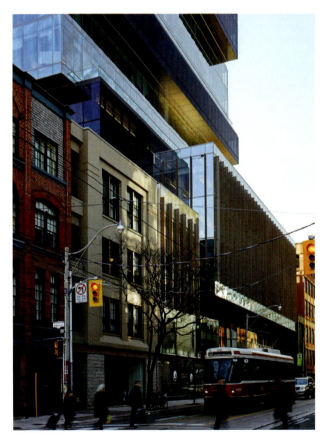

Opposite: The stacked-and-shifted box design affords numerous viewing terraces around the perimeter of the building.

Left: Floor plans show the pedestrian pass-through (Level 1– bottom) and varying sizes of floor plates and terraces (levels 3 and 13 – middle and top) afforded by the stacked-box design.

Top Right: The sky deck near the top of the building affords views of Lake Ontario and the Toronto skyline.

Bottom Right: Though a larger building than its neighbors, it preserves the prevailing scale by "nesting" into the street wall.

53

Three Alliance Center
Atlanta, United States

Completion Date: April 2017
Height: 107 m (351 ft)
Stories: 29
Area: 50,172 sq m (540,047 sq ft)
Primary Function: Office
Owner: Three Alliance Buckhead, L.P.
Developer: Tishman Speyer Properties
Architects: Mack Scogin Merrill Elam Architects (design); Smallwood, Reynolds, Stewart, Stewart (peer review)
Structural Engineer: Stanley D. Lindsey & Associates, Ltd. (design)
MEP Engineer: AHA Consulting Engineers (design); Smallwood, Reynolds, Stewart, Stewart (peer review)
Project Manager: Tishman Speyer Properties
Main Contractor: Turner Construction Company
Other CTBUH Member Consultants: AECOM (civil); URS Corporation (civil); Van Deusen & Associates (vertical transportation)
Other CTBUH Member Suppliers: Harmon, Inc. (cladding); thyssenkrupp (elevator)

Three Alliance Center is the final piece of a three-tower office complex in the Buckhead area of Atlanta, at the junction of Lenox Road and Highway 400, adjacent to a MARTA (metro) station.

The most distinguishing design feature of the building is the array of faceted windows that cascade down the building's glass façade. The faceted windows were specifically designed to interact with the surrounding urban lights when viewed from a moving vehicle, setting up a display of flittering light patterns to passersby. Displayed in checkered patterns along the blue curtain wall, the windows create a sense of geometric asymmetry. The south façade, facing onto the forecourt, presents a slower dynamic, where the protruding windows taper off toward the bottom of the tower.

Subtly pushing back against the rectilinear glass box typology, the lobby is contained in a double-height glass pop-out, within which an abstract, milky-white opaque soffit drops gradually toward the marble floor as the visitor advances. Its layered planes work in concert with rippling, curving walls to direct pedestrians toward the wood-paneled elevator lobbies. Light fills the space, entering via the glass box and directed into the interior by the cloud-like canopy, or by way of the floor lights that reflect off the canopy above. Outside is a generous courtyard shared between the three towers in the Alliance Center complex.

Opposite: The faceted windows were specifically designed to interact with the surrounding urban lights when viewed from a moving vehicle.

Top Left: A generous plaza is provided at the tower's base.

Bottom Left: The sweeping entry sequence and doors set into the curving wall are evidenced in the ground floor plan.

Top Right: A sculpted ceiling plane directs visitors through the lobby.

Bottom Right: The protruding windows are particularly dense near the top of the tower and taper off toward the bottom.

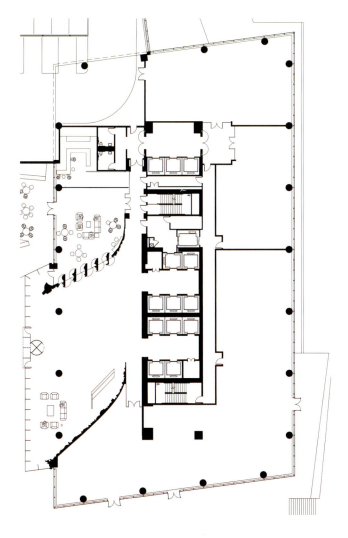

Torre KOI

San Pedro Garza García, Mexico

Completion Date: July 2017
Height: 279 m (916 ft)
Stories: 65
Area: 1,900 sq m (20,451 sq ft)
Primary Functions: Residential / Office
Owner/Developer: Internacional de Inversiones
Architect: VFO Arquitectos (design)
Structural Engineers: Thornton Tomasetti (design); Stark + Ortiz (design)
MEP Engineer: Esa Consultoria e Ingenieria (design); Instalaciones Sanitarias Hidraulicas y Soldaduras (design); Vizafire (design); Surtidora Electrica del noreste (design)
Project Manager: PMP Consultores
Main Contractors: Aluvisa; Constructora DOCSA

Soaring above its urban landscape, Torre KOI is the tallest building in Mexico. The glassy, mixed-use tower in San Pedro Garza Garcia was designed to reflect its physical environment and its relationship with the surrounding city. The first 15 floors, as well as the top five, are dedicated to office space, while 36 floors between contain apartments.

The blue-green façade reflects the surrounding mountains, with panels that differ in style as the building rises to its pinnacle. Its inclined crown recalls the chiseled mountaintops that define the Monterrey area. Floor-to-ceiling windows offer tenants bright, naturally lit spaces. On the 22nd floor, the building's dramatic setback features a cut in its parapet, revealing an infinity pool that offers views of the valley in which the tower is nestled, as well as the city's burgeoning skyline.

The site planning for the tower, part of the three-tower VAO complex, is well suited to the surroundings. Torre KOI is placed on the corner of the property, affording a welcoming, broad entrance to the street, while making room for extensive landscaping and a swooping-roofed commercial building over a nine-level parking garage. The undulating roof of the commercial building leads the eye gradually upwards to take in the full height of the tower.

In the heart of Mexico's most industrialized metropolis, Torre KOI acts as a national example for the implementation of sustainable operational practices, including support facilities for bicycles and electric vehicles. Finally, in consideration of the local economy, the tower's construction used as many local materials as possible.

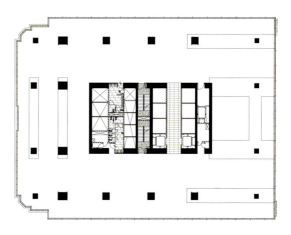

Opposite: Torre KOI draws attention to the VAO complex, which also has substantial podium-top landscaping and a commercial building with an undulating roof.

Top: The chiseled crown and setbacks of the tower reference the mountains that surround the Monterrey area.

Bottom Left: Interior spaces are sophisticated and understated.

Bottom Right: Typical office floors (top) and residential floors (bottom), illustrate the angled views and balcony spaces achieved by the chiseled façade.

57

University of Chicago Campus North Residential Commons

Chicago, United States

Completion Date: September 2016
Height: 50 m (164 ft)
Stories: 15
Area: 37,161 sq m (399,998 sq ft)
Primary Functions: Residential / Retail
Owner/Developer: University of Chicago
Architects: Studio Gang (design, architect of record); Hanbury (design)
Structural Engineer: Magnusson Klemencic Associates (design)
MEP Engineer: dbHMS (design)
Main Contractor: Mortenson Development Company Inc.
Other CTBUH Member Consultants: Jensen Hughes (code); Transsolar Energietechnik GmbH (sustainability)

Featuring a mix of student residences, dining amenities, classrooms, green spaces, and retail, the Campus North Residential Commons is designed as new "front door" for the University of Chicago—a welcoming portal that strengthens connections between the campus and nearby neighborhoods.

The design situates three slender bar buildings within an urban fabric of plazas, gardens, walkways, and courtyards, forming a central quadrangle that comprises inviting outdoor spaces for students and neighbors. The central quadrangle is anchored by a public landscaped plaza, surrounded by active programming including retail, classrooms, and a café. The buildings are scaled to their context, with the tallest structure completing the urban edge of a busy thoroughfare, while the shorter structures are more attuned to the adjacent residential neighborhood. The white precast concrete façade emulates the language of the collegiate Gothic limestone buildings that define the University's core campus, while updating the traditional architecture with new material technology and construction methods.

The residences are organized around three-story "house hubs," cozy, home-like spaces that bring together 100 undergraduates with distinct spaces for gathering, studying, cooking, and relaxing, connected by cascading stairs and seating tribunes. Importantly, the project also provides an active street presence to a neighborhood that was previously closed off from the University by a four-meter wall.

Opposite Top: The buildings' arrangement opens up the quad to the rest of the campus.

Opposite Bottom: "House hubs" are common spaces intended for smaller groups of students within the buildings, making them seem more intimate.

Above: The arrangement of the towers places the highest towards the busy street, while channeling pedestrians from the corner into the site.

Below: The site orientation of the three towers creates a permeable threshold that integrates the complex with both the neighborhood and campus, while the interior organization presents differently scaled gathering spaces.

Wilshire Grand Center
Los Angeles, United States

Completion Date: June 2017
Height: 335 m (1,100 ft)
Stories: 73
Area: 187,026 sq m (2,013,137 sq ft)
Primary Functions: Hotel / Office
Owner: Hanjin International Corporation; Korean Air
Developer: Martin Project Management
Architect: AC Martin (design)
Structural Engineer: Thornton Tomasetti (design); Brandow & Johnston Inc (engineer of record)
MEP Engineer: Glumac (design)
Main Contractor: Turner Construction Company
Other CTBUH Member Consultants: Fortune Shepler Consulting (vertical transportation); Lerch Bates (façade maintenance); RWDI (wind)

As the tallest building west of the Mississippi River, Wilshire Grand Center rises prominently in downtown Los Angeles. The tower is composed of 890 rooms of the InterContinental Hotel that sits atop 18 office floors. Its podium includes hotel convention spaces — ballrooms, meeting rooms, and break-out areas, along with retail spaces, restaurants, and a health club.

As a multi-program building in an earthquake-prone area, a thorough seismic reinforcement design was necessary. Wilshire Grand represents one of the best examples of performance-based seismic design (PBSD), which goes beyond the prescriptive codes with a custom solution optimized for the building's specific conditions. Since the floor plan and reinforced concrete core plan are elongated, three sets of outriggers connect the core to 10 of the perimeter concrete-filled steel box columns to supplement core transverse stiffness for occupant comfort, helping to resist transverse overturning under strong winds and absorb energy in seismic events.

The tower is also notable for being the first high-rise building in Los Angeles to have an articulated rooftop since the implementation of the city's helipad ordinance in 1974, requiring that buildings over a certain height incorporate helipads, and thereby flat roofs. The crown structure, referred to the project team as a "sail," gives way to an ornamental spire and has a narrow profile that acts as a natural wind shield for an outdoor rooftop lounge.

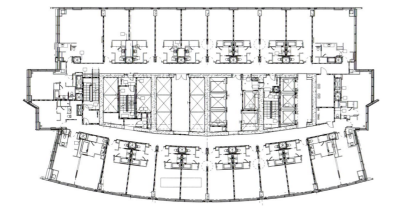
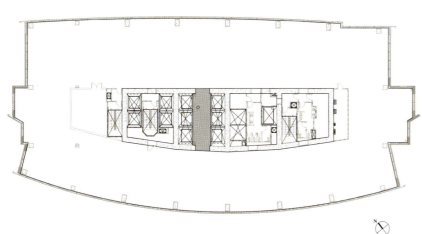

Opposite: The curved sides and crown, as well as the height of Wilshire Grand make it one of the most distinctive buildings in Los Angeles, which for years mandated flat-topped high-rises.

Top Left: The hotel lobby, situated at the top of the building, features soaring open spaces.

Top Right: A wide, flowing staircase and swooping canopy invite street life deep into the complex.

Bottom: The elongated central core allowed for sufficient column-free office floor plans (bottom) as well as single-loaded hotel corridors (top) that allowed most of the services to be placed at the center.

1 | 30 Park Place
New York City, United States

Completion Date: September 2016
Height: 282 m (926 ft)
Stories: 67
Area: 63,453 sq m (683,002 sq ft)
Primary Functions: Residential / Hotel
Developer: Silverstein Properties
Architects: Robert A.M. Stern Architects (design); SLCE Architects (architect of record)
Structural Engineer: WSP Cantor Seinuk (design)
MEP Engineer: WSP Flack + Kurtz (design)
Main Contractor: Tishman Construction
Other CTBUH Member Consultants: Langan Engineering (geotechnical); Vidaris, Inc. (building monitoring, energy concept, façade, roofing)

2 | 88 Scott
Toronto, Canada

Completion Date: December 2017
Height: 198 m (650 ft)
Stories: 58
Area: 54,438 sq m (585,966 sq ft)
Primary Function: Residential
Developer: Concert Properties Ltd.
Architect: IBI Group Architects (design)
Structural Engineer: Jablonsky, Ast and Partners (design)
MEP Engineer: MV Shore Associates (design)
Main Contractor: Bird Construction

3 | 609 Main at Texas
Houston, United States

Completion Date: May 2017
Height: 230 m (755 ft)
Stories: 48
Area: 98,259 sq m (1,057,651 sq ft)
Primary Functions: Office
Owner/Developer: Hines
Architects: Pickard Chilton (design); Kendall/Heaton Associates (architect of record)
Structural Engineer: Cardno Haynes Whaley, Inc. (engineer of record)
MEP Engineer: ME Engineers (engineer of record)
Main Contractor: Harvey Builders
Other CTBUH Member Consultants: Cerami & Associates (acoustics); Curtain Wall Design and Consulting, Inc. (façade); OJB Landscape Architecture (landscape); RWDI (wind); Walter P. Moore (civil)
Other CTBUH Member Supplier: Harmon, Inc. (cladding)

4 | 615 South College
Charlotte, United States

Completion Date: May 2017
Height: 79 m (260 ft)
Stories: 19
Area: 34,467 sq m (371,000 sq ft)
Primary Function: Office
Owner/Developer: Portman Holdings
Architect: John Portman & Associates (design)
Structural Engineer: John Portman & Associates (engineer of record)
MEP Engineer: Barrett Woodyard & Associates (engineer of record)
Main Contractor: Holder Construction Company
Other CTBUH Member Consultants: Fisher Marantz Stone (lighting); Fortune Shepler Saling Inc. (vertical transportation)

5 | AQWA Corporate
Rio de Janeiro, Brazil

Completion Date: October 2017
Height: 95 m (312 ft)
Stories: 22
Area: 223,000 sq m (2,400,352 sq ft)
Primary Functions: Office
Owner/Developer: Tishman Speyer Properties
Architects: Foster + Partners (design); RAF Arquitetura (architect of record)
Structural Engineers: JKMF (design); Beltec Estrutura Metalica (design)
MEP Engineers: MHA Engenharia Ltda. (design); Teknika (design)
Main Contractor: Hochtief do Brasil
Other CTBUH Member Consultant: Arup (lighting)

6 | Biscayne Beach
Miami, United States

Completion Date: May 2017
Height: 168 m (550 ft)
Stories: 52
Primary Function: Residential
Owner: Two Roads Development
Developers: Two Roads Development; GTIS Partners
Architects: WHLC Architecture (design); BC Architects (design)
Structural Engineer: GCI Consultants (design)
MEP Engineer: Langan Engineering (design)
Main Contractors: Moss & Associates LLC; Plaza Construction Corporation
Other CTBUH Member Consultant: Langan Engineering (civil, environmental, geotechnical)

7 | BRIC Phase 1
San Diego, United States

Completion Date: April 2016
Height: 53 m (173 ft)
Stories: 17
Area: 41,743 sq m (449,318 sq ft)
Primary Function: Hotel
Owner/Developer: LPP Lane Field, LLC
Architect: John Portman & Associates (design)
Structural Engineer: Integrated Design Engineers (design)
MEP Engineers: McParlane & Associates, Inc. (design); Michael Wall Engineering (design); tk1sc (design)
Project Manager: John Portman & Associates
Main Contractor: Hensel Phelps Construction Co.
Other CTBUH Member Consultants: Fortune Shepler Saling Inc. (vertical transportation); Jensen Hughes (life safety)

8 | CF Calgary City Centre Phase I
Calgary, Canada

Completion Date: June 2016
Height: 160 m (524 ft)
Stories: 37
Area: 86,200 sq m (927,849 sq ft)
Primary Functions: Office
Owner/Developer: Cadillac Fairview Corporation Ltd
Architect: Zeidler Partnership Architects (design)
Structural Engineer: Read Jones Christoffersen Ltd (design)
MEP Engineers: Mulvey & Banani (design); Smith + Andersen (design)
Main Contractor: PCL Construction Management Inc.
Other CTBUH Member Consultant: WSP (LEED)

9 | Cielo
Seattle, United States

Completion Date: 2015
Height: 102 m (335 ft)
Stories: 32
Primary Functions: Residential
Developer: Laconia Development
Architects: Kwan Henmi Architecture Planning (design)
Structural Engineer: DCI Engineers (engineer of record)
Main Contractor: PCL Construction Services, Inc.

10 | Equus 333
San Pedro Garza García, Mexico

Completion Date: February 2016
Height: Tower 1 & 2: 112 m (368 ft); Tower 3: 96 m (316 ft)
Stories: 24
Total Area: 65,883 sq m (709,160 sq ft)
Primary Function: Tower 1 & 2: Office; Tower 3: Residential
Owner/Developer: Legado Corporativo Inmobiliaria, S.A. DE C.V.
Architects: Duda | Paine Architects (design); Pladis Arquitectura + Inteligencia (architect of record)
Structural Engineers: Postensa (design); Socsa (peer review)
MEP Engineer: SENSA (engineer of record)
Main Contractor: IP PROYECTOS
Other CTBUH Member Consultants: Curtain Wall Design and Consulting, Inc. (façade); Kinetica (roofing); RWDI (wind)
Other CTBUH Member Supplier: Lerch Bates (elevator)

11 | Hotel Las Americas Golden Tower
Panama City, Panama

Completion Date: December 2016
Height: 152 m (498 ft)
Stories: 31
Area: 34,699 sq m (373,497 sq ft)
Primary Function: Hotel
Owner: Grupo Inversiones Talarame
Developer: Promotora Las Americas Golden Tower SA
Architects: Carlos Ott Architect (design); Eduardo A. Delgado Acosta (architect of record)
Main Contractor: Constructa Ingenieros Panama S.A.

12 | INDX Condominiums
Toronto, Canada

Completion Date: July 2016
Height: 178 m (585 ft)
Stories: 54
Area: 47,051 sq m (506,453 sq ft)
Primary Function: Residential
Owner: Lifetime Developments
Developers: CentreCourt Developments; Lifetime Developments
Architect: IBI Group Architects (design)
Structural Engineer: Jablonsky, Ast and Partners (engineer of record)
MEP Engineer: Able Engineering Inc. (engineer of record)

13 | Jade Signature
Sunny Isles Beach, United States

Completion Date: December 2017
Height: 194 m (636 ft)
Stories: 57
Area: 91,000 sq m (979,516 sq ft)
Primary Function: Residential
Owner: Fortune International Group
Developer: Fortune International Reality
Architects: Herzog & de Meuron Architekten (design); Stantec Ltd. (architect of record)
Structural Engineer: McNAMARA • SALVIA (design)
MEP Engineer: Stantec Ltd. (design)
Main Contractor: Suffolk Construction Company, Inc.
Other CTBUH Member Consultant: Pierre-Yves Rochon, Inc. (interiors)
Other CTBUH Member Supplier: KONE (elevator)

14 | L'Avenue
Montreal, Canada

Completion Date: March 2017
Height: 184 m (605 ft)
Stories: 51
Area: 590,300 sq m (6,353,936 sq ft)
Primary Functions: Residential / Office
Developer: Broccolini Construction
Architects: IBI Group Architects (design); Beique Legault Thuot Architectes (architect of record)
Structural Engineer: NCK Inc. (design)
MEP Engineer: Dupras Ledoux (design)
Main Contractor: Broccolini Construction

15 | Level BK
New York City, United States

Completion Date: December 2017
Height: 134 m (438 ft)
Stories: 40
Area: 58,556 sq m (630,292 sq ft)
Primary Functions: Residential
Owner/Developer: Douglaston Development
Architect: Stephen B. Jacobs Group P.C. Architects and Planners (design)
Structural Engineer: WSP Group (design)
MEP Engineers: Stantec Ltd. (design); Edwards & Zuck Engineers (design)
Main Contractor: Levine Builders
Other CTBUH Member Consultant: Gilsanz Murray Steficek (façade)

11

12

13

14

15

16 | Northwestern Mutual Tower and Commons
Milwaukee, United States

Completion Date: August 2017
Height: 169 m (554 ft)
Stories: 32
Area: 61,270 sq m (659,505 sq ft)
Primary Functions: Office
Owner: Northwestern Mutual
Developer: Hines
Architects: Pickard Chilton (design); Kendall / Heaton Associates (architect of record)
Structural Engineer: Magnusson Klemencic Associates (engineer of record)
MEP Engineer: Alvine Engineering (engineer of record)
Main Contractors: CG Schmidt; Gilbane Building Company
Other CTBUH Member Consultants: Buro Happold (LEED); Cerami & Associates (acoustics); Entuitive (façade); OJB Landscape Architecture (landscape); RWDI (wind)
Other CTBUH Member Supplier: CAST CONNEX (steel)

17 | Optima Signature
Chicago, United States

Completion Date: June 2017
Height: 179 m (587 ft)
Stories: 57
Area: 59,674 sq m (642,326 sq ft)
Primary Functions: Residential
Owner: Optima Center Chicago II, LLC.
Developer: Optima, Inc.
Architect: David C. Hovey, FAIA (design)
Structural Engineer: CS Associates, Inc. (design)
MEP Engineers: KJWW Engineering Consultants (design); FE Moran (engineer of record); Nova Fire Protection (engineer of record); Cosentini Associates (peer review)
Main Contractor: Optima, Inc.
Other CTBUH Member Supplier: AMSYSCO (post-tensioning)

18 | Park Avenue West
Portland, United States

Completion Date: March 2016
Height: 164 m (537 ft)
Stories: 30
Area: 56,908 sq m (612,553 sq ft)
Primary Functions: Residential / Office
Owner/Developer: TMT Development
Architect: TVA Architects (design)
Structural Engineer: KPFF Consulting Engineers (engineer of record)
MEP Engineer: Interface Engineering (engineer of record)
Main Contractor: Hoffman Construction Company

19 | Ten Thousand
Los Angeles, United States

Completion Date: December 2016
Height: 147 m (483 ft)
Stories: 40
Area: 71,279 sq m (767,241 sq ft)
Primary Function: Residential
Owner/Developer: Crescent Heights
Architect: Handel Architects LLP (design, architect of record)
Structural Engineer: Magnusson Klemencic Associates (design, engineer of record)
MEP Engineers: Cupertino Electric Inc. (engineer of record); Critchfield Mechanical Inc. (engineer of record); All Area Plumbing (engineer of record); C & B Consulting Engineers (peer review)
Main Contractor: Swinerton Builders
Other CTBUH Member Consultants: Arup (façade); Edgett Williams Consulting Group Inc. (vertical transportation)

20 | The Collection, Tower
Honolulu, United States

Completion Date: November 2016
Height: 129 m (422 ft)
Stories: 43
Area: 75,499 sq m (812,664 sq ft)
Primary Functions: Residential
Owner/Developer: The Collection LLC
Architects: Pappageorge Haymes Partners (design); Design Partners, Inc. (design)
Structural Engineer: Sowlat Structural Engineers (design)
MEP Engineer: Insynergy Engineering, Inc. (engineer of record)
Main Contractor: Hawaiian Dredging & Construction Company
Other CTBUH Member Consultants: Sato & Associates, Inc. (civil)

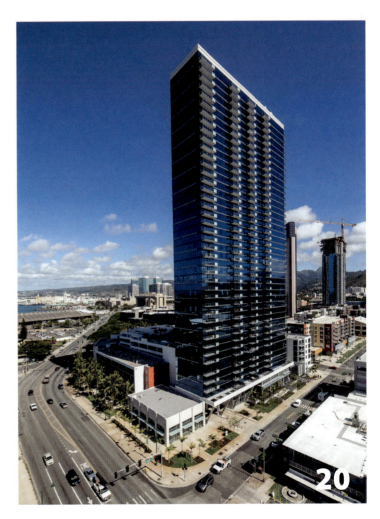

21 | The Encore
New York City, United States

Completion Date: July 2016
Height: 162 m (533 ft)
Stories: 48
Area: 30,611 sq m (329,494 sq ft)
Primary Function: Residential
Owner/Developer: West 60th Street LLC
Architect: Stephen B. Jacobs Group P.C. Architects and Planners (design)
Structural Engineer: Rosenwasser/Grossman Consulting Engineers P.C. (engineer of record)
MEP Engineers: I. M. Robbins P.C. (engineer of record); Stantec Ltd. (engineer of record)
Project Managers: Glenwood Management; West 60th Development LLC
Other CTBUH Member Supplier: thyssenkrupp (elevator)

22 | The Hub
New York City, United States

Completion Date: March 2016
Height: 185 m (607 ft)
Stories: 53
Area: 67,772 sq m (729,924 sq ft)
Primary Function: Residential
Owner/Developer: Steiner NYC
Architects: Richard Dattner & Associates (architect of record); Hill West Architects (design)
Structural Engineer: DeSimone Consulting Engineers (design)
MEP Engineer: Cosentini Associates (design)
Main Contractor: New Line Structures

ASIA & AUSTRALASIA

Asia has been the epicenter of skyscraper construction for more than a decade. In the dizzying blur of completions, there is much monotony. But there are also signs of the regional tall boom coming of age, as the rush to modernize is tempered with the desire to provide green space, respect and perpetuate local cultural context, and form distinctive regional and city identities. The region continues to impress, and as it matures, raw spectacle is being subtly supplanted by sophistication and place-making for future generations.

1 William Street

Brisbane, Australia

Completion Date: October 2016
Height: 260 m (852 ft)
Stories: 46
Area: 126,800 sq m (1,364,864 sq ft)
Primary Function: Office
Owner: Cbus Property; ISPT Core Fund
Developer: Cbus Property
Architects: Woods Bagot (design)
Structural Engineer: Hyder Consulting (engineer of record)
MEP Engineer: EMF Griffiths (engineer of record)
Main Contractor: Multiplex
Other CTBUH Member Consultants: Altitude Façade Access Consulting Pty Ltd (façade); Aspect Studios (landscape); JLL (property management); Windtech Consultants Pty Ltd (wind); WSP Group (vertical transportation); WT Partnership (quantity surveyor)
Other CTBUH Member Supplier: Yuanda (cladding)

A major catalyst project for Brisbane's waterfront precinct, the 1 William Street commercial tower was developed to establish an engaging and unified workplace for 5,000 employees of the Queensland Public Service. The project was also seen as an opportunity to reintegrate an undervalued section of the foreshore back into the physical and social fabric of the city.

The project site is surrounded on three sides by the Riverside Expressway and its access ramps, with only one side facing a city street with pedestrian access. The building was constructed with a generous street-facing lobby, while its river-facing side smoothly curves alongside the highway on-ramps to face the river like the prow of a ship. The site shape is reflected in the tower's extrusion, which carries a strong cleft up its middle, separating its two halves. This is topped by a spire, guiding the eye over the sloping, louvered roof.

The tower's façade references an archetypal feature of Queensland architecture through the provision of horizontal and vertical louvers. Considering solar impact, the length of the louvers varies in relation to the aspect of the building, resulting in a façade expression that transitions as one moves around the building.

Connectivity on and between floors is achieved via full-height atria enabling a non-hierarchical, inclusive workspace with a mix of individual and team-based settings.

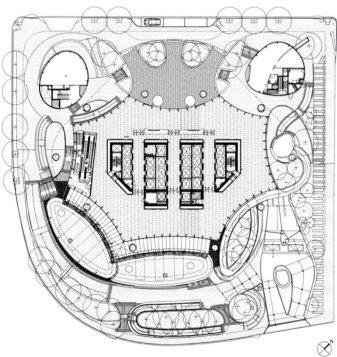

Opposite: The tower's shape responds to its site condition, with highway on-ramps wrapping three sides.

Above: Interfloor connectivity via atria and stairs reinforce that this is a non-hierarchical workplace.

Bottom Left: The ground floor plan of the tower demonstrates the inclusiveness of the scalloped façade beneath the tower's 6-sided overhang.

Bottom Right: The tubular steel element that terminates the extended façade mullions becomes an expression of the central "cleft" on the main body of the tower.

35 Spring Street

Melbourne, Australia

Completion Date: March 2017
Height: 164 m (539 ft)
Stories: 44
Area: 56,976 sq m (613,285 sq ft)
Primary Function: Residential
Owner/Developer: Cbus Property
Architect: Bates Smart (design)
Structural Engineer: Robert Bird Group (engineer of record)
MEP Engineer: Umow Lai (engineer of record)
Project Manager: RCP
Main Contractor: Multiplex

35 Spring Street helps define the edge of the city, demarcating Melbourne's downtown grid from the parklands and suburbs beyond. The tower incorporates 241 luxury apartments which are generously sized and often customized, featuring contemporary design and bespoke finishes.

Situated on the corner of Spring Street and Flinders Lane, the design was inspired by its location. Flinders Lane is a cultural destination within the city today; however, in the 1880s, the lane was home to Melbourne's fabric industry. The façade interprets the warp and weft weaving of fabric, referencing the history of Flinders Lane, as well as the ashlar patterns found in the stonework of nearby historic buildings. The vertical and horizontal pattern of the façade creates a woven veil on the surface of the building. This helps to soften the threshold between inside and outside, creating a sense of privacy for residents.

The tower was designed with three different vertical sections, in order to respond to the different site conditions. Along Flinders Lane, the tower steps back to avoid overshadowing the fine-grained nature of the laneway. At midlevel the tower steps back again, this time in order to respond to the height of the surrounding buildings. The sense of openness created from the Treasury Gardens opposite and the fact that Spring Street forms the edge of Melbourne's downtown grid, meant that the tower did not require a setback at street level. This enhanced the sculptural quality of the tower and helped the building complete the high-rise edge along Spring Street when approaching the city from the east.

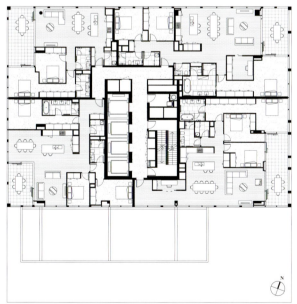

Opposite: The façade pulls back from the framed elements as the tower rises.

Top: The project helps define the edge of the downtown CBD (at right) where it meets the civically-oriented area of Parliament Reserve, the Old Treasury and Fitzroy Gardens (to the left).

Bottom Left: This plan of Level 37 shows how the setbacks within the façade frame create substantial outdoor spaces at the corners.

Bottom Right: A detail view of the façade shows the "weft and weave" of the fabric-inspired design.

161 Sussex Street

Sydney, Australia

Completion Date: September 2016
Height: 103 m (338 ft)
Stories: 26
Area: 23,655 sq m (254,620 sq ft)
Primary Functions: Office / Hotel / Exhibition
Owner/Developer: M&L Hospitality
Architect: Cox Architecture (design)
Structural Engineer: Taylor Thomson Whitting (design)
MEP Engineers: Aurecon (design); AECOM (design)
Project Manager: Savills
Main Contractor: Multiplex
Other CTBUH Member Consultants: Bates Smart (interiors); JBA Urban Planning Consultants Pty Ltd (planning); WT Partnership (quantity surveyor)

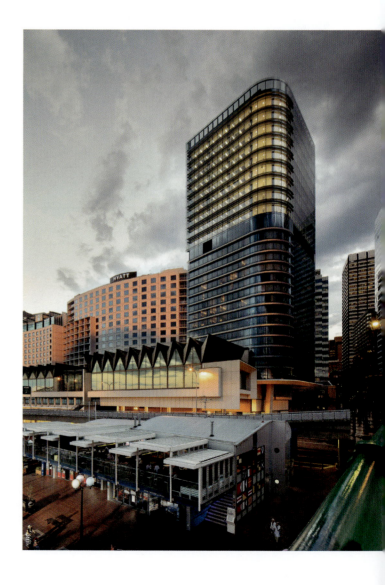

This revitalization of a hotel occupying an entire city block includes a significant expansion of rooms in a new tower element, and new conferencing facilities in a new horizontal element, both of which straddle an active highway and lacked a suitable ground plane on which to build. By using air-space over the existing highway, the project posits a new way for cities to "re-occupy" otherwise wasted space over infrastructure, creating new commercial and urban opportunities.

On the opposite side of the building, the interface with Sussex Street has been thoughtfully reconsidered — a 1980s "faux-heritage" frontage was removed, revealing authentic brick buildings that date back to the early days of colonial Sydney. Some of the buildings were incorporated into the hotel lobby and reception areas, providing street-level meeting space and a transition from street to tower. The new podium reinforces the alignment and street wall of Sussex Street, while extending the public domain onto the site itself. The ground plane is treated as an extension of the public domain, open to hotel and conference facility users. A through-building link positively invites the public to traverse the site and connects the city core to Darling Harbour.

During construction, measures were taken to avoid unnecessary disruption to this busy location. Structures that would straddle the highway were pre-fabricated where possible, to minimize construction time over a live roadway. The hotel was continuously occupied during construction.

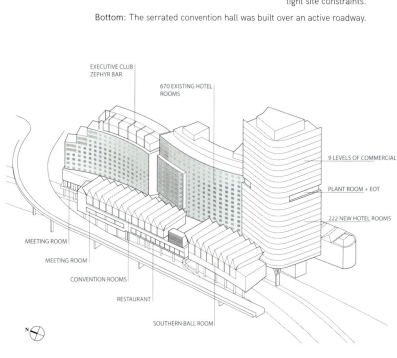

Opposite: Overview of the new 161 Sussex Street, with convention hall in the foreground and new tower to the right. Darling Harbour waterfront promenade is in the foreground.

Top Left: A "faux-heritage" façade was replaced with a plaza that interpolates with actual heritage buildings at the property line.

Top Right: The expanded and reconfigured complex worked within very tight site constraints.

Bottom: The serrated convention hall was built over an active roadway.

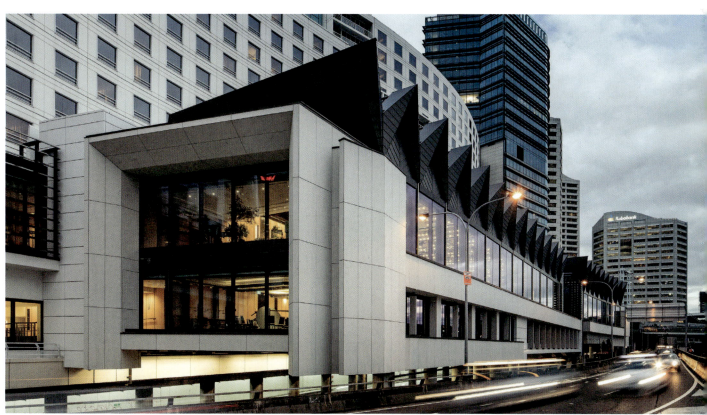

Chaoyang Park Plaza

Beijing, China

Chaoyang Park Plaza is set on the edge of Beijing's largest public park, and has been envisioned as an extension of its green space, moving the typology beyond becoming just another set of box-like towers.

The scheme expresses the "Shanshui City" philosophy, derived from the East Asian perception of a world imbued with an affinity for nature. The design translates natural elements found in classical Shanshui landscape painting into a large sculptural art form that evokes a spiritual resemblance to nature on a city scale. The two main towers reference "the mountains"; the space between them "the valley"; and the low-rise commercial and residential buildings, which are also part of the master plan, as "rocks," forming "the creek."

The towers' façades are composed of single-curved, cold-bent, dark, reflective glass that gives the feeling that the architectural complex is naturally growing out of the ground, rather than having been built, while evoking the aesthetic resonance of a Chinese ink painting. The vertical fins on the exterior emphasize the smoothness and verticality of the towers, while also functioning as an energy-efficient ventilation system, drawing fresh air indoors. At the base of the buildings, a pond works as an air-cooling system in the summertime. Air flows over the water before entering the building through the vertical fins, naturally cooling down the overall temperature of the interior. Thus, the ideal of nature is not only embodied in the aesthetics of the design, but in the innovation and integration of green technology as well.

Historically, Beijing was designed so that there was no definition between the urban and natural space. The city's functionality was interwoven with the natural aesthetics, so that they never felt like they existed as separate entities. The design of Chaoyang Park re-evaluates how industrialization has made us forfeit our natural environment, and reconsiders how Beijing can be imbued with a natural spirit and cultural energy once again. This spirit is reinforced by framed views of nature outside,

Completion Date: August 2017
Height: Tower 1: 129 m (423 ft); Tower 2: 122 m (399 ft)
Stories: Tower 1: 27; Tower 2: 26
Area: 223,009 sq m (2,400,449 sq ft)
Primary Function: Office
Owner: Smart-hero (HK) Investment Development Ltd.
Developer: Beijing Jingfa Properties Co., Ltd.
Architect: MAD Architects (design)
Structural Engineer: CCDI Group (design)
MEP Engineer: Parsons Brinckerhoff Consultants Private Limited (design)
Main Contractor: China Construction Eighth Engineering Division Corp. Ltd.

as well as planted sky lobbies indoors. The top-floor atrium space under a sculpted glass dome provides a particularly airy setting, allowing occupants to gaze out upon the cityscape while standing amidst trees. Several smaller, two-story skyspaces are placed throughout the building, offering moments of repose and serenity.

The Chaoyang Park Plaza complex has become a new public space for locals to meet — simultaneously within nature and in a high-density commercial urban area. Amidst a sea of rectilinear, drab and monotonous tower blocks, Chaoyang Park Plaza's smoothly textured buildings and its meandering interior pathways and serene water features distinguish the project in terms of its spiritual, as well as physical proximity to the park itself. This is particularly well-reinforced at the ground level, where occupants can view the naturalistic site through full-height windows from the comfort of the indoors, where the smooth stones characteristic of Chinese gardens have been brought inside, and serve as benches.

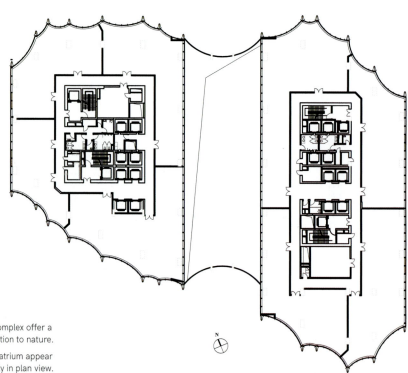

Above: The ground floor and courtyard of the complex offer a serene sense of continuity and connection to nature.

Right: The vertical fin pattern and interconnecting atrium appear prominently in plan view.

Opposite Left: Detail views of the exterior fins show how water-cooled air passes through.

Opposite Top Right: Meandering, bamboo-lined paths reinforce the "mountains-in-the-city" motif.

Opposite Bottom Right: The towers seem to meld with the park's greenery while standing apart from typical residential blocks.

The vertical fins on the exterior emphasize the smoothness and verticality of the towers, while also functioning as an energy-efficient ventilation system, drawing fresh air indoors.

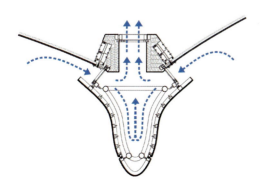

City Center Tower

Taguig City, Philippines

Completion Date: December 2016
Height: 122 m (400 ft)
Stories: 30
Area: 56,820 sq m (611,605 sq ft)
Primary Functions: Office
Owners: Hyopan Land Phils., Inc.; Ticino Holdings Inc.
Developer: W Group
Architects: CAZA (design); Esteban Y. Tan and Gavino L. Tan Partners (architect of record)
Structural Engineer: R.S. Ison & Associates (design)
MEP Engineers: Isagani M. Martinez Consulting Engineers (design); RGJ Electrosystem Consultants Inc. (design)
Main Contractor: Manny SY Associates

The design for the City Center Tower seeks to advance the geometric limits of the standard "core-and-shell" office building by introducing a series of concentric circles within the traditional rectangular structure. The result of this marriage between a parabola and a rectangular volume is an architectural language that mixes structured and free-form shapes, which in turn elicits both efficiency and playfulness. The building satisfies tenant requirements, while at the same time producing a façade populated by a cascading terrace of balconies and bulging metallic mullions that help typically isolated offices maintain visual connections with the outside.

The building pays homage to mid-century Modernist tower design, while looking to push this tradition forward. The design stacks simple rectangular volumes with a gridded surface, creating a tower that floats over its podium. The play between volume and surface dematerializes the size of the tower, while color and shape heighten the sense of fluidity. The solid rectangular shape appears to be sliced open by a parabola. Perforated steel caps give way to the exposed edges of concrete floor plates, while the color of the glass frit pattern that frames each window changes to define the carved void.

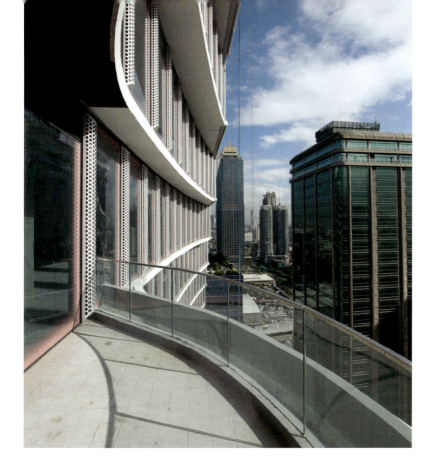

Opposite: The otherwise gridded, rectilinear façade is interrupted by a parabolic curve.

Top Left: Balconies extend where the parabolic "carve" hits the façade.

Middle Left: A colored glass-frit gradient and perforated metal help to articulate the façade's transitions.

Bottom left: While it achieves a dramatic effect, the "carve" in the building reduces floor space and shifts the column grid only slightly.

Bottom right: Viewed from below, the carve appears as a subtle dimple and ridge pattern.

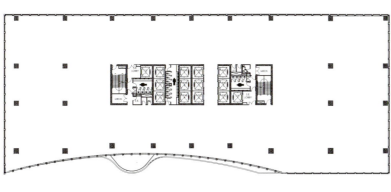

Eq. Tower
Melbourne, Australia

Completion Date: April 2017
Height: 202 m (663 ft)
Stories: 63
Area: 55,487 sq m (597,257 sq ft)
Primary Function: Residential
Developers: ICD Property; Sino-Ocean Land
Architect: Elenberg Fraser (design)
Structural Engineer: Robert Bird Group (design)
MEP Engineer: Murchie Consulting (design)
Project Manager: Sinclair Brook
Main Contractor: Multiplex
Other CTBUH Member Consultant: Altitude Façade Access Consulting Pty Ltd (access); BG&E (façade); Cardno (traffic); Vipac Engineers & Scientists (acoustics)
Other CTBUH Member Supplier: KONE (elevator)

Eq. Tower is cloaked in a glass façade that was designed using a parametric equation, which gives the building its unique form. The result is a slender, and sculptural "bottle-shaped" building that uses an integrated design language between the podium, low-rise and high-rise tower elements. The slick, glazed finish of the tower is achieved with the assistance of enclosed winter gardens, while a sense of movement is achieved through shaping and curved edges. The form of the tower is also textured and punctuated through a series of balcony openings, which taper out as the tower rises.

The seemingly complex form of the tower evolved through simple translation of three varied floor plan arrangements. The beauty manifests from the transitions from one to the other, as convex becomes concave, balcony becomes winter garden and urban becomes panoramic. The various folds in the façade derive from the urban analysis of prevailing solar and wind conditions, and maximizing views and building setbacks.

The building nurtures the city's laneway culture by weaving Melbourne's latest arcade directly through the middle of the building below. At the street scale, it presents a dramatic 6-to-9-meter-high street canopy with a series of glass boxes below announcing the retail, lobby and arcade entrances off A'Beckett Street. The 40-meter podium features activated apartments that conceal the car parking behind, allowing the pink glass tower to reach towards the street by extending its materiality down to the street canopy.

Opposite: The tower's bottle-like shape is derived from a parametric equation.

Top Right: Interior amenity space.

Bottom Left: The ground floor creates an arcade through the middle, carrying on the city's "laneway culture"

Bottom Right: On its lower half, the tower's sleek façade is peeled open to allow for gill-like balconies.

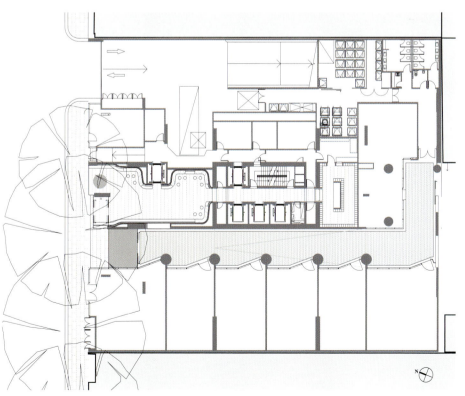

FV

Brisbane, Australia

Completion Date: August 2017
Height: 95 m (312 ft)
Stories: 30
Area: 93,400 sq m (1,005,349 sq ft)
Primary Function: Residential
Owner/Developer: GURNER TM
Architect: Elenberg Fraser (design)
Structural Engineer: Webber Design (design)
MEP Engineer: ADP Consulting (design)
Main Contractor: Multiplex
Other CTBUH Member Consultants: Vipac Engineers & Scientists (wind)

Flatiron, part of the FV (Flatiron + Valley House) development, is a modern re-imagining of New York's iconic skyscraper in the Brisbane context, trading offices for high-end residential use, and substituting stone for a striking bronze mesh surface. Like its predecessor, it holds the corner of Barry Parade and Alfred Street with its iconic curved profile. Sliding metal screens wrap around the façade, recalling the wrap-around verandas of a Queenslander, providing solar protection. The tower has a burnished glow that reflects — both literally and metaphorically — the long rays of afternoon sun that are a hallmark of the capital of the Sunshine State.

The façade is broken up into three distinct sections. The lower band contains full-height glass, with retail shops beyond. The middle band hides the structured parking by way of perforated metal panels arrayed in vibrant colors. The panels are flush to the building surface, picking up the flow of traffic around the "prow" of the building facing the main road, and "bunch up" — begin to pivot outwards — towards the middle of the elevation, marking the entrances to the retail space on Barry Parade and the residential pedestrian and vehicle entrances on Albert Street. The top band consists of the apartment floors, whose repetitive motif is diversified by the constantly changing pattern of screens.

Perhaps most intriguing is the space between these sections - a "cut out" floor above the podium level, makes the upper and bottom halves of the building appear to float independently of each other. The "floating" theme is carried through to the resident facilities at this level, including a horizon infinity pool wrapping the tower's perimeter — complete with a swim-up bar.

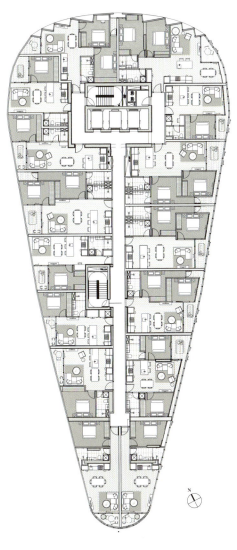

Opposite: The tower invokes the shape of New York's Flatiron Building.

Top: The amenity floor takes advantage of the "point" in plan to create a dramatic space for the outdoor infinity pool.

Bottom left: The smooth exterior's sliding screens make way for a serrated enclosure line, affording intimate and private balconies for the units.

Bottom right: The differing tower and podium façade treatments are separated by a gap indicating the amenities floor.

Guangzhou CTF Finance Centre
Guangzhou, China

Completion Date: October 2016
Height: 530 m (1,739 ft)
Stories: 111
Area: 398,000 sq m (4,284,036 sq ft)
Primary Functions: Hotel / Residential / Office
Owner: Chow Tai Fook Enterprises
Developer: Guangzhou Xinyu Real Estate Development Co., Ltd.
Architects: Kohn Pedersen Fox Associates (design); Leigh & Orange (architect of record); Guangzhou Design Institute (architect of record)
Structural Engineers: Arup (design); Leslie E. Robertson Associates (peer review)
MEP Engineer: WSP | Parsons Brinckerhoff (design)
Project Manager: New World China Land Co. Ltd.
Main Contractor: China State Construction Engineering Corporation
Other CTBUH Member Consultants: ALT Limited (façade); Arup (fire, geotechnical, security); BMT Fluid Mechanics Ltd. (wind); Lighting Planners Associates (lighting); Rider Levett Bucknall (cost); RWDI (wind); Wordsearch (marketing); WSP | Parsons Brinckerhoff (LEED)
Other CTBUH Member Suppliers: CoxGomyl (façade maintenance equipment); Dow Corning Corporation (sealants); Hitachi, Ltd. (elevator)

The CTF Finance Centre is the third-tallest building in China and the seventh-tallest in the world at the time of completion. The design of the tower derives from an efficient integration of program and a sensitive response to urban context. Four major transition points sculpt the form of the tower: from office to residential, to hotel, to crown, and to sky. To accommodate the smaller floor plates required for different programs, the tower sets back at four angled parapets, allowing for lush sky terraces and dramatic skylights.

On the façade, the terracotta panels mask operable vents that allow building users access to fresh air, even at considerable heights where daily use of operable windows would otherwise be impossible. This smart skin lowers the building's energy use by allowing access to fresh unconditioned air and limiting the use of glass, but also by creating shade with angled piers that preserve floor-to-ceiling views while providing generous shading on the exterior. This offers a much more thermally comfortable environment than an all-glass curtain wall. Additionally, the embodied energy of terracotta is far less than aluminum, glass, or steel. Moreover, it can be produced in many locations throughout China, reducing the environmental impact of shipping during the construction process.

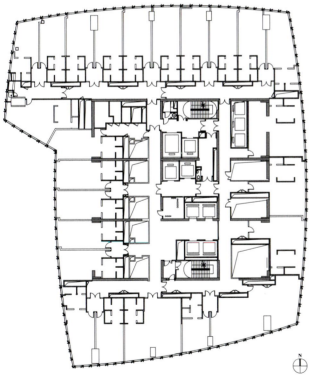

Opposite: The tower provides a distinct point of reference for those wandering Huacheng Square.

Top: The tower steps back as it rises with four angled parapets.

Bottom Left: A typical floor plan shows the effect of the tapering setbacks in the upper half of the tower.

Bottom Right: Detail view of the terracotta panels that provide shade and cover operable vents allowing fresh air.

Hangzhou Gateway

Hangzhou, China

Completion Date: April 2017
Height: 60 m (197 ft)
Stories: 16
Area: 23,650 sq m (254,566 sq ft)
Primary Function: Office
Owner: Hakim Information Technology Co Ltd
Developers: Hakim Information Technology Co Ltd; Hangzhou Xintiandi Group LTD
Architects: Mudi (design); China CUC (design); JDS Architects (design)
Structural Engineer: China CUC (engineer of record)
MEP Engineer: China CUC (engineer of record)

The Hangzhou Gateway creates a connection between two prominent parts of the city. A path under the building establishes and enhances a connection throughout the overall master plan, transforming the building from a hindering wall of office space to a geometry that facilitates circulation; the design of this social amenity gives the building its unique identity. By excavating a portion of the built mass, a diagonal passage is forged through the site, which at the same time articulates a shaded rest area below. The double curved surface of the arch and the graphic pattern of green space invites passersby to meander through. Landscaped terraces on the executive floors, patterned after Chinese terraced rice fields, serve as a recreational park and rainwater retention device, which helps to cool the building.

By carving out voids, the building offers spaces at a human scale with specific qualities. The design engages with Hangzhou's rich and diverse architectural history by reinterpreting the traditional Chinese gateway and reconnecting with the city's tradition of proximity to nature.

The conceptual aspirations of the project began manifesting soon after construction completed, as the excavated arch at ground level has become the natural path for pedestrians meandering through the city block. For the owner Hakim, the "H"-shaped building is an obvious extension of identity that has strengthened and consolidated the brand of the building as its new headquarters.

Opposite: The form of the building seems to twist to the side to sweep pedestrians through the site.

Top left: The façade steps back to support planters and small terraces.

Top right: The "gateway" effect is most obvious in this whimsical arch over a public walkway.

Below: Lines of movement are reinforced by the site paving patterns.

Huangshan Mountain Village

Huangshan, China

A UNESCO World Heritage Site, the region of Huangshan in eastern China borders many ancient villages using traditional architecture and embedded with a deep history. The site of the Huangshan Mountain Village is on a hillside, with a rolling landscape that offers a great view towards Taiping Lake, and the famous Huangshan Mountain. With this in mind, the design team organized the buildings of this residential project in a linked configuration across the southern slope of the lake, so that they form a dynamic relationship with the site and each other, establishing a new type of village landscape: one where architecture becomes nature, and nature becomes architecture.

The design affirms the inherent significance of the site's precious landscape in Huangshan — an area known for its rich, verdant scenery and distinct granite peaks. Considering the cultural and environmental significance of the area, the design team broke down a typical high-rise typology into 10 smaller buildings. Diverse in height and appearance, each has been composed in deference to the local topography, whereby the contour lines of the landscape continue into the shape of each volume, so that they appear to be "growing" out of the mountainous terrain.

Each residential unit has been envisioned as a quiet retreat, boasting generous balconies whose organic lines seem to have been sculpted by wind and water, with no two the same. These extend the interior to the exterior, providing plenty of outdoor space that offers inhabitants unrivaled access to one of China's most famous landscapes. Communal amenities and walking paths encourage residents to wander among the buildings, with the unique floors of each building accessed from these shared social spaces.

Much emphasis has been put on the outdoor space, through the integration of expansive terraces and elevated footbridges, in order to give residents the feeling that they are not just observers of the scenery that surrounds them, but actually immersed within it — creating a dialogue with the mountains, lake and sky.

Completion Date: May 2017
Height: Village 4: 45 m (148 ft); Village 6: 82 m (268 ft); Village 8: 51 m (167 ft)
Stories: Village 4 & 8: 12; Village 6: 22
Area: 14,809 sq m (159,403 sq ft)
Primary Function: Residential
Owner: Greenland Group
Developers: Greenland Group; Wang Weixian
Architect: MAD Architects (design)
Structural Engineer: HSArchitects (design)
MEP Engineer: HSArchitects (design)
Main Contractor: China Construction Eighth Engineering Division (Village 6 & 8)

To achieve the "mountain-like" effect in the buildings, the designers used concrete in an innovative way, which is best demonstrated by the design of the balconies. To achieve their signature organic lines, concrete molds were rationalized in a 3D drawing program, so that repeatable shapes could be designed. But the shapes were smoothed to such a degree that no joints would be visible, giving the appearance of having been sculpted with free-flowing lines that look hand-drawn.

The buildings have been designed to minimize impact on the site topography. Grading and soil dislocation was kept to an absolute minimum, resulting in varied entrance levels for each volume. The incorporation of additional landscaping is intended as an integrative move, recovering the site's original forest in a way that allows the architecture to become a part of the landscape.

Residents have expressed how close they feel with nature, because of the balance of indoor and outdoor space in each unit. They do not feel as if they are living in a high-density environment, but rather, floating over the forest. While much of the project's program is residential, local villagers often come to walk around the elevated bridges to explore the architecture and experience the landscape in a new way.

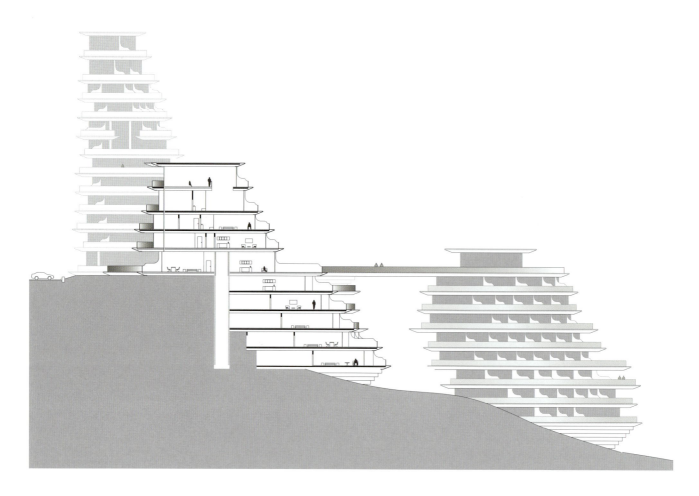

Each building has been composed in deference to the local topography, whereby the contour lines of the landscape continue into the shape of each volume.

Above: The mountainous site presented numerous challenges around grading and access.

Right: Broad balconies extend from the buildings so that residents can enjoy the natural context.

Opposite Top: The mountains themselves were the primary form-giving cues for the design of the towers.

Opposite Bottom: Open spaces within the towers maintain the sense of porosity and connection with the landscape.

Light House

Melbourne, Australia

Completion Date: August 2017
Height: 218 m (715 ft)
Stories: 69
Area: 48,836 sq m (525,666 sq ft)
Primary Function: Residential
Owner/Developer: Hengyi Pacific Pty Ltd
Architect: Elenberg Fraser (design)
Structural Engineer: WSP Group (design)
MEP Engineer: Murchie Consulting (design)
Project Manager: Gallagher Jeffs
Main Contractor: Multiplex Constructions
Other CTBUH Member Consultants: AECOM (façade); Cardno (traffic); Norman Disney & Young (lighting); Winward Structures (civil)
Other CTBUH Member Suppliers: KONE (elevator); Studco Australia Pty Ltd (ceiling)

The Light House has a sculptural presence along the Melbourne skyline. Designed to create a prismatic effect, the skin of the building catches and plays with the sunlight. At certain times of day, its faceted surfaces of glass appear to tumble from the sky, creating a mosaic of color and reflection.

The exterior facets are not merely decorative flourishes, but a considered urban response driven by the marriage of architecture and interior design. They create a form that addresses all aspects; maximizing natural light and ventilation, while carefully balancing privacy and views. Each room is pronounced in the façade, offering the occupant exclusive panoramic views framed by bay windows that look out beyond the immediate context. Together with the orientation of these windows, the interiors create an experience where apartments are as unique as their owners, as every room accentuates a different outlook over the Melbourne landscape.

Appearing to turn on its trajectory, the building has no corners. This three-dimensional kaleidoscope not only twists and undulates on its axis; its façade is a moving object. The effect of constant motion is amplified by the multi-chromic directional paint system applied to the surface, which reflects and draws the building up into the sky.

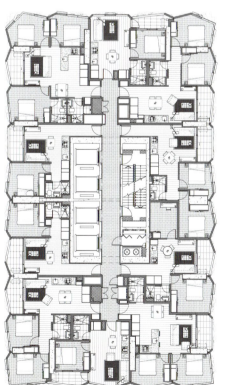

Opposite: The faceted façade dissolves the corners of the building

Top: On the narrow faces, solid-color panels interrupt the glazing.

Bottom Left: The facets provide obliquely angled views from the bedrooms and balconies adjacent to living areas.

Bottom Right: The pool area offers a different interpretation of the tower's crystalline themes.

Lotte World Tower
Seoul, South Korea

Joining the ranks of the world's top 10 tallest buildings, at number 5 at the time of completion, Lotte World Tower offers one of the world's most complex stacks of mixed-use programming. The development is an example of success in the quest to reconcile the programmatic spectrum of the city into a "vertical village." Components within the tower and adjacent podium and connected buildings in the complex include: a transit center, parking, public square, lakeside park, generous indoor public spaces, retail, aquarium, movie theaters, concert hall, food and beverage services, healthcare, roof gardens, conference spaces, office space, hotel, residences, and an observation deck. A network of 121 elevators strings together this array of programs. Over 10,000 people work in the tower, several hundred live in the tower, and an estimated 110,000 visit the complex every day for retail and entertainment.

As a major presence on the Seoul skyline, the building aspires to represent the sweep of Korean artistry and technology, referencing both the country's artistic traditions and its prominence in the technology and electronics sector. The design of the tower offers a strong, simple, and coherent architectural statement, with a sleek and subtle compound curve, emphasized by mullions running from the ground up the tapered body of the building. The curved line of the building references the gracefulness of dynastic periods in Korean art, inspired by traditional Celadon ceramic vases, bowls, and cups.

A coordinated design process was essential for the complex to successfully host such a diversity of interconnected programs. For instance, a 2,036-seat concert hall — normally a feature that would be placed on the ground floor — is placed atop the eighth floor of the retail podium. Careful interior circulation planning ensures that it functions well amidst all the other uses converging on the site. Visual continuity is established through its use of the same curved geometries as the tower's exterior and the scoop of public space at the ground level.

Some tall building critics have observed that the emphasis on verticality may come at a price: the fragmentation of cities into soaring towers divorced from any sense of neighborhood context or community. In the case of Lotte World Tower, the client and project team went to great lengths to frame the development, not as a self-contained city, but as an integrated part of its surroundings, woven into the fabric of Seoul rather than simply affixed to it. With its elevated "sky street" and abundance of vertical and horizontal connections, the development encourages connectivity to the urban environment with its walkability and major public spaces, including a landscaped lakeside park ringed by restaurants and seating and a major roof garden on top of the podium.

The tower reflects sustainability concerns by providing leadership in energy conservation and environmental stewardship. The development generates up to 14.5 percent of its own energy consumption through several innovative features, including wind turbines at the top of the building, an array of photovoltaic cells on the podium roof, and a geothermal mass system that uses the constant earth temperature 200 meters below the site to warm the complex in winter and cool it in summer. In the interest of structural efficiency and material economy, the tower is supported by a combination of the core and eight megacolumns located on the perimeter, in conjunction with a blended lateral force-resisting system, which consists of shear walls, outrigger trusses, and bracing.

Completion Date: April 2017
Height: 555 m (1,819 ft)
Stories: 123
Area: 304,081 sq m (3,273,101 sq ft)
Primary Functions: Hotel / Residential / Office / Retail
Owner/Developer: Lotte Property & Development
Architects: Kohn Pedersen Fox Associates (design); BAUM Architects (architect of record)
Structural Engineers: Leslie E. Robertson Associates (design); Chang Minwoo Structural Consultants (engineer of record); Thornton Tomasetti (peer review)
MEP Engineers: SYSKA Hennessy Group (design); WSP | Parsons Brinckerhoff (peer review)
Main Contractor: LOTTE Engineering & Construction
Other CTBUH Member Consultants: ALT Limited (façade); Aon Fire Protection Engineering (fire); Fortune Shepler Consulting (vertical transportation); Lerch Bates (façade maintenance); Rider Levett Bucknall (cost); RWDI (wind); WSP | Parsons Brinckerhoff (energy concept, LEED)
Other CTBUH Member Supplier: Otis Elevator Company (elevator)

Left: Lobby areas are paneled in smooth, arcing wood surfaces.

Right: Plans showing the tapering effect of the tower as it rises: Prime office floor (bottom), Serviced apartments (second from bottom), Hotel floor (third from bottom), and observation deck at Level 118 (top).

Opposite top: The tallest building in South Korea, the tower dominates the Seoul skyline.

Opposite bottom: The "sky street" links the multiple programs of the complex.

With its elevated "sky street" and abundance of vertical and horizontal connections, the development encourages connectivity to the urban environment with its walkability and major public spaces.

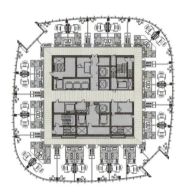
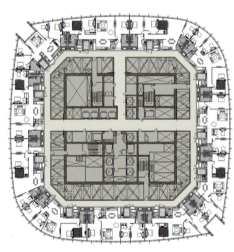
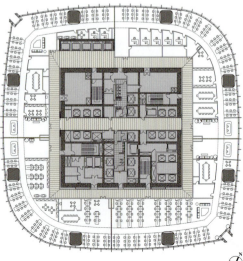

Marina One
Singapore

Marina One, a high-density, mixed-use building complex in the heart of Singapore's new Marina Bay financial district, complements the Urban Redevelopment Authority's (URA) vision of making Singapore a "City in a Garden." Marina One comprises three high-rise buildings, which accommodate office, residential and retail functions. Most strikingly, they contain an abundance of communal green space, with the multitude of functional spaces strategically paired to promote connectivity and community within the green areas.

The office tower features sky gardens and "high-density floors" on levels 28 and 29, making them the largest grade-A office floors in Singapore. These are occupied by the trading operations of Mitsubishi UFJ Financial Group (MUFG). Restaurants and cafés, a fitness club, a food court, a large supermarket, and event spaces are located on several public terraces, creating a vibrant communal destination.

While the outer faces of the towers strictly follow the city grid, the inner faces create a free-formed three-dimensional space. The organic shape of the building complex, with its louvers, and the generous planting within, contribute to an improvement of the microclimate and increase biodiversity. Inspired by Asian paddy field terraces, the green center formed by the towers — with its multi-story three-dimensional gardens — contains diverse tropical flora and creates a new habitat. The color scheme of the interior and the building façade features calm and earthy bronze shades to support the harmonious atmosphere.

The orientation of the buildings around the central space constitutes a reinterpretation and scaling-up of the classic courtyard-building model that has served warm-weather communities for generations. The visual and sensory excitement results from extrapolating this comfortable model to an urban high-rise context; it comes from the realization that tall buildings can not only be "green," but can also be as intimate and subtly layered as they are physically massive.

Completion Date: December 2017
Height: Tower 1: 225 m (740 ft); Tower 2 & 3: 141 m (462 ft)
Stories: Tower 1, 2 & 3: 34
Primary Function: Tower 1: Office; Tower 2 & 3: Residential
Owner/Developer: M+S Pte Ltd
Architects: ingenhoven architects (design); Architects 61 (architect of record)
Structural Engineers: KK Lim & Associates Pte Ltd (design - Tower 1); Magnusson Klemencic Associates (design - Tower 1); Beca Carter Hollings & Ferner (SE Asia) Pte. Ltd. (design - Tower 2 & 3/engineer of record - Tower 1)
MEP Engineer: Beca Carter Hollings & Ferner (SE Asia) Pte. Ltd. (design)
Project Managers: UEM Sunrise Berhad; Mapletree Project Management Pte Ltd
Main Contractors: Hyundai Engineering & Construction; GS E&C
Other CTBUH Member Consultants: Arup (façade, lighting); Windtech Consultants Pty Ltd (wind)
Other CTBUH Member Supplier: Schindler (elevator)

The interaction between the geometry of the buildings, penetrated by air wells and slots, and the garden facilitates natural ventilation and generates an agreeable microclimate. Within the Marina One site, the largest public landscaped area in the Marina Bay Central Business District, recreation space close to nature is provided. The usable area of the green space represents 125 percent of the original site surface area.

The compact and efficient design is complemented by energy-saving ventilation systems, highly effective external solar screening devices, and glazing that reduces solar radiation into the building. Direct connections to four of Singapore's six Mass Rapid Transport (MRT) lines, bus stops, bicycle parking facilities, and electro-mobile charging stations ensure that exhaust emissions caused by private transport are significantly reduced. Centrally provided recycled water is used for toilet flushing, while a rainwater harvesting system reduces further water consumption. In addition, carefully positioned photovoltaic cells make use of the sun's energy.

Inspired by Asian paddy field terraces, the green center formed by the towers – with its multi-story three-dimensional gardens – contains diverse tropical flora and creates a new habitat.

Opposite Top: The louver pattern continues to the roof deck.

Opposite Bottom: The undulating louvers form a bowl-like garden space between the towers.

Top: The public realm at the project's center is enhanced by plantings, increasing the site's green plot ratio to 125 percent.

Bottom Left: A section view indicates of the "valley" between the towers and the locations of greenery throughout.

Bottom Right: The curvaceous office tower contrasts with its rectilinear residential neighbor.

Namdaemun Office Building
Seoul, South Korea

Completion Date: January 2017
Height: 98 m (322 ft)
Stories: 14
Area: 5,779 sq m (62,205 sq ft)
Primary Function: Office
Owner/Developer: Heungkuk Life Insurance Co., Ltd.
Architect: Mecanoo Architecten (design)
Structural Engineer: Donglim Co Ltd (engineer of record)
MEP Engineer: Donglim Co Ltd (engineer of record)
Main Contractor: Donglim Construction Co Ltd

The Namdaemun Market is the oldest and largest market in South Korea and has become an important 24-hour destination for trade and a popular tourist attraction. The market's history and regional traditions informed the design for a contemporary office building. Maximizing land allocation, the slim Namdaemun building sits on a corner plot opposite the market. Its restrained, monochromatic appearance acts as a counterbalance to the colorful frenzy of the market's nonstop activity.

The building's defining feature is its stark black façade of various linear patterns. The role of the frame extends beyond decoration, continuously creating different atmospheres, filtering incoming light and making shadows across the interior spaces. The façade is composed of varying prefabricated aluminum panels, placed to create a rhythm that defines the building.

The relationship between the building and its surroundings reflects the passing of time, changing from day to night. During the day, the façade material reflects the sunlight, whereas at night, the building glows from within, revealing its characteristic façade pattern to the market and beyond.

Due to site constraints, the tower footprint is rather small, and with its 230-square-meter-per-level occupancy, it allows for natural ventilation. The glass façade components are designed to avoid extreme solar gains coming from east and west. Solar panels on the rooftop provide hot water for the entire building, making it totally independent from street-level gas distribution pipelines.

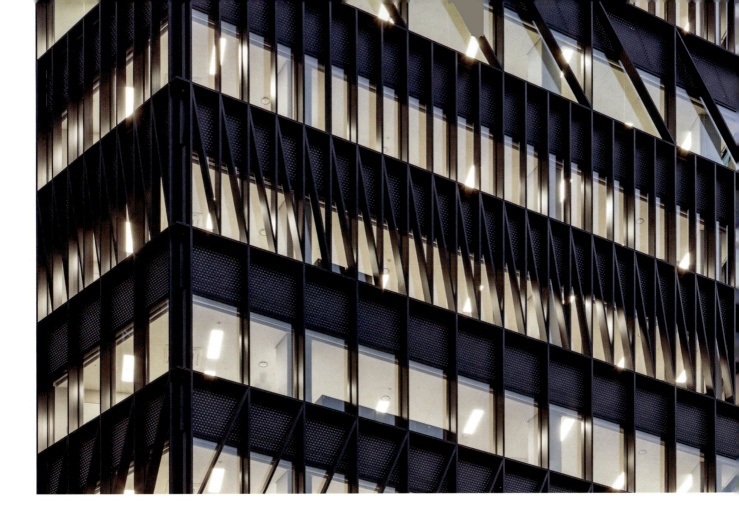

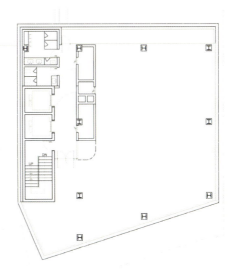

Opposite: The building's black paneling and angled façade braces emphasize its chamfered corner and strong profile.

Above: On closer inspection, three angles of inclination are visible on the alternating rows of diagonals.

Bottom Left: The understated building acts as a counterbalance to the colorful frenzy of the adjacent market.

Bottom Right: A typical office floor plan showing all core and service functions along one edge.

Ping An Finance Center

Shenzhen, China

The Shenzhen Ping An Finance Center (PAFC) is a transit-integrated supertall building occupying a major node in the increasingly connected megacity of Hong Kong-Shenzhen-Guangzhou. It is the second-tallest building in China and the fourth-tallest in the world at the time of completion. Its stretched, obelisk-like shape is streamlined with continuously tapering corners for aerodynamic performance, visual effect, and space efficiency.

As the hub of Shenzhen's central business district, PAFC plugs into a vast three-dimensional network of subways, pedestrian footbridges, and street-level connections. Notwithstanding its density (it has a floor-area-to-site ratio of more than 20-to-1), the impact of the project at street level is surprisingly humane. Sheltered arcades, broad canopies, and human-scale elements create a walkable and vibrant atmosphere.

Given the tower's dominant presence on the skyline, the primary design objective was to create a feeling of lightness. PAFC's design came to symbolize its owner's image and title — "Ping An" is the combination of the Chinese characters for "peaceful" and "safety," while evoking the entrepreneurial spirit of Shenzhen. The balance between stability and aspiration led to the metaphor of a tower pulled taught by opposing forces of gravity and lift, uniquely in equilibrium.

The streamlined shape of the tower was designed specifically to optimize wind performance while creating an efficient and regular interior. The long vertical contours of the aerodynamic form are traced by eight stainless-steel columns, which converge to a point at the tower's apex. Stainless-steel piers are drawn vertically up the façade, enhancing the tower's stretched form. Stone-clad "talons" anchor the base of the columns to create the dynamic tension of an object ready to "take flight." The building features the largest stainless-steel façade in the world to date, to preserve its appearance in the salty coastal atmospheric conditions of Shenzhen. Jet mist granite, hand-selected from Virginia for its beauty and durability, complements the steel and glass portions of the façade.

The tower is predicted to sustain an 18.25 percent energy savings beyond ASHRAE standards, and a 46 percent

Completion Date: December 2016
Height: 599 m (1,965 ft)
Stories: 115
Area: 459,187 sq m (4,942,648 sq ft)
Primary Functions: Office
Owner/Developer: Ping An Financial Center Construction & Development
Architects: Kohn Pedersen Fox Associates (design); CCDI Group (architect of record)
Structural Engineers: Thornton Tomasetti (design); CCDI Group (engineer of record); China Academy of Building Research (peer review)
MEP Engineers: J. Roger Preston Limited (design); CCDI Group (engineer of record)
Main Contractor: China Construction First Group Construction & Development Co., Ltd.
Other CTBUH Member Consultants: ALT Limited (façade); Arup (façade, LEED, sustainability); Beijing Fortune Lighting System Engineering Co., Ltd. (lighting); Fortune Shepler Consulting (vertical transportation); Jones Lang LaSalle, Inc. (property management); Lighting Planners Associates (lighting); Rider Levett Bucknall (cost); RWDI (wind); Sandu Environmental Signage (way finding)
Other CTBUH Member Suppliers: Dow Corning Corporation (sealants); Grace Construction Products (fire proofing); Hilti AG (cladding); KONE (elevator); Otis Elevator Company (elevator); Outokumpu (cladding); Schindler (elevator); Shenyang Yuanda Aluminium Industry Engineering Co.,Ltd. (cladding)

annual savings in energy costs over a conventionally constructed commercial office building of the same scale. This is accomplished partly by using heat recovery systems (enthalpy wheels), ice storage, and water recovery systems, and regenerative lift drives. Notably, PAFC utilizes Internet of Things technology — "smart building" sensors which monitor outdoor and indoor environments, with actuators to dynamically adapt the HVAC, lighting, and façade shading systems. In addition, 428 sensors are deployed as part of its structural health monitoring system, to measure the tower's horizontal displacement, vertical settlement, and stress on key structural elements.

Standing directly at the intersection of Shenzhen's primary east-west and north-south planning axes, which also serve as the city's main arteries linking Shenzhen to the wider Pearl River Delta region by high-speed rail, PAFC plugs seamlessly into a vast, mostly below-ground transit network. At the same time, the project preserves the ground level for pedestrian experiences — tree-lined lanes, sheltered arcades, and street cafés.

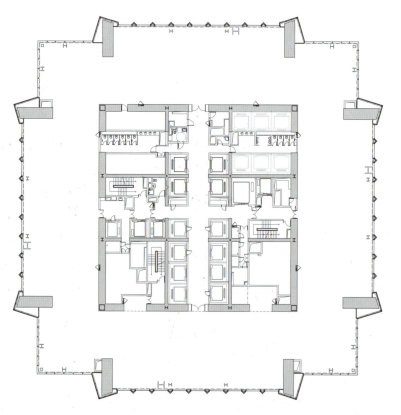

Ping An Finance Center features the largest stainless façade in the world to date, to preserve its appearance in the salty coastal atmospheric conditions of Shenzhen.

Opposite Top: Office furnishings and fit-outs align to the many view angles available from the building.

Opposite Bottom: A typical floor plan demonstrates the role of the megacolumns in defining the façade.

Above: Overhead view emphasizes the diamond-tipped crown and its relationship with the overall skin of the building.

Left: Horizontal louvers define striations in what is otherwise a predominantly vertically oriented façade.

Poly International Plaza
Beijing, China

Poly International Plaza is the first structure of its kind — incorporating a four-story super-diagrid frame without perimeter columns. Through its technical and spatial innovation, it redefines the speculative high-rise office experience, offering a unique, environmentally high-performance workplace, in contrast to the typical center-core office building. The project site comprises a main tower and two smaller supporting towers positioned along a direct axis to the center of Beijing, and acts as a central focus in the landscape. The elliptical footprint of the three towers frees the buildings from the rigid geometry of the adjoining urban fabric, and invites the community into the site by fluidly merging the landscaped public parks and open spaces on either side. Walls and planted mounds establish a sculpted site topography that defines diverse spaces in the landscape, from separate arrival courts to shared strolling gardens, which unfold and evolve as one moves through the site.

Inspired by Chinese paper lanterns, the design of the main tower's exterior is formed by a continuous diagrid pattern, with a jewel-like faceted façade that reflects light and the urban environment. The design embodies a deep integration of architecture and structure, achieving a strong daylight-filled visual openness, due to the long spans enabled by the diagrid frame. To address climatic and air quality challenges, an actuated double skin envelops the interior. The interstitial space between the inner and outer envelopes creates daylit communal areas that accommodate meetings and foster social interaction, while establishing connectivity between floors. At the building's narrow ends, the interstitial space expands to create two 29-story atria, which pull in daylight and harness expansive downtown views. Elevator lobbies open directly toward the atria, providing geographic orientation by way of external views.

The long-span structural design not only opens up the interior, creating a column-free work environment, but also employs a highly sustainable architectural/mechanical approach to address Beijing's climatic and air quality challenges. Mechanically, this semi-climatized interstitial space mediates exterior temperature extremes, reducing the overall building energy consumption by 23 percent and carbon emissions by 18 percent. Many advanced analytical studies were performed on this custom structure to validate the design. Scaled testing of prototypical portions of the diagrid system was performed to validate its behavior and performance under dynamic loads.

An insulative layer at the exterior of the building acts as a thermal blanket during the coldest winter period. Interior operable blinds provide glare control under all conditions and reduce incoming solar radiation. The inherent nature of the double façade greatly reduces noise transmission from the exterior. Floor-to-ceiling glass provides the maximum possible connection to the outdoors while maintaining comfort, playing a substantial role in building user satisfaction, comfort and productivity.

The progressive design of the interior spaces features communal lounges, meeting rooms, a bamboo roof garden, open stairs, and high atriums that encourage interaction and create a sense of connectivity among those who work in the building.

Completion Date: July 2016
Height: 161 m (529 ft)
Stories: 31
Area: 61,223 sq m (658,999 sq ft)
Primary Function: Office
Owner/Developer: Poly Real Estate Group Co. Ltd.
Architects: Skidmore, Owings & Merrill LLP (design); Beijing Institute of Architectural Design (architect of record)
Structural Engineer: Skidmore, Owings & Merrill LLP (engineer of record)
MEP Engineer: WSP Flack + Kurtz (design)
Main Contractor: China Construction Third Engineering Bureau Co., Ltd.
Other CTBUH Member Consultants: Edgett Williams Consulting Group Inc. (vertical transportation); Schindler (vertical transportation); SWA Group (landscape); WSP Built Ecology (sustainability)
Other CTBUH Member Supplier: Schindler (elevator)

Poly International Plaza is the first structure of its kind – incorporating a four-story super-diagrid frame without perimeter columns.

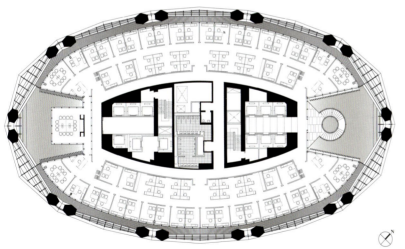

Opposite Top: The main tower builds on the elliptical form of the two smaller towers in the complex.

Opposite Bottom: The folded geometry of the diagrid exoskeleton carries down to the the ground-level entrance.

Top: The building seems to hover above its light-filled lobby.

Bottom Left: A typical floor plan shows the location of voids, affording interior views of the diagrid frame.

Bottom Right: A spiral staircase visually orients occupants through the void toward the outer grid and affords lines of sight into adjacent office spaces.

Raffles City Hangzhou

Hangzhou, China

Completion Date: March 2017
Height: 258 m (845 ft)
Stories: Tower 1: 60; Tower 2: 59
Area: 187,119 sq m (2,014,132 sq ft)
Primary Functions: Tower 1: SOHO/Serviced apartments/Office/Retail; Tower 2: Residential/Hotel/Office/Retail
Owner/Developer: CapitaLand China
Architects: UNStudio (design); China United Engineering Corporation (architect of record)
Structural Engineer: Arup (design)
MEP Engineer: Shanghai SAIYO Construction Engineering Co.,Ltd (design); Arup (design)
Main Contractor: Shanghai Construction No.4 (Group) Co., Ltd.
Other CTBUH Member Consultants: Access Advisors Ltd. (façade maintenance); Arup (fire, LEED); Davis Langdon (quantity surveyor); Davis Langdon & Seah (cost); Meinhardt (façade); Permasteelisa Group (façade); Shenyang Yuanda Aluminium Industry Engineering Co.,Ltd. (façade)
Other CTBUH Member Supplier: Hilti AG (cladding)

Situated in Qianjiang New Town, this mixed-use development has become a major landmark along the green axis of the city's new CBD. A rich mix of 24/7 functions occupies the substantial site, within two streamlined towers set atop a striking podium and landscaped plaza. The high-rises contain residential units, Grade A offices, the Conrad Hotel and a rooftop helipad; while the six-story podium accommodates retail, restaurants, leisure facilities and parking, and has a direct underground connection to the metro.

Situated diagonally opposite the civic center, the corner site borders both the urban built-up context and green axis/city park that connects West Lake to the Qiantang River. The twisted form of the two towers can be interpreted as bending to recognize the vibrant urban context in one direction and the legendary landscape of Hangzhou in the other.

The plan is organized as two diagonal and intersecting figure-of-eights. The main entrance to the south appears as a prominent gateway from the city park and civic center. A terraced plaza merges the site with the green surroundings, where four distinct landscape courtyards flow from the periphery of each quadrant to the inner atrium, forming the main access points and external courtyards of the podium. The north and south entrances lead visitors towards the inner atrium. The east and west nodes spiral downwards into outdoor sunken plazas.

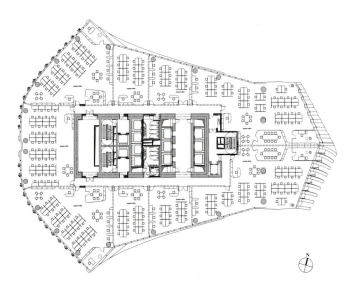

Opposite: The expressionistic, amorphous towers look remarkably different depending on the view angle.

Left: Floor plans from different heights in Tower 1 demonstrate the range of spaces accommodated within. From bottom, Level 11 - office; Level 34 - SOHO apartment; and Level 58 - SOHO apartment.

Top Right: A gateway bridge with a shimmering metal underside draws visitors down the landscaped stairs into the retail area.

Bottom Right: The significant splaying of the towers from the centerline is most obvious when viewed from above.

Tencent Seafront Towers
Shenzhen, China

Considering the rapid growth of mobile and online services in both the domestic and global market, Tencent, one of China's leading internet companies, needed a new headquarters building with a unique, distinctive appearance and an extremely versatile workplace with easily reconfigurable spaces.

The Tencent Seafront Towers were constructed in a special zone of Shenzhen, the Software Industry Base. The project represents a new vision of the workplace, one that is more interconnected and flexible than hierarchical. The north and south towers are connected by three sections of joined floors, which fully embody the characteristics of the essential connection of the Internet era — the "Link."

These "linked towers" symbolically represent the links that connect each distant corner of the Internet, in the same sense that employees of Tencent are linked together through skybridges, more effectively than would be possible in a single, traditional high-rise building. As symbols of Tencent's values, the three linking bridges — Cultural Link, Health Link, and Knowledge Link — contain shared functions of the North and South towers. These shared functions help to promote opportunities for closer communication and interaction. These humanized design elements, optimized for learning, innovation and creative work, also fully reflect the characteristics of products provided by Tencent to their customers.

The Culture Link is the closest to the ground level and supports a range of activities and public spaces. It starts on the first floor and houses the lobby and reception area, meeting rooms, retail, an exhibition space, a cantilevered auditorium and restaurants. There is a lower, two-story section and an upper, three-story section. Connecting these two sections creates on open atrium that enhances the connectivity between the two buildings, by way of a smooth, continuous space.

The Health Link begins at Floor 21 and features a running track, gym, full-sized basketball court, stadium, and more (including a swimming pool at the top of the north tower). There is also a juice bar and cafe. The Health Link is prominently at the heart of the campus — for Tencent, the health of the employee is key to the health of the company. Healthy food options in dining areas, exercise and fitness facilities, and even on-site doctors and therapists all combine to create an integrative approach to health and wellness.

Employee learning is one of Tencent's critical values. Thus, the third Link starts on Floor 34, symbolically at the top or "head" of the tower, and emphasizes knowledge. There are rooftop gardens, conference rooms, an upscale dining hall, a training center called Tencent University, as well as meditation rooms and a library.

"Sustainable design" in its broadest interpretation refers to the integration of the sustainability of environment, economy, and society, which serves to fulfill the users' goals and needs. Tencent Seafront Towers adopt sustainable design techniques to achieve energy savings, emission reductions, water conservation and other objectives, thereby providing a healthy and comfortable working environment. According to the guiding ideology of suiting local conditions, economic feasibility, and technical maturity, the design mainly uses passive strategies while supplementing the proactive strategy of economic rationality. Specific methods include the optimized orientation of buildings; the control of the window-to-wall ratio; the implementation of a high-performance curtain wall; the targeted use of natural ventilation; platform ventilation and heat recovery systems; high-efficiency lamps; water-saving sanitary fixtures; and rainwater recycling. The total effect of these strategies is to reduce annual energy consumption by approximately 20 percent and water use by 50 percent, compared to a conventional project of the same size.

Completion Date: 2017
Height: Tower 1: 246 m (806 ft); Tower 2: 195 m (639 ft)
Stories: Tower 1: 50; Tower 2: 38
Primary Function: Office
Owner/Developer: Tencent Technology Company Limited
Architects: NBBJ (design); Tongji Architectural Design (Group) Co., Ltd. (design); Shenzhen Tongji Architects (design)
Structural Engineers: AECOM (design); Tongji Architectural Design (Group) Co., Ltd. (design); Shenzhen Tongji Architects (design)
MEP Engineers: Shenzhen Tongji Architects (design); Tongji Architectural Design (Group) Co., Ltd. (design); WSP Group (design)
Main Contractor: China Construction Second Engineering Bureau Ltd.
Other CTBUH Member Consultants: Arup (traffic); Atkins (LEED); Gensler (interiors); Inhabit Group (façade); NBBJ (landscape); Thornton Tomasetti (façade); WT Partnership (cost)
Other CTBUH Member Supplier: Armstrong World Industries (ceiling–Tower 1); Schindler (elevator)

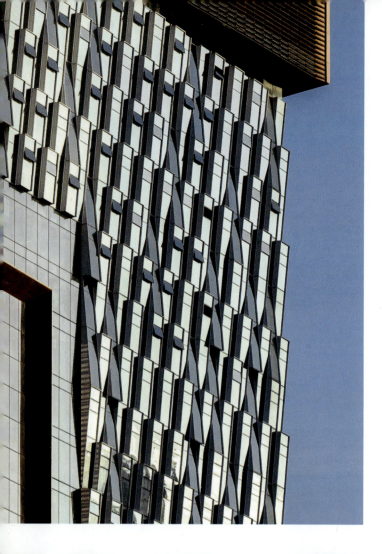

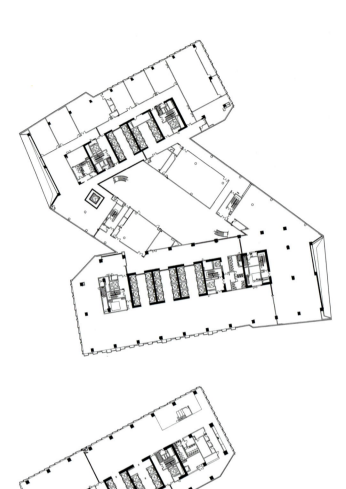

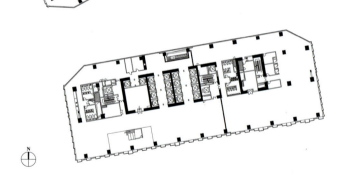

Top Left: The hooded façade modules of the standard office floors contrast with the red-louvered protrusion and smooth-glass indentation indicating the location of two of the three "link" structures connecting the two towers.

Top Right: Plans for Floor 35 (top), "The Knowledge Link" and 15 (bottom) show the two towers' configurations on connected and separated floors.

Left: Multi-floor skybridge "links" create opportunities for collaborative elements, like this communicating stair.

Opposite Top: The Health Link, located at Level 22, includes extensive fitness facilities, including a climbing wall.

Opposite Bottom: The Knowledge Link at level 35 contains green spaces for brainstorming and quiet contemplation.

The project represents a new vision of the workplace, one that is more interconnected and flexible than hierarchical.

The Tembusu

Singapore

Completion Date: August 2016
Height: 59 m (194 ft)
Stories: 18
Area: 29,920 sq m (322,056 sq ft)
Primary Function: Residential
Owner/Developer: Wing Tai Holdings Limited Singapore
Architect: ARC Studio Architecture & Urbanism (design)
Structural Engineer: P & T Consultants Pte Ltd (design)
MEP Engineer: United Projects Consultants Pte Ltd (design)
Main Contractor: Shimizu Corporation
Other CTBUH Member Consultant: Rider Levett Bucknall (quantity surveyor)

The client's objective was to create both an ecological and a community project. As such, the architecture is closely integrated with the landscape and water features. The strategies deployed create a close connection with nature at varying scales. The project wraps gardens on the building façade to create the sensation of low-rise apartment living's proximity to nature. From the small window and balcony gardens, to the large sky gardens and environmental decks, nature is freely accessible, complex and varied. The planting is physically extended on the façade through delicate thread-like filaments that serve as supports for epiphytes and creepers to hold on, bringing landscape closer to each residential unit.

The "thick skin" of greenery surrounding the towers is an environmental mediator as well as a powerful expression of the project's identity. To further support the ecological community underpinnings of the project, the rainwater drainage system is integrated into the landscape, so it that forms a water remediation system that captures, filters and integrates water throughout.

The wellness of inhabitants was also considered during the design process. Building blocks are aligned to face the north and south directions to maximize solar exposure, with thoughtfully organized layouts, in order to maximize distant views for the units. Through the landscaping, sky pods, sky links between buildings, and the herb garden on the 18th floor, an additional 6,000 square meters of communal space has been created, much of it at height.

Opposite: The towers are wrapped by elevated walkways, facilitating easy transfers and pleasant strolling for inhabitants.

Top: Extensive hanging greenery adds to the forest-canopy-like atmosphere of the complex.

Bottom: A perimeter bioswale and internal ponds provide respite from the surrounding urbanized environment.

Tsinghua Ocean Center

Shenzhen, China

Completion Date: December 2016
Height: 63 m (207 ft)
Stories: 14
Area: 15,880 sq m (170,930 sq ft)
Primary Function: Education
Owner: Graduate School at Shenzhen, Tsinghua University
Developer: Bureau of Public Works of Shenzhen Municipality
Architect: OPEN Architecture (design)
Structural Engineer: Shenzhen Institute of Building Research Co., Ltd (design)
MEP Engineer: Shenzhen Institute of Building Research Co., Ltd (design)
Main Contractor: Sichuan Huashi Group Co., LTD

The Ocean Center is a laboratory and office building designed for the newly established deep-ocean research base of Tsinghua University. As a critique of the "instant university towns" mushrooming in China, which are often over-scaled and lacking in humanistic considerations, this building actively engages the campus life with an open and welcoming attitude. Abundant public spaces are injected into this vertical campus building, transforming a research center into a lively social hub where intelligent minds meet and interdisciplinary exchanges happen naturally.

The architectural language of the building is born out of the local climate, which is warm and humid most of the year. Numerous semi-outdoor spaces regulate the building's micro-climate, while the thin-slab typology maximizes natural daylight and ventilation. Exterior shading devices efficiently restrict the heat gain while offering good views from the lab and offices.

Mechanical rooms and shafts for the laboratories, along with the vertical structural cores, form the vertical infrastructure at both ends of the building; various mechanical systems are then delivered horizontally through the ceilings of the central corridor to different laboratories. This configuration leaves the research floors open and allows for flexible repartition if other changes are needed in the future.

1. Experimental Cistern
2. Equipment Room
3. Lobby
4. Exhibition Hall
5. Convenient Store
6. Multimedia Space
7. Lecture Hall
8. Conference Room
9. Reference Room
10. Public Floor
11. Labs
12. Roof Garden

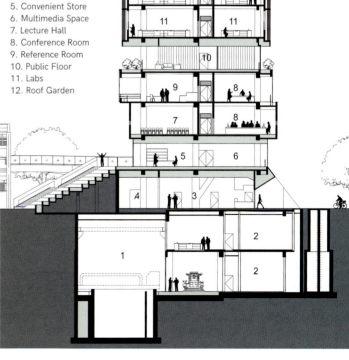

Opposite: The long side has a strong "open" face, while the shorter side has a more opaque character.

Top: Interpolating stairs and landings provide plenty of opportunities for interaction.

Bottom Left: The extruded and recessed boxes, as well as varying façade treatments, pack a great deal of variety into a compact building.

Bottom Right: The diversity of programming and spatial conditions is expressed in section.

Zhengzhou Greenland Central Plaza

Zhengzhou, China

Completion Date: 2017
Height: 284 m (931 ft)
Stories: 63
Primary Functions: Office
Owner/Developer: Greenland Group
Architects: von Gerkan, Marg and Partners Architects (design); Tongji Architectural Design (Group) Co., Ltd. (architect of record)
Structural Engineers: Schlaich Bergermann und Partner (design); Tongji Architectural Design (Group) Co., Ltd. (engineer of record)
MEP Engineers: Parsons Brinckerhoff Consultants Private Limited (design); Tongji Architectural Design (Group) Co., Ltd. (engineer of record)
Main Contractors: Zhongtian Construction Group Co., Ltd.; Shanghai Construction No.2 Group Co., Ltd.
Other CTBUH Member Suppliers: Armstrong World Industries (ceiling); KONE (elevator)

The Central Plaza project, together with the East Railway Station, forms the urban spine of the Zhengzhou Integrated Transportation Hub, a new mixed-use urban quarter in the constantly growing capital of China's Henan Province. Like a city gate, the twin towers are positioned along the central axis of the station. This urban axis is executed as a generous public park flowing through the gate defined by the twin towers.

The Grade-A office spaces are enriched by special meeting, communication and break areas in the double-height sky lobbies, which provide open-air terraces. The tower's top atria attract people by way of three-story "Sky Commerce" centers, offering exclusive restaurants, shops and spa.

The shape of the buildings is a reference to the dynamic of the Traffic Hub and to the Yellow River, whose winding river bed passes Zhengzhou. The morphology of the river shapes the outlines of the floor plans, but at the same time is turned into the vertical: the massive volume of the towers is gently meandering upwards, shaping several setbacks and generating a vivid and varied sculpture. The leftover cavities are used as semi-public multi-floor spaces for meeting, communication, food & beverage, culture and leisure. The unique functional extension of the program is visually expressed by the neatly embedded lobbies.

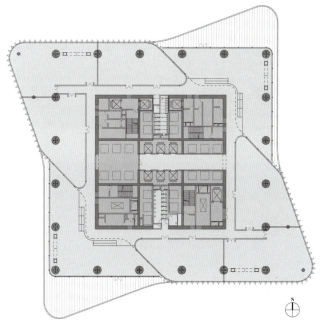

Opposite: The massive volume of the towers gently meanders upwards, shaping several setbacks and generating a vivid and varied sculpture.

Above: The tower pair bookends a long, grand promenade from the city's East Railway Station.

Left: A sky lobby at level 16, showing large communal spaces and exterior terraces.

Top Right: View upwards through a corner void near the tower crown.

Bottom Right: A translucent corner piece, with void beyond, marks the top of one of the towers.

1 | 1 Parramatta Square
Parramatta, Australia

Completion Date: January 2017
Height: 65 m (213 ft)
Stories: 16
Area: 28,362 sq m (305,286 sq ft)
Primary Functions: Office / Education / Retail
Owner/Developer: Charter Hall
Architect: Architectus (design)
Structural Engineer: Arcadis (engineer of record)
MEP Engineer: WSP (engineer of record)
Project Manager: Charter Hall
Main Contractor: John Holland Group Pty Ltd
Other CTBUH Member Consultants: Architectus (planning); Aspect Studios (landscape)

2 | 177 Pacific Highway
Sydney, Australia

Completion Date: August 2016
Height: 125 m (410 ft)
Stories: 32
Area: 45,455 sq m (489,274 sq ft)
Primary Function: Office
Owner/Developer: Suntec Real Estate Investment Trust
Architect: Bates Smart (design)
Structural Engineer: Arcadis (engineer of record)
MEP Engineer: AECOM (engineer of record)
Project Manager: Leighton Properties
Main Contractor: CPB Contractors
Other CTBUH Member Consultants: AECOM (acoustics, fire, sustainability, traffic); Aspect Studios (landscape); Inhabit Group (façade maintenance); JBA Urban Planning Consultants Pty Ltd (urban planner)
Other CTBUH Member Supplier: Yuanda (façade maintenance equipment)

3 | Aquaria Grande Tower B
Mumbai, India

Completion Date: July 2016
Height: 164 m (538 ft)
Stories: 41
Area: 18,500 sq m (199,132 sq ft)
Primary Function: Residential
Owner/Developers: The Wadhwa Group
Architect: James Law Cybertecture International (design)
Structural Engineer: Mahimtura Consultants Pvt. Ltd. (design)
MEP Engineer: MEP Consulting Engineers (design)
Main Contractor: The Wadhwa Group

4 | Chinachem Central
Hong Kong, China

Completion Date: Central I: November 2016; Central II: July 2017
Height: Central I: 134 m (438 ft); Central II: 138 m (452 ft)
Stories: 27
Area: Central I: 7,593 sq m (81,730 sq ft); Central II: 8,587 sq m (92,430 sq ft sq ft)
Primary Functions: Office / Retail
Owner/Developer: Chinachem Group
Architect: Dennis Lau & Ng Chun Man Architects & Engineers (HK) Ltd. (DLN) (design)
Structural Engineer: AECOM (design)
MEP Engineer: Man Lick Engineering and Trading Co. Ltd. (design); Skyforce Engineering Limited (design - Central II)
Main Contractor: China Overseas

5 | Golden Eagle International Shopping Center
Nanjing, China

Completion Date: December 2016
Height: 220 m (722 ft)
Stories: 44
Area: 183,291 sq m (1,972,928 sq ft)
Primary Functions: Office / Hotel / Retail
Owner/Developer: Nanjing Golden Eagle International Group Co., Ltd.
Architect: Lab Architecture Studio (design)
Structural Engineer: Jiangsu Provincial Architectural D&R Institute Ltd (design)
MEP Engineer: Jiangsu Provincial Architectural D&R Institute Ltd (design)
Main Contractor: China Nulcear Industry Huaxing Construction Co., Ltd

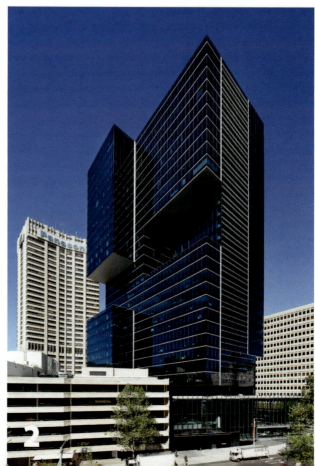

6 | Gravity Tower
Melbourne, Australia

Completion Date: July 2017
Height: 99 m (323 ft)
Stories: 30
Area: 15,055 sq m (162,051 sq ft)
Primary Function: Residential
Developer: Blue Earth Group
Architect: Plus Architecture (design)
Structural Engineer: Mordue Engineering (engineer of record)
MEP Engineer: Lucid Consulting Australia (engineer of record)
Project Manager: Fusion Project Management
Main Contractor: Hamilton Marino
Other CTBUH Member Consultant: Olsson Fire & Risk (fire)

7 | Green Residences
Hangzhou, China

Completion Date: 2017
Height: 102 m (335 ft)
Stories: 33
Total Area: 189,500 sq m (2,039,761 sq ft)
Primary Function: Residential
Owner/Developer: Hangzhou Jiahe Real Estate GmbH
Architect: Peter Ruge Architekten (design)
Structural Engineer: Zhejiang Zhongshe Engineering Design Co. Ltd. (design)
MEP Engineers: Zhejiang Zhongshe Engineering Design Co. Ltd. (design)
Main Contractor: Zhejiang Kun hung Construction Co., Ltd.

8 | IM tower
Tokyo, Japan

Completion Date: July 2016
Height: 80 m (262 ft)
Stories: 14
Area: 5,400 sq m (58,125 sq ft)
Primary Function: Office
Owner/Developer: IM property
Architect: Maeda Corporation (design)
Structural Engineer: Maeda Corporation (engineer of record)
MEP Engineer: Maeda Corporation (engineer of record)
Main Contractor: Maeda Corporation

9 | Kyobashi EDOGRAND
Tokyo, Japan

Completion Date: October 2016
Height: 170 m (559 ft)
Stories: 32
Area: 85,995 sq m (925,642 sq ft)
Primary Functions: Office / Retail
Owner: Kyobashi 2-chome West District Redevelopment Associates
Developers: NIPPON TOCHI-TATEMONO Co., Ltd.; Tokyo Tatemono Co., Ltd.
Architect: NIKKEN SEKKEI LTD (design)
Structural Engineer: NIKKEN SEKKEI LTD (design)
MEP Engineer: NIKKEN SEKKEI LTD (design)
Main Contractor: Shimizu Corporation

10 | Nakanoshima Festival Tower West
Osaka, Japan

Completion Date: March 2017
Height: 199 m (654 ft)
Stories: 41
Area: 151,146 sq m (1,626,922 sq ft)
Primary Functions: Hotel / Office
Owners/Developers: The Asahi Shimbun Company; Takenaka Corporation
Architect: NIKKEN SEKKEI LTD (design)
Structural Engineers: NIKKEN SEKKEI LTD (design); Takenaka Corporation (design)
MEP Engineer: NIKKEN SEKKEI LTD (design)
Main Contractor: Takenaka Corporation

6

7

8

9

10

11 | Ningbo Bank of China
Ningbo, China

Completion Date: 2016
Height: 246 m (808 ft)
Stories: 50
Area: 107,787 sq m (1,160,210 sq ft)
Primary Functions: Office
Owner: Ningbo Eastern New City Development Investment Ltd.
Architect: Skidmore, Owings & Merrill LLP (design)
Structural Engineer: Skidmore, Owings & Merrill LLP (design)
MEP Engineer: Skidmore, Owings & Merrill LLP (design)
Other CTBUH Member Supplier: Schindler (elevator)

12 | One Avighna Park
Mumbai, India

Completion Date: April 2017
Height: 247 m (810 ft)
Stories: 61
Area: 61,873 sq m (665,995 sq ft)
Primary Function: Residential
Owner/Developer: Nish Developers Pvt Ltd
Architect: Neo Modern Architects Pvt. Ltd (design)
Structural Engineer: Mahimtura Consultants Pvt. Ltd. (design)
MEP Engineer: Elemec UAE (design)
Main Contractor: Simplex Infrastructures Ltd.
Other CTBUH Member Consultant: BMT Fluid Mechanics Ltd. (wind)
Other CTBUH Member Supplier: Schüco (aluminium); UltraTech Cement Lanka (Pvt.) Ltd. (concrete)

13 | Parnas Tower
Seoul, South Korea

Completion Date: September 2016
Height: 185 m (607 ft)
Stories: 39
Area: 104,374 sq m (1,123,472 sq ft)
Primary Functions: Hotel / Office
Owners: GS Retail; Parnas Hotel
Developer: GS Engineering & Construction
Architects: KMD Architects (design); Chang-Jo Architects (architect of record)
Structural Engineer: Dong Yang Structural Engineers (engineer of record)
MEP Engineer: Buro Happold (engineer of record)
Main Contractor: GS E&C

14 | Rosewood Sanya and Sanya Forum
Sanya, China

Completion Date: August 2017
Height: 207 m (680 ft)
Stories: 46
Area: 103,813 sq m (1,117,434 sq ft)
Primary Functions: Serviced apartments / Hotel
Owner/Developer: Poly Real Estate Group Co. Ltd.
Architect: Goettsch Partners (design); Guangzhou Design Institute (architect of record)
Structural Engineer: RBS Architectural Engineering Design Associates (engineer of record)
MEP Engineer: Parsons Brinckerhoff Consultants Private Limited (engineer of record)
Main Contractor: China State Construction Engineering Corporation

15 | Shenyang K11
Shenyang, China

Completion Date: 2017
Height: Tower C: 224 m (736 ft); Tower D: 176 m (578 ft); Tower E: 218 m (714 ft); Tower F: 113 m (371 ft); Tower G: 116 m (381 ft)
Stories: Tower C: 57; Tower D: 42; Tower E: 55; Tower F: 26; Tower G: 24
Total Area: 196,462 sq m (2,114,699 sq ft)
Primary Function: Serviced Apartments (Tower C, D & E); Hotel (Tower F & G)
Developer: New World Development Company Limited
Architect: Dennis Lau & Ng Chun Man Architects & Engineers (HK) Ltd. (DLN) (design)
Structural Engineer: AECOM (design)
MEP Engineer: WSP | Parsons Brinckerhoff (design)
Main Constractor: Hip Hing Construction (China) Co. Ltd.
Other CTBUH Member Consultants: Access Advisors Ltd. (façade maintenance); BMT Fluid Mechanics Ltd. (wind); Meinhardt Facade Technology (S) Pte. Ltd. (façade)
Other CTBUH Member Supplier: JORDAHL (cladding)

11

12

16 | Talan Towers
Astana, Kazakhstan

Completion Date: 2017
Height: Tower 1: 146 m (478 ft); Tower 2: 120 m (393 ft)
Stories: Tower 1: 30; Tower 2: 26
Total Area: 126,472 sq m (1,361,333 sq ft)
Primary Functions: Tower 1: Office / Retail; Tower 2: Residential / Hotel / Retail
Owner/Developer: Tower 1: Astana Property Management LLC; Tower 2: Verny Capital
Architects: Dizayn Group (design - Tower 1); Skidmore, Owings & Merrill LLP (architect of record)
Structural Engineers: Dizayn Group (design); Skidmore, Owings & Merrill LLP (engineer of record)
MEP Engineers: Dizayn Group (design); AKFA (design)
Project Manager: Turner International LLC
Main Contractors: Tower 1: Yrys Batys LLP; Metal Yapi; KUKBO; Interium Srl.; Energoprojekt; Renaissance Construction Company; Tower 2: Turner International LLC
Other CTBUH Member Consultants: CallisonRTKL (interiors - Tower 1); Jones Lang LaSalle, Inc. (maintenance - Tower 1); Perkins+Will (interiors - Tower 1); Van Deusen & Associates (vertical transportation - Tower 1); Wacker Ingenieure (wind)
Other CTBUH Member Suppliers: CoxGomyl (façade maintenance equipment - Tower 1); KONE (elevator - Tower 1); Hilti AG (cladding - Tower 2)

17 | Telkom Landmark Tower 2
Jakarta, Indonesia

Completion Date: July 2017
Height: 220 m (722 ft)
Stories: 46
Area: 64,550 sq m (694,810 sq ft)
Primary Function: Office
Owner/Developer: Telkom Group
Architects: Woods Bagot (design); PDW Architects (architect of record)
Structural Engineer: PT. Haerte (design)
MEP Engineer: 134 PT Arnan Pratama Consultants (design)
Main Contractor: PT Adhi Karya
Other CTBUH Member Consultants: JLL (property management); Meinhardt Facade Technology (S) Pte. Ltd. (façade); Windtech Consultants Pty Ltd (wind)

18 | The Summit - Plot 554
Suzhou, China

Completion Date: June 2017
Height: 167 m (547 ft)
Stories: 39
Area: 95,300 sq m (1,025,801 sq ft)
Primary Functions: Serviced apartments / Office / Retail
Owner/Developer: Tishman Speyer Properties
Architects: Goettsch Partners (design); Suzhou Institute of Architectural Design Co., Ltd. (architect of record)
Structural Engineers: WSP (design); Suzhou Institute of Architectural Design Co., Ltd. (engineer of record)
MEP Engineers: WSP (design); Suzhou Institute of Architectural Design Co., Ltd. (engineer of record)
Other CTBUH Member Consultants: Broadway Malyan (interiors); Faithful+Gould (LEED); Inhabit Group (façade); Permasteelisa Group (façade)
Other CTBUH Member Supplier: Permasteelisa Group (cladding)

19 | The Suzhou Modern Media Plaza
Suzhou, China

Completion Date: 2016
Height: Tower 1: 215 m (705 ft); Tower 2: 165 m (541 ft)
Stories: Tower 1: 42; Tower 2: 38
Area: 323,724 sq m (3,484,536 sq ft)
Primary Function: Tower 1: Office; Tower 2: Hotel / Residential
Owner/Developer: Suzhou Broadcasting System
Architects: ARTS Group Co, Ltd. (design - Tower 1); NIKKEN SEKKEI LTD (design)
Structural Engineer: NIKKEN SEKKEI LTD (design)
MEP Engineer: NIKKEN SEKKEI LTD (design)
Main Contractor: Zhongyifeng Construction Group Co., Ltd.
Other CTBUH Member Consultants: Aurecon (façade); Shenyang Yuanda Aluminium Industry Engineering Co.,Ltd. (façade)
Other CTBUH Member Supplier: KONE (elevator)

16

17

18

19

20

20 | Upper West Side
Melbourne, Australia

Completion Date: 2016
Height: 170 m (558 ft)
Stories: 53
Primary Function: Residential
Developer: Far East Consortium International Limited
Architect: Cottee Parker Architects (design)
Structural Engineer: WSP Structures (design)
MEP Engineers: Hydrautech (design); Wood and Grieve Engineers (design)
Main Contractor: Multiplex
Other CTBUH Member Consultants: BG&E (façade); Rider Levett Bucknall (quantity surveyor); WSP (civil)

21 | Urbana Tower
Kolkata, India

Completion Date: 2017
Height: Tower 1, 4, 5, 6 & 7: 152 m (500 ft); Tower 2 & 3: 165 m (541 ft)
Stories: Tower 1, 4, 5, 6 & 7: 41; Tower 2 & 3: 46
Area: 45,000 sq m (484,376 sq ft)
Primary Function: Residential
Owner/Developer: Bengal NRI Pvt Ltd
Architect: aCTa asia private limited (design)
Structural Engineer: NES Structures (design)
MEP Engineer: Meinhardt (design)
Main Contractor: Larsen & Toubro

22 | Zhongzhou E-ClASS
Shenzhen, China

Completion Date: August 2016
Height: 160 m (526 ft)
Stories: 40
Area: 85,000 sq m (914,932 sq ft)
Primary Functions: Residential / Retail
Developer: Zhongzhou Baocheng Real Estate Co., Ltd.
Architect: PT Architecture Design (Shenzhen) Co., Ltd. (design)
Structural Engineer: Zhubo Design (design)
MEP Engineer: Zhubo Design (design)
Main Contractor: Jiangsu Province Huajian Construction Co., Ltd.

EUROPE

The comparatively ancient and traditionally low-rise cities of Europe have historically had a hot-and-cold relationship with skyscrapers. But, as in the Americas, here skyscrapers have now been on the skyline for several generations, and the inventiveness of its designers and developers is showing an increasing affection for repurposing dated towers that gave a poor impression of skyscrapers to some Europeans the first time around. New-build towers are also striking the balance between reaffirming the strength of the existing urban grain and the demands of dynamic populations.

A'DAM Toren

Amsterdam, Netherlands

Completion Date: May 2016
Height: 94 m (308 ft)
Stories: 22
Area: 16,000 sq m (172,223 sq ft)
Primary Functions: Office / Hotel
Owner: A'DAM Toren
Developers: Lingotto; Hans Brouwer; Duncan Stutterheim; Sander Groet
Architects: Felix Claus en Dick Van Wageningen Architecten (design); OZ (architect of record)
Structural Engineer: Royal Haskoning DHV (design)
MEP Engineer: Huygen Installatie Adviseurs (design)
Main Contractor: Aanneming Maatschappij J.P. van Eesteren
Other CTBUH Member Consultants: Deerns (vertical transportation)
Other CTBUH Member Supplier: KONE (elevator)

In 2009, the Shell Tower, a well-known building designed in the 1960s and located on the northern banks of the IJ River, was vacated by Shell. A developer and three entrepreneurs in the music industry set out to transform this mono-functional and closed-off office building into a public tower that operates 24/7 and provides a vibrant functional mix.

The project consists of an observation deck (including the "Over the Edge" swing), multiple bars and restaurants (including a revolving restaurant), a boutique hotel, an underground dance club, and public parking. A'DAM is also home to several leading companies in the music industry.

Specific to the building are the many functions that are vertically incorporated on a very small footprint. This offered challenges during the design, building and management process, but it also paved the way for innovation. Preserving the iconic Sixties architecture, originally designed by Arthur Staal, was a priority. As the building was in poor technical shape, a drastic renovation was in order. To preserve the original idea of a robust, dark-colored tower set on sturdy columns, with a diagonal white crown, the original concrete façade was replaced with a new one, based on the same grid. To enhance the view, the windows were made bigger. The crown and canopy were replaced by a full-size observation deck. The original plinth was modified to accommodate multiple entrance routes. Originally designed for 350 people, A'DAM now welcomes 3,500 people a day.

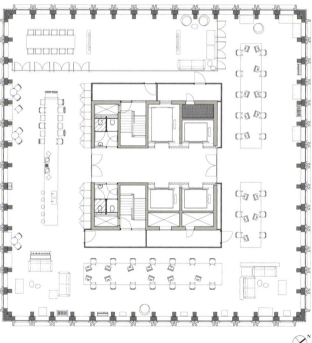

Opposite: The A'DAM Toren was originally an office building for Royal Dutch Shell (bottom). Its refashioning into a cultural center has preserved some of its 1960s-era "space age" flourishes (top).

Top: The tower's interiors have been remodeled to suit the "look and feel" of music-focused tenants.

Bottom Left: The 15th floor plan shows how a typical floor has been turned into an office space attuned to the working style of an entertainment company.

Bottom Right: The addition of features like the "Over the Edge" swing ride transformed the former office tower into a vibrant public destination.

Angel Court

London, United Kingdom

Angel Court is located within the Bank of England Conservation Area, where no new high-rise buildings are permitted. However, by stripping an existing 1970s tower to its core, and replacing it with an intelligent and characterful building that responds to statutory, environmental, functional and aspirational requirements, Angel Court has become a contemporary tower that integrates into its historic surroundings.

Given its sensitive location, Angel Court had to ensure it related to its context at both ground level and in the sky. At its base, a former service road and its neighboring public street, formerly a dark alleyway reaching through a hole in the wall, has been transformed into an attractive pedestrian street, lined with shops and restaurants, which catch the midday sun, creating additional public realm and the chance for an increase in economic activity. The tower stands off its podium base, with new entrances created off Angel Court addressing visitors from north and south. The new street, with its shops and restaurants, adds 30 percent more space to the public realm.

With the client and city planners' engagement, the design team carried out extensive studies that examined new-build, re-build and refurbishment options for the design. Settling on retention of only the original core, the re-designed building has two distinct forms. The sculpted, lower garden floors with deep-set windows, faced in rough-hewn Carlow Blue limestone, sit comfortably in their context, and contrast with the softly curved tower, which is faced in a light opal-fritted glass, wrapping around the walls of the original, irregular octagonal form. The translucent, ethereal tower, its skin flowing as a continuously curved surface across its entire volume, blends into its surroundings by appearing entirely translucent during the day, drawing the sky down to earth; as external light fades and internal lights take over, the building becomes grounded with its base. At night, the tower transforms to reveal a simple, square grid to match the lower buildings, unifying the whole composition.

Completion Date: February 2017
Height: 101 m (330 ft)
Stories: 26
Area: 46,020 sq m (495,355 sq ft)
Primary Functions: Office
Owners/Developers: Mitsui Fudosan Co. Ltd.; Stanhope
Architect: Fletcher Priest Architects (design)
Structural Engineer: Waterman Group (design)
MEP Engineer: Waterman Building Services Ltd (design)
Main Contractor: Mace Limited
Other CTBUH Member Consultants: Arup (traffic)
Other CTBUH Member Suppliers: Hilti AG (fire proofing)

Internally, visitors enter a double-height lobby, with the service core at the center of the building. The lower "garden floors" contain private terraces for tenants to enjoy. On the tower's "sky floors," 360-degree floor plates provide unparalleled views of the City of London and beyond. The city planner's aspiration was for a glass tower that did not appear to be "glassy." This provided the design team with an opportunity to adopt advanced façade techniques, including a type of glass with a unique "double-frit", a one-millimeter-diameter ceramic dot that was screen-printed onto an inside face of the double-laminated glass panels to provide 27 percent solidity. The dot is white on the outer face of the glass and black on the inside, so that its outer appearance is translucent and light in tone during the day. The ceramic frit contributed to a total 60 percent solidity of the tower façade, which significantly limits solar gains, while appearing virtually transparent for occupiers looking out.

The design also increases floor space by over 60 percent without increasing the tower height, through the relocation of service floors and enlargement of floor plates. Generous tenant amenities, including external terraces over five different levels, and a centerpiece communal lounge leading onto a mature garden at the midpoint of the building, all contribute to a building that responds to the health and well-being requirements of its modern tenants.

Angel Court strips an existing 1970s tower to its core, replacing it with an intelligent and characterful building that responds to statutory, environmental, functional and aspirational requirements.

Top Left: The renovation preserves the octagonal shape of the original building but substitutes a new skin, among other improvements.

Top Right: The ground-level public realm has also been improved, through adding a new pedestrian laneway.

Left: The ceramic frit of the new envelope contributed to a total 60-percent solidity of the tower façade, which significantly limits solar gains, while appearing virtually transparent for occupiers looking out.

Opposite Top: From the inside, the frit pattern is invisible, but controls solar gain, and views are unobstructed.

Opposite Bottom: The 2nd (left) and 9th-floor (right) plans show how the lettable space was extended from the tower into neighboring buildings, and the roof of the adjoining structure has become a planted, inhabitable terrace.

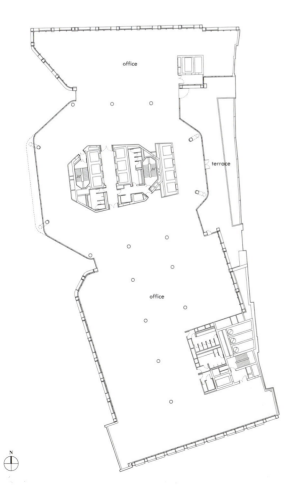
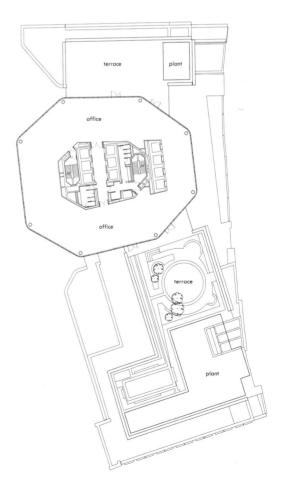

Axis
Frankfurt, Germany

Completion Date: June 2016
Height: 61 m (200 ft)
Stories: 19
Area: 19,500 sq m (209,896 sq ft)
Primary Function: Residential
Owner/Developer: Wilma Wohnen Süd GmbH
Architect: Meixner Schlüter Wendt Architekten (design)
Structural Engineers: Bollinger + Grohmann (design); DBT Ingenieursozietät (peer review)
MEP Engineer: ITG Consult Atlas AG (engineer of record); Planungsgruppe für technische Gebäudeausrüstung GmbH & Co (engineer of record)
Main Contractor: Grontmij GmbH
Other CTBUH Member Consultants: Wacker Ingenieure (wind)

Bookending a grand boulevard at the center of a large development west of downtown Frankfurt, Axis sets a precedent for a new generation of urban living in Germany. The building's architectural context is inherent in the site's prominent location as a gateway to this new district. Clad in white limestone with slender, floor-to-ceiling windows, the residential tower stands out amongst the mid-rise blocks that line the development's central park. Along the southern façade, balconies protrude and retract at varying angles above a green courtyard, giving the building an asymmetric rippling effect.

On the outside, the extensive façade cladding with white limestone creates a contemporary, monolithic structure that belies the quietude of the inner portion. The free play of the two-storied, combined window apertures generates a differentiated lattice structure which, by avoiding a clear readability of the individual stories, intriguingly inhibits a clear perception of proportions. In contrast to the smooth urban outer façade, inside the building ring, a soft, polygonal inner world emerges, offering a calmer, more domestic scale.

In a country that has codified ambitious climate goals into law, the building offers a plethora of green features. Wide, permanently installed plant containers provide generous greening of the open spaces. A wastewater heat pump derives heat from the energy contained in the municipal wastewater system, generating 100 percent of the energy required for heating and cooling the tower's apartments. The building was also constructed to meet the very high KfW 55 Efficiency House standard, which is comparable to Passivhaus in terms of ecological footprint.

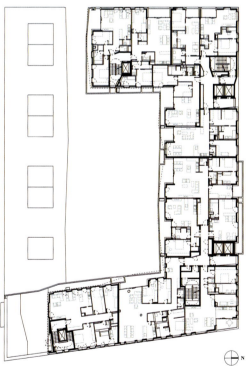

Opposite: The project is situated on the broad Europa-Allee.

Top: The intimately-scaled inner courtyard contrasts with the intensity of the street side.

Bottom Left: The oblique angles of the overall floor plate and of the overhangs makes each unit balcony a different experience.

Bottom Right: The tesselating balconies break down the scale of the tower facing the courtyard.

Canaletto

London, United Kingdom

The Canaletto residential tower, located halfway between the City of London and Angel in Islington, is immediately identifiable by its wraparound curvilinear ribbon-like façade. The design for the tower incorporates the curvilinear façade, a streamlining of the building's mass and a contrasting of scale and detail that is atypical of a residential tower.

The pattern of the façade clusters groups of two to three floors together, bookended by forward and reverse "letter-C"-shaped extrusions, forming vertical communities that relate more closely to the small scale of neighboring buildings than to a typical high-rise. The wrapping frames are mirrored to emphasize the verticality along the spines of the building. By "scaling down" what is quite a large building, the organization of exterior elements emphasizes the intimate residential experience within. Contrasting materials are employed within each grouping, where the "outer" smooth metallic element is complemented by an "inner" use of textured materials. Throughout the building, the cluster concept of the façade allows for a maximum level of transparency, thereby lending the tower a softer and more nuanced silhouette.

The interplay of the balcony, the cowled overhang, and the asymmetrical floor plates creates highly nuanced outdoor spaces for the individual units, some of which are rounded in three dimensions, that cleverly blend sensations of enclosure and exposure. In some units, a balcony overhead intersects with one of the C-shaped pieces to create a porthole-like effect; in others, the enclosure line steps back from the balcony and provides a seamless view from the interior through a single piece of curved glass.

On the ground level, a generous canopy wraps around the building, further integrating it with the street. The building interacts with the vibrant neighborhood by way of a landscaped garden on Wharf Road, which provides access to the residential lobby, while its City Road side cants inwards from the intersection to provide access to a plaza overlooking the City Road Basin of the Regent's Canal.

The composition of residences includes studios, one- and two-bedroom apartments, a number of three-bedroom apartments and one distinct penthouse with a full rooftop. Outside of the privacy afforded by the 190 individual living units, the Canaletto tower caters to a variety of collective leisure activities by way of shared amenities, where the residents can enjoy healthy leisure pursuits or relax in areas designed for gathering and socializing. These include a restaurant, swimming pool, health club, media room and club lounge, with a terrace on the 24th floor.

Several sustainable and innovative strategies are evident in the building. The frame articulating the building form acts as passive solar shading device. The projected profiles prevent excessive amounts of solar heat gain and balance good daylight penetration to the interior space. They also mitigate wind downdrafts, to create a comfortable microclimate at ground level. Energy-efficient MVHR (mechanical ventilation and heat recovery) systems are implemented in all apartments together with fan coil units (FCUs) to provide cooling. A waste management plan provides dedicated residential and commercial refuse areas. All plants and associated equipment are chosen to reduce energy consumption and minimize waste and pollutants; all wood in the project is FSC/COC Certified. Finally, to reduce material, a post-tensioned slab system is used. This allows for an increased floor-to-ceiling height at an optimal structural strength.

Completion Date: March 2017
Height: 96 m (314 ft)
Stories: 31
Area: 21,732 sq m (233,921 sq ft)
Primary Function: Residential
Owner: Orion City Road Trustee Limited
Developer: Groveworld
Architect: UNStudio (design); Axis Architects (architect of record)
Structural Engineer: URS (design)
MEP Engineer: Hoare Lea (design)
Main Contractor: Ardmore Ltd
Other CTBUH Member Consultants: Buro Happold (façade); EC Harris (cost); RWDI (wind)

The extruded "ribbons" on the façade cluster several floors together at a time, forming groups of vertical communities that relate more closely to the small scale of neighboring buildings.

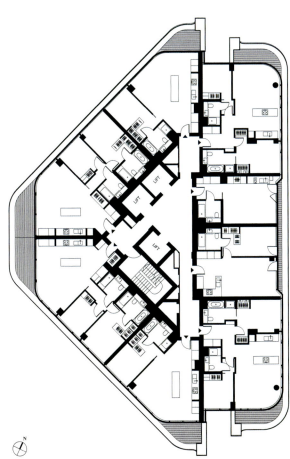

Opposite Top: The short, prow-like end of the tower is articulated by offset pairs of "C"-shaped panels.

Opposite Bottom: Inside one of the "C"-shapes; an intimate balcony space.

Above: The exclusive "Club Canaletto" on the 24th floor is one of many residential amenities in the building.

Left: The rounded triangular shape of the tower creates opportunities for several unusual curving balcony types.

Dollar Bay

London, United Kingdom

Completion Date: April 2017
Height: 109 m (357 ft)
Stories: 31
Area: 14,500 sq m (156,077 sq ft)
Primary Function: Residential
Owners/Developers: Mount Anvil; One Housing Group
Architect: SimpsonHaugh & Partners (design, architect of record)
Structural Engineer: WSP Group (design, engineer of record)
MEP Engineers: WSP Group (design)
Main Contractor: Mount Anvil

Dollar Bay rises like a beacon at the head of South Dock in London, signaling the area's redevelopment while enhancing the public space on a constrained yet prominent site. The taut geometry and rippling, glazed façades evoke a cascading waterfall, while adjustable louvers and operable windows create a constantly changing surface. Where its chiseled form rests lightly on the ground, a new public space encircles it. Residents, locals and passersby now enjoy fully accessible pathways to a rejuvenated waterfront area, landscaping, outdoor seating and public art.

Rising as two crystal-like forms fused together by a joint circulation core, Dollar Bay respects its low-rise neighbors, standing at a modest 31 stories compared to Canary Wharf's towers nearby. The building's small footprint and location make way for the new promenade around its base, transforming the previously neglected quayside into a public space and providing safe passage to neighboring areas. By designing the building to be shorter than neighboring towers and locating it as far west as possible on the site, its impact on neighboring low-rise residences is minimized.

Inside the tower, the east-west orientated floorplate maximizes internal space, allowing most homes to enjoy double or triple aspects. Generous winter gardens provide residents with additional flexible space and offer thermal insulation. A unique dock-water cooling solution — the first time London dock-water has been used to cool a residential building — reduces the carbon footprint, saves homeowners money and ensures no unsightly plant equipment is externally visible.

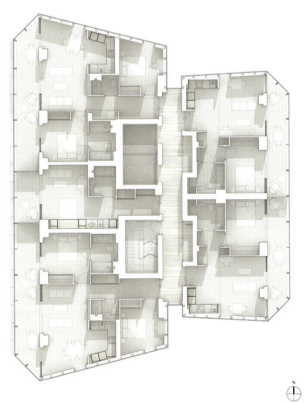

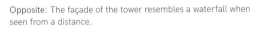

Opposite: The façade of the tower resembles a waterfall when seen from a distance.

Top: Apartment interiors give way to a partially enclosed, louvered balcony.

Bottom Left: The building is split into two distinct halves, with a circulation spine down the middle.

Bottom Right: At street level, the faceted curtain wall forms an enclosure over the entrance.

New'R

Nantes, France

Completion Date: January 2017
Height: 55 m (180 ft)
Stories: 20
Area: 10,350 sq m (111,406 sq ft)
Primary Function: Residential
Owner/Developer: Kaufman & Broad
Architect: Hamonic + Masson & Associés (design)
Structural Engineer: BETAP (design)
MEP Engineer: ALBDO (design)
Project Manager: Polytec
Main Contractor: Polytec

Composed of curves and surrounded by undulating balconies, New'R pays homage to Oscar Niemeyer, the architecture of the 1970s French Riviera, and the hedonistic fantasy of Miami Beach. Sensual and multi-directional, the building is located at a pivotal point between an existing and a new neighborhood currently being developed alongside rail infrastructure. There are 40 differing typologies for 156 apartments, meaning the repetition inherently found in housing projects is offset by the tower's undulating form.

There was a strong focus on the connection between the building, its users, and the city throughout the design process. The differing scales introduce a richness and intricacy, turning the building into a narrative with a genuine identity. One of the main aims was to promote a communal lifestyle and encourage the building's inhabitants to get to know one another through sharing common spaces, including a shared greenhouse.

The question of public space and its extension through the project was a prerequisite; the resulting condition not only invites different activities and interactions, but also establishes a strong link between the shared public space of the road and the building. The city's flow of pedestrians, cars and bicycles and the mixed program (parking, retail, office space and housing) interweave and embellish the ground floor, creating a "pedestrian-level volume." The building's transparency, depth and various perspectives engender a dynamism and liveliness around the perimeter of the project, consequently enriching the surrounding environment.

Opposite: The design references Oscar Niemeyer, the 1970s French Riviera, and Miami Beach archetypes.

Top: The ground floor entrance is demarcated by a raising a portion of the tower on pilotis.

Bottom Left: The unusual shape of the plan affords extra space for a greenhouse and shared terrace on the 10th floor.

Bottom Right: The interplay of the wall corrugation, patterned flooring, and curving balustrade enriches the balcony experience.

The Silo

Copenhagen, Denmark

The Silo is the largest industrial building in the redeveloped neighborhood of Nordhavn (North Harbor) in Copenhagen. It has been transformed from a grain container, constructed in 1962, into a residential building. The lower floor is a public event space, while the top floor is a public restaurant. This mix of functions ensures that The Silo will be active at all times. The spatial variation within the original silo is immense, due to the various functions of storing and handling grain, creating 38 unique apartments with floor heights of up to seven meters. The interior has been preserved as raw and untouched as possible, while a façade made of galvanized steel has been installed on the exterior of the former concrete silo to serve as a climate shield. The new facade's bright and reflective surface enhances The Silo's original monolithic character — a beacon in the field of transformation and an urban focal point for the new development of the Nordhavn area.

In many ways it would have been easier tearing down the outmoded industrial structure, but it was and still is an important landmark. It tells a relevant story about the industrial past of Nordhavn as a former industrial harbor area worth preserving. The Silo represents a built resource, and by revitalizing what many people looked upon as industrial waste, it has been turned into a valuable and treasured urban feature.

The transformation is done by deliberately leaving historical traces, recalling The Silo's past; while the overall act of recycling supports contemporary goals for sustainable building. Inhabitants and neighbors can easily acknowledge its former identity and heritage. By giving it a new façade, but keeping the original structure and height, the distinctive slender shape of The Silo is preserved, along with its history.

All apartments have floor-to-ceiling windows and balconies with a view of Copenhagen's skyline. The balconies function as wind shields, providing the inhabitants with a more private outdoor space. On top of The Silo, a new, box-like addition has been constructed and covered with reflective glass, setting a different tone from the variegated main façade.

Completion Date: June 2017
Height: 65 m (213 ft)
Stories: 17
Area: 10,000 sq m (107,639 sq ft)
Primary Function: Residential
Owners/Developers: Klaus Kastbjerg; NRE Denmark
Architect: COBE (design)
Structural Engineer: Balslev and Wessberg (design)
MEP Engineer: Balslev and Wessberg (design)
Main Contractor: NRE Denmark

The common ground floor is closely connected to the immediate environment due to the visual connection provided by its large openings and the landscape pavement. The pavement and urban furniture are made of actual concrete fragments from the former silo, emphasizing the coherence between building and site context. Corridors contain traces of former industrial uses, including steel chutes for distributing grains.

Updating The Silo to the current energy standards was a crucial requirement of the design process, alongside preserving the original materiality to the greatest extent possible. This involved developing and constructing a new façade system that would allow the building to sustain residential occupancy. The added assembly contains a triple-glazed window, galvanized steel cladding over two hollow rectangular steel beams, a wall insulation panel and an integrated blind, all outside of the existing concrete wall. The mix of functions is a matter of social sustainability, creating spaces for social interactions in the entire building. Furthermore, keeping original structures in our cities is a matter of sustainability, and an ethical and visionary approach to cultural heritage, emphasizing the importance of creating a long-lasting and robust design.

Left: The benefit of adding the galvanized steel modules to the exterior of the original building becomes clear in plan; living units gain extra outdoor space.

Right: The Silo before (above) and after (below) renovation; its essence remains "industrial" but it is clearly transformed.

Opposite Top: Interior surfaces were left "raw" to link inhabitants to the building's industrial past.

Opposite Bottom: The galvanized modules being added to the sides of the building during construction. The modules brought solar control and insulation to the concrete building, as well as extra space.

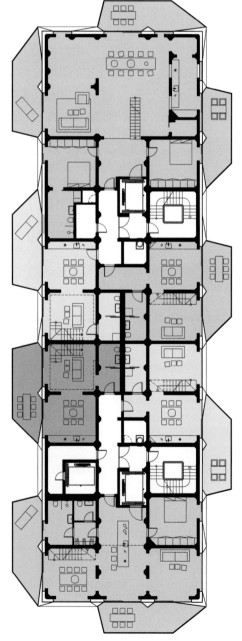

By giving it a new façade, but keeping the original structure and height, the distinctive slender shape of The Silo is preserved, along with its history.

Tribunal de Paris

Paris, France

The new Paris Courthouse accommodates up to 8,000 people per day. The building consists of a plinth five-to-eight-stories high, on top of which stands a tower of three superimposed parallelepipeds, whose section diminishes as the tower gets higher, creating a distinctive stepping profile.

The plinth gathers the public services, including 90 courtrooms. The building is entered at the ground floor level, from the piazza, into the monumental public lobby, where the flow of visitors and employees are greeted and directed. This rectangular space is the full height of the plinth, up to 28 meters, and is notable for its slender steel columns and the amount of natural light that enters via skylights and through the glazed façade that looks onto the piazza. Via this monumental room and the two small atria on either side of it, natural light can penetrate the heart of the building. Meanwhile, the eighth floor has a 7,000 square-meter planted terrace; the staff restaurant opens onto this large garden. The tower's outline breaks in two places, on the 19th and 29th floors, where "hanging gardens" have been created.

When the competition for the project was first launched, the French government suggested dividing the law courts into two separate buildings: one for the public functions and the second for the offices. The key idea from the design team was to house all these spaces in one single, important building, which would be capable, by its size and importance, of becoming the starting point for the redevelopment of the area around the Porte de Clichy.

One of the other design ideas was to build a courthouse that would be in line with a new vision of Justice that is modern and humanistic. The façades' transparency, as well as the lobby's dimensions, enable the public spaces to be open and communicate service to the citizens. Both the general public and users benefit from warm spaces, in particular the public cafeteria and the exterior green terraces.

The building rises out of an L-shaped site, between the city ring road (Peripherique) and Martin Luther King Park. The principal building's axis follows the north-south diagonal of the Park, giving structure to the Clichy-Batignolles development area. The south façade turns towards

Completion Date: July 2017
Height: 160 m (524 ft)
Stories: 38
Area: 17,500 sq. m (188,368 sq. ft)
Primary Function: Office
Owner: Bouygues Batiment International
Developer: Arélia
Architect: Renzo Piano Building Workshop (design)
Structural Engineer: Setec TPI (design)
MEP Engineers: Setec Bâtiment (design); Berim (design)
Main Contractor: Bouygues Batiment International
Other CTBUH Member Consultants: MovvéO Ltd. (vertical transportation); Permasteelisa Group (façade)
Other CTBUH Member Suppliers: Bouygues Batiment International (concrete, façade maintenance equipment); Epexyl (interior partition); KONE (elevator)

Paris, and the north façade towards Clichy. This diagonal terminates a "visual corridor" that leads towards the north, between the east façade of the building and the Maison des Avocats, extending to Clichy. The office façades on the eastern and western sides give views towards Montmartre and the Eiffel Tower; the north and south facades, which are narrower, look towards central Paris or towards Clichy and Mont-Valérien. Thanks to this orientation, the building symbolically opens onto the City.

Sustainable development was one of the main concerns of the project. In terms of energy, the building is high-performing, thanks to thermal inertia, natural ventilation, and the integration of 2,000 square meters of photovoltaic panels. These add a distinctive interruption to the smooth glass of the façade, and express the government's commitment to sustainable electricity generation in a clear design move.

This low-energy building uses about 70kWh/m^2/year, and in some parts even 50kWh/m^2/year, which is about half of the consumption of the most recent office buildings in La Défense. The building is the first high-rise in France to meet the "Plan Climat Paris" requirements.

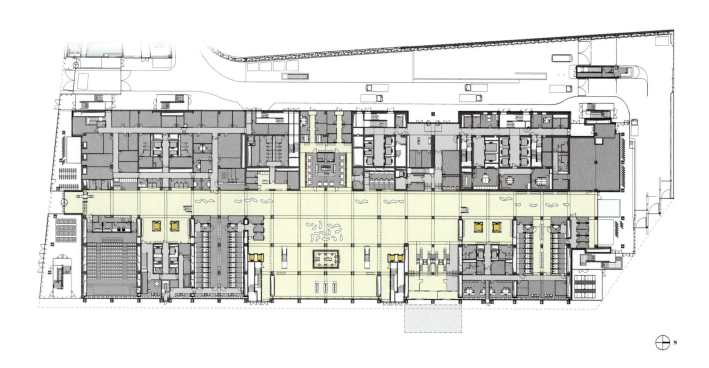

The façades' transparency, as well as the lobby's dimensions, enable the public spaces to be open and communicate service to the citizens.

Opposite Top Left: During breaks in judicial proceedings, citizens and employees can enjoy the 7,000 square meter planted terrace.

Opposite Top Right: Arriving in the lobby, visitors are greeted by smooth, thin columns, and daylight flooding the oversized space.

Opposite Bottom: Ground-floor plan, showing circulation corridor at the center and secure loading area at the rear.

Above: The imposing scale of the building is interrupted by planted decks separating each of the four cubes.

Right: Solar panels are arrayed to emphasize and complement the setbacks between the "floating" blocks forming the overall composition of the building.

Upper West
Berlin, Germany

Completion Date: July 2017
Height: 119 m (390 ft)
Stories: 35
Area: 66,990 sq m (721,074 sq ft)
Primary Functions: Office / Hotel / Retail
Owner: SIGNA Prime Selection AG
Developers: Strabag Real Estate GmbH; RFR Realty LLC
Architects: Langhof (design); KSP Jurgen Engel Architekten (architect of record)
Structural Engineer: Ed. Züblin AG (design)
MEP Engineers: Gesellschaft für Städtebau und Projektentwicklung (design); DS-Plan GmbH (design); enuTEC Energietechnik und Umweltmanagement GmbH (design)
Main Contractor: Ed. Züblin AG

Hand in hand with the rediscovery of the center city as a desirable place to live as well as work, Berliners' interest has been growing in mixed-use high-rises. As the uses change within, the building's shape and façade morph from a strict, geometric and angular volume into an amorphous figure, characterized by curves the higher it gets.

The first 18 floors of the Upper West tower comprise a hotel with 582 guest rooms. The 14 floors above are optimized for use as offices, and can be flexibly divided into between one and three rental units. The building is crowned on the 35th floor by a sky bar, complete with rooftop terrace. There is a separate entrance lobby and set of elevators for each use. Contained within a compact core, five elevators are reserved for hotel guests. A further five elevators take employees from the office lobby to their workplaces, while two lifts transport visitors from the relevant entrance area to the sky bar. This is possible owing to dual-sided lift access and intelligent electronic controls.

The challenge in terms of planning lies in finding a structural, functional and economically viable solution that combines all the requirements set by the different uses. To this end, at Upper West, an unusual structural grid of 2.86 meters was developed, which fulfills the requirements of all potential users — offices, hotel, hospitality, and retail outlets, and an underground car park — and at the same time is compatible with the prescribed expressive shape of the floor plan and the building overall. As a result, overall space utilization exceeds 80 percent of each floor's total area.

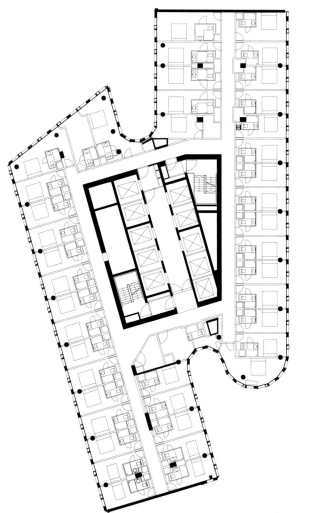

Opposite: Upper West directly abuts Kantstrasse, a main road that forms the development's northern perimeter.

Top: The tower's office space can be flexibly divided between one and three rental units.

Bottom Left: The column spacing for the tower, as shown in this hotel floor plan, follows an atypical 2.86-meter structural grid.

Bottom Right: Tight angles give way to additional curvature along the tower's height.

White Collar Factory

London, United Kingdom

Completion Date: February 2017
Height: 75 m (247 ft)
Stories: 17
Area: 31,600 sq m (340,140 sq ft)
Primary Function: Office
Owner/Developer: Derwent London
Architect: Allford Hall Monaghan Morris (design)
Structural Engineer: AKTII (design)
MEP Engineer: Arup (design)
Project Manager: Jackson Coles
Main Contractor: Multiplex
Other CTBUH Member Consultant: AECOM (quantity surveyor)

White Collar Factory is the built iteration of an eight-year research project led by its developer and architect. The project took inspiration from factories and warehouses built in the 19th century, with an eye to accommodating the needs of fast-growing 21st-century manufacturing industries. The "industrial" motif is obvious starting at the lobby, with its exposed structure, ductwork and raceways, and a reception desk atop a scissor lift. But the building is industrial in substance as well as style.

Beginning in 2008, the team set out five principles for the project: it needed to have tall ceilings, "smart servicing" (responsive but efficiently built MEP systems), a simple, passive façade, a deep plan and a concrete structure. This investigation led first to a full-scale baseline prototype structure, which was tested for a year before the design was finalized. The result is that the new tower utilizes concrete in several ways: it provides the structure, carries the servicing and offers thermal mass, and it gives a highly expressive finish.

Space cooling is provided by a concrete core cooling system, where chilled water pipes are embedded in the reinforced concrete slab, enhancing the natural effect of the thermal mass to regulate internal temperatures and provide radiant cooling.

The glazing is interspersed with metal panels punched with "portholes" and banded with anodized aluminum panels. Operable windows are provided throughout the building, allowing 70 percent of the floor plate to be naturally ventilated. In conjunction with thermal mass and chilled slabs, the mechanical ventilation can be switched off for half of the year.

Opposite: The White Collar Factory takes its shape from the chamfered corner of Old Street and City Road in the heart of the Islington high-tech district.

Top: Operable "porthole" windows provide extra incentive for occupants to naturally ventilate the building.

Bottom Left: The pattern set by the large "porthole" windows near the top is repeated down the façade by way of metal screens with smaller circular perforations.

Bottom Right: The industrial/nautical "porthole" theme is carried through to the interior, including desks and doors.

1 | Arena Tower
London, United Kingdom

Completion Date: March 2017
Height: 149 m (489 ft)
Stories: 45
Area: 22,575 sq m (242,995 sq ft)
Primary Function: Residential
Owner: Frogmore
Developers: Frogmore; Galliard Homes; LBS Properties
Architect: Skidmore, Owings & Merrill LLP (design)
Structural Engineer: WSP (design)
MEP Engineer: Whitecode Design Associates (design)
Main Contractor: C J O'Shea Group Ltd

2 | De Verkenner
Utrecht, Netherlands

Completion Date: May 2016
Height: 50 m (164 ft)
Stories: 16
Area: 12,500 sq m (134,549 sq ft)
Primary Function: Residential
Owner/Developer: Mitros
Architect: Mei architects and planners (design)
Structural Engineer: Pieters Bouwtechniek (design)
MEP Engineer: J. van Toorenburg BV (engineer of record)
Main Contractor: ERA Bouw

3 | Federation Tower
Moscow, Russia

Completion Date: October 2017
Height: 374 m (1,226 ft)
Stories: 93
Area: 442,915 sq m (4,767,497 sq ft)
Primary Functions: Residential / Office
Owner/Developer: ZAO Bashnya Federatsiya
Architects: Rimax Design (design); SPEECH (design); nps tchoban voss (architect of record)
Structural Engineer: Thornton Tomasetti (engineer of record)
MEP Engineer: Ebert-Ingenieure (design)
Project Manager: Turner International LLC
Main Contractors: China State Construction Engineering Corporation; thyssenkrupp; Schindler; Renaissance Construction Company; Stolitsa
Other CTBUH Member Consultants: Schindler (vertical transportation); thyssenkrupp (vertical transportation)
Other CTBUH Member Suppliers: ArcelorMittal (steel); CoxGomyl (façade maintenance equipment); Schindler (elevator); Shenyang Yuanda Aluminium Industry Engineering Co.,Ltd. (cladding); thyssenkrupp (elevator)

4 | Millennium Center 1
Sofia, Bulgaria

Completion Date: May 2017
Height: 115 m (378 ft)
Stories: 32
Primary Function: Hotel
Owner/Developer: NIKMI JSC
Architect: Amfion (design)
Structural Engineer: Amfion (design)
MEP Engineer: Amfion (design)
Main Contractor: NIKMI JSC

5 | Q22 Tower
Warsaw, Poland

Completion Date: June 2016
Height: 155 m (509 ft)
Stories: 42
Area: 53,000 sq m (570,487 sq ft)
Primary Function: Office
Owner: Invesco Real Estate
Developer: Echo Investment
Architect: Kuryowicz & Associates (design)
Structural Engineer: BuroHappold Engineering (design)
MEP Engineer: BuroHappold Engineering (design)
Main Contractor: Modzelewski & Rodek
Other CTBUH Member Consultant: BuroHappold Engineering (BREEAM)

3

4

5

MIDDLE EAST & AFRICA

In this region with some of the world's youngest populations, nations and economies, the ground is fertile and the sky seems the limit. While it is difficult to generalize about a tall building culture across such a vast area, from this collection it is clear that a sense of history, recognition of the importance of cultural signifiers, and enthusiasm for new techniques and concepts is driving the best of what the region's skylines have to offer.

Azrieli Sarona

Tel Aviv, Israel

The Azrieli Sarona Tower is the first "twisted tower" built in Israel and the second-tallest building constructed in the country to date. The fundamental design approach was to produce two independently rotated, twisted building masses that are carefully controlled in their proportions, angle of rotation, overall layout and detailing of the skin.

As the tower rises, the combination between its geometric form and its double-skin façade creates a dynamic and refined appearance. The double-skin façade, with its interior layers of rectangular white elements oriented to the vertical, and smooth, clean transparent glass on the exterior, whose mullions lean at a soft angle parallel to the building edge, increases the complexity of the exterior appearance while cutting down on interior cooling loads. The tower skin hints and relates to the existing Azrieli Towers nearby.

The rotated plan of the building is derived from its location between a main road on the east and Sarona Park, which contains several small Templar buildings, to the west. Two trapezoid masses, each rotating around a different pivot point, results in their being separated by different distances on each floor, coming to an even balance at the tower's midpoint. The rotated plan is aligned on its base with the Sarona Park grid, and as the tower rises, the rotated plan starts to relate to the surrounding towers and the broader cityscape. The shopping mall levels connect between the park level and the street level — which is one story lower than the park — with several entrances; at street level, the landscape allows for wider pedestrian access paths through welcoming piazzas.

In addition to providing an identifiable profile in the skyline, the cleft between the two halves of the building, and the resulting diverging façade planes, also creates opportunities for twice the number of "corner offices" in a standard rectilinear office building.

Great efforts have been made during the project's design and construction to minimize its impact on the environment while improving occupants' well-being. The design includes wastewater and HVAC condensation water recycling, energy-efficient lighting, occupancy and daylight sensors, highly efficient cooling towers (with variable-speed-drive fans and variable-speed pumps), as well as efficient vertical transportation with energy-recovery devices.

The double-skin façade reduces heat loss in the winter as well as unwanted solar heat gain in the summer by way of its air cavity and integrated interior blinds, saving about 26 percent of HVAC energy compared to the 2007 ASHRAE baseline. The cooling effect is achieved mainly by natural ventilation in the void between the layers. Natural ventilation is assisted by the interplay of the tower's location and its double-skin façade design. Wind velocities at the top of the tower are as much as 2.2 times those recorded at 10 meters above grade, which should allow for more than 35 air changes per hour (ACH). A mechanical fan cooling system is automatically operated and provides auxiliary ventilation in the event of low winds and extreme heat conditions.

Completion Date: June 2017
Height: 238 m (782 ft)
Stories: 56
Area: 2,350 sq m (25,295 sq ft)
Primary Function: Office
Owner/Developer: Azrieli Group
Architect: Moshe Tzur Architects and Town Planners (design)
Structural Engineer: David Engineers Ltd. (design)
MEP Engineers: Yosha Amnon Consulting Engineers Ltd (design); Bar Akiva Engineers Ltd (design); M. Doron - I. Shahar & Co. Consulting Engineers Ltd. (design)
Project Manager: Waxman Govrin Geva Engineering LTD.
Main Contractor: Elhar Engineering Construction Ltd.

   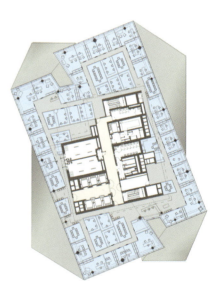

Top: The double-skin façade features interior layers of rectangular white elements oriented vertically, and transparent glazing on the exterior, increasing the complexity of the tower's appearance while cutting down on interior cooling loads.

Bottom: Three floor plans, for levels 12 (left), 33 (center), and 57 (right), demonstrate the dynamic effects of the rotated plan and vertical cleft on two faces, including the provision of additional corner office spaces.

Opposite Top: The tower has a distinctive cleft down its center and a twisting profile, based on a rotated plan extrusion that responds to a main road and a park on its perimeter.

Opposite Bottom: The lobby of Azrieli Sarona extrapolates the angles and dynamics of the exterior.

The double-skin façade's air cavity and integrated interior blinds reduce winter heat loss and unwanted summer solar heat gain, saving about 26 percent of HVAC energy over a standard building.

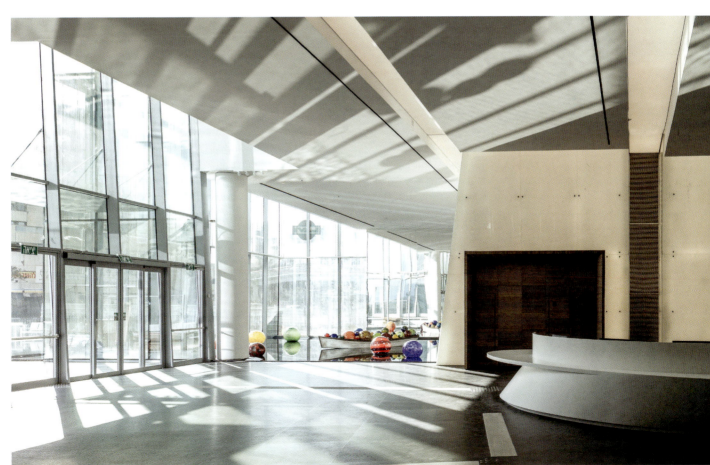

Beirut Terraces

Beirut, Lebanon

Beirut Terraces is a waterfront residential tower in Beirut Central District (BCD) that progresses the city's reputation for indoor/outdoor living experiences through the introduction of extended terraces to the "vertical village" concept. The project is surrounded on the north by the sea, on the south by low-rise residences, and on the east by a 45-meter-wide green pedestrian corridor. In contrast to many other residential high-rises around the world, the tower externally expresses the unique qualities of each living unit through the recession or extension of enclosed space across irregular, shifting floor plates.

The concept rests on the extensive terraces created by this shifting geometry, where customized planters, extended perforated slabs, and green walls provide privacy, shade, and a unique terrace character. Meanwhile, on the ground level, a surface pond surrounding the driveway under shade provides relief from the intense sunshine and hard surfaces, but also reinforces the project's proximity to the sea and indoor/outdoor seamlessness.

Beirut Terraces offers simplexes, duplexes, and penthouses, each with a unique layout and size, making each apartment more akin to a single-family home, each complemented by dedicated parking, generous storage space, a private pool, and a gym. Street-level retail is also available, satisfying the requirements of upscale brands that seek exposure in one of the most prestigious residential areas of Beirut.

Individual apartments are grouped on different levels in "mini-village" formations. Blending art with landscaping provides a consistently "green" atmosphere, and balances the immediate environment by providing an active set of "lungs" for the building. The floor-to-ceiling windows ensure rooms are bathed in natural light, offering residents scenic views of the sea, the mountains, and the city, while deep overhangs cut down on glare and provide a sense of protection. Vegetated screens throughout the building's terraces provide shade and guarantee the necessary privacy for each household. The poignant identity established by the tower's unique profile during daytime is further reinforced at night through an integrated, state-of-the-art lighting system that highlights the slabs' fenestrations.

Completion Date: June 2016
Height: 119 m (392 ft)
Stories: 27
Area: 79,200 sq m (852,502 sq ft)
Primary Function: Residential
Owners: DIB Tower Sal; TOWN Tower Sal
Developer: Benchmark
Architect: Herzog & de Meuron Architekten (design)
Structural Engineer: Khatib & Alami (engineer of record)
MEP Engineer: Khatib & Alami (engineer of record)
Project Manager: Hill International
Main Contractor: MAN Enterprise
Other CTBUH Member Consultants: Arup (lighting); Davis Langdon (cost)

Significant measures were undertaken to ensure Beirut Terraces' environmental performance. These include the use of pre-insulated, foam-based ductwork to reduce energy consumption, and water-cooled A/C systems that consume less power than air-cooled systems. Rainwater is collected for reuse, and grey water drainage is treated and reused. On the building's exterior, low-E, double-glazed, triple-glass façades absorb noise and light, while planters recycle air and reduce solar gain. Importantly, the irrigation systems for the terrace planters are carefully programmed and sequenced to avoid sun exposure and, consequently, unnecessary evaporation.

The "U-Boot" voided slab system was used for the structure of the terraces themselves. This innovative system utilizes polypropylene formworks during concrete pouring to incorporate voids into the slabs, which enhances their structural performance in a number of ways. The system ultimately resulted in faster construction, more spacious rooms, improved acoustic behavior, considerable fire resistance and no toxic emissions.

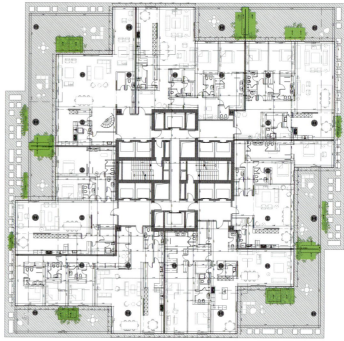

The tower externally expresses the unique qualities of each living unit through the recession or extension of enclosed space across irregular, shifting floor plates.

Left: Customized planters, extended perforated slabs, and green walls provide privacy, shade, and a unique terrace character.

Above: A typical floor plan shows the extent to which each unit's space is devoted to balconies/terraces.

Opposite Top: Many of the terraces have substantial plantings and extensive views of the Mediterranean Sea.

Opposite Bottom: The shaded surface pond at the base provides relief from the intense sunshine and hard surfaces of the tower's surroundings, and reinforces the project's indoor/outdoor coherence.

Rothschild Tower

Tel Aviv, Israel

This residential tower is anchored to Rothschild Boulevard in the heart of Tel Aviv's White City, a UNESCO World Heritage Site. The area is filled with thousands of Bauhaus buildings dating back to the 1930s and 1940s, designed by German Jewish architects who began immigrating to Israel before World War II. The prominent corner site is the intersection of the gracious civic promenade that is Rothschild Boulevard with the commercial corridor of Allenby Street.

The Rothschild Tower rests on a retail base, with connectivity to its own restored through-block retail arcade under resident amenities, firmly embedding the building and its residents in the pulse of the neighborhood. For such a large building in a sensitive setting, lightness and transparency are primary goals, in order not only to reduce scale and mass in the context of the low-to mid-rise neighborhood and scale-less reflective local towers, but to express the optimism and energy of secular, modern Tel Aviv. Those goals are accomplished with clear glass, protected in this desert climate by a delicate louver screen that acts as an elegant white "veil," inspired by the ventilated layers of traditional Middle Eastern clothing. It both defines and obscures the distinction between the public image of the building and the private realm within.

Bauhaus principles inspired a functionality and economy of means, while still using modern mass-produced materials, and in this case, a repetitive planning module. An efficient assembly of "served" and "service" spaces around the core maximizes ventilation, the quality of light in the plan, and views to the sea.

The tower is designed to recognize its role as a citizen in the city, with gestures to different scales at the base, shaft, and top of the building. At the scale of the street, it is deliberately lifted on graceful piloti, with an undulating glass lobby and retail wall in deference to the importance of the intersection of Rothschild and Allenby. Its lofty openness contributes to a vibrant streetscape. At the scale of the neighborhood, the louver elements of the building's screen texture have architectural precedents in the ubiquitous "treeseem," the sliding louver blinds enclosing open air porches or negative spaces common to existing Bauhaus buildings. At the scale of the city, the top of the building has "signature" gestures to Tel Aviv and the sea in the terraced design of penthouse apartments behind a large "urban window" facing the Mediterranean Sea.

The corner site is connected to public transportation and a bike-share program outside the main entrance — within walking distance of the sea and neighborhood commercial zone. The building's simple massing and small floor plates relegate service and wet areas to the core, liberating the periphery to maximize ventilation, views, and light. The layered façade is a bioclimatic response to the desert sun, and is comprised of a louvered screen and high-performance unitized glazed curtain wall façade that effectively eliminates solar radiation and glare and allows air movement across the façade, substantially reducing the cooling load. Simple building systems initiatives also conserve energy. Low-flow, high-efficiency plumbing fixtures are used in all bathrooms. Light and occupancy sensors control LED lighting. Mechanical equipment is "right-sized," and each apartment has a "smart home" system to conserve energy and maximize control. Recycled and recyclable materials are used extensively.

Completion Date: March 2017
Height: 154 m (505 ft)
Stories: 42
Area: 27,000 sq m (290,626 sq ft)
Primary Function: Residential
Owner/Developer: Berggruen Residential Ltd.
Architects: Richard Meier & Partners Architects (design); Barely Levitzky Kassif Architects (architect of record)
Structural Engineer: David Engineers Ltd. (engineer of record)
MEP Engineers: R. Cohen & Associates (engineer of record); D. Hahn Consulting Engineers LTD (engineer of record)
Project Manager: Waxman Govrin Geva Engineering LTD.
Other CTBUH Member Supplier: KONE (elevator)

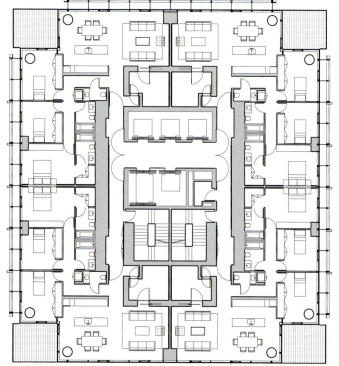

Above: The Rothschild Tower holds a commanding presence along its eponymous boulevard and builds on the tradition of Bauhaus buildings in its surroundings.

Left: A typical floor plan shows the highly private corner balconies and the screen protecting three sides of the building.

Opposite Top: The building's signature louvers are clearly visible in this poolside view.

Opposite Bottom: In the lobby, the building's interwar-era design influences are clear.

The louver elements of the building's screen texture have architectural precedents in the "treeseem": the ubiquitous sliding blinds common to existing Bauhaus buildings.

Zeitz MOCAA
Cape Town, South Africa

Since 1924, one of the most identifiable structures in Cape Town, South Africa, was a massive grain storage and silo complex, constructed by the South African Railways and Harbours Company on the downtown waterfront. The building had sat unused since 2001, as the owners and community sought out a way to repurpose it. Shortly after a design concept was developed, an initiative began to create Africa's first international museum dedicated to contemporary African art. It was decided that the grain silo could be transformed into a new home for the Zeitz Foundation's art collection, which could act as a founding collection upon which the new museum could build. The top portion of the taller building was transformed into a luxury hotel, while the bottom portion of the elevator building and the storage annex would become the new museum.

The two major parts of the complex were connected by a central atrium carved from the silo's cellular structure. Main circulation routes are housed within the atrium, via cylindrical lifts that run inside two bisected concrete tubes. The remaining internal tubes were removed to make space for 80 climate-controlled gallery spaces that were deliberately pared back to create a platform for the art on show.

By focusing on the history of the structure, specifically the many billions of kernels of grain that journeyed through the building over the decades, it was decided that the form of the atrium's volume should take the shape of a grain of corn. The shape was scaled up to fill the 27-meter-high volume and translated into thousands of coordinates. In order for the building to retain its structural integrity, a new concrete building had to be cast inside the old shell. The 170-millimeter-thick concrete tubes were lined with inner sleeves of reinforced concrete, following the atrium shape to reveal the curved geometries of the 4,600 cubic-meter space.

Retaining existing steel and concrete allowed for limited additional wall and ceiling finishes, and is in accordance with international best practice for sustainable museum design. When a survey uncovered that the original walls

Completion Date: September 2017
Height: 58 m (190 ft)
Stories: 14
Primary Functions: Museum
Owner/Developer: Victoria and Alfred Waterfront
Architects: Heatherwick Studio (design); Jacobs Parker Architects (architect of record); Rick Brown Associates (architect of record); Van Der Merwe Miszewski Architects (architect of record)
Structural Engineers: Arup; Sutherland
MEP Engineers: Arup; Solution Station
Main Contractor: Mace Limited
Other CTBUH Member Consultants: Arup (façade, fire)

were not perfectly vertical, it was decided to cast the new walls with varied widths to achieve a fixed vertical inside of the tube. New walls were cast in the final atrium shape and used as a guide to trim the old walls by using handheld double-disk saws.

The cut sweeps through the concrete at varying angles. Numerous iterations were explored to ensure that none of the angles were too oblique, which could have caused the concrete to chip during the cutting process. Small chamfers were applied to sharp edges and gradually tapered out as the angle grew in width. Both surfaces were polished together into one continuous surface. The old and new concrete can be identified by the varying textures resulting from the difference in historic and modern aggregate mixtures. The almost archaeological attempt to showcase the original silo's exposed spaces and textures was made possible through the use of modern construction materials and techniques.

From the outside, the greatest visible change to the building's original structure is the addition of the glass windows inserted into the geometry. These multi-faceted windows bulge outward as if gently inflated. By night, this transforms the building into a glowing beacon in Table Bay.

Above: Voids cutting through some of the individual grain silos bring light into deep interior spaces and provide a unique viewing opportunity for the all-glass elevator runs.

Top Right: The structure as it appeared in 1925, when it was still in use as a grain silo.

Right: Entrance, showing cut-away form of the original silos.

Opposite Top: The window frame patterns are reflected on the floor of the roof deck.

Opposite Bottom: The relationship between the dramatic atrium, gallery spaces, and hotel above are revealed in section.

By focusing on the structure's history, specifically the many billions of kernels of grain that journeyed through it, it was decided that the atrium's volume should take the shape of a grain of corn.

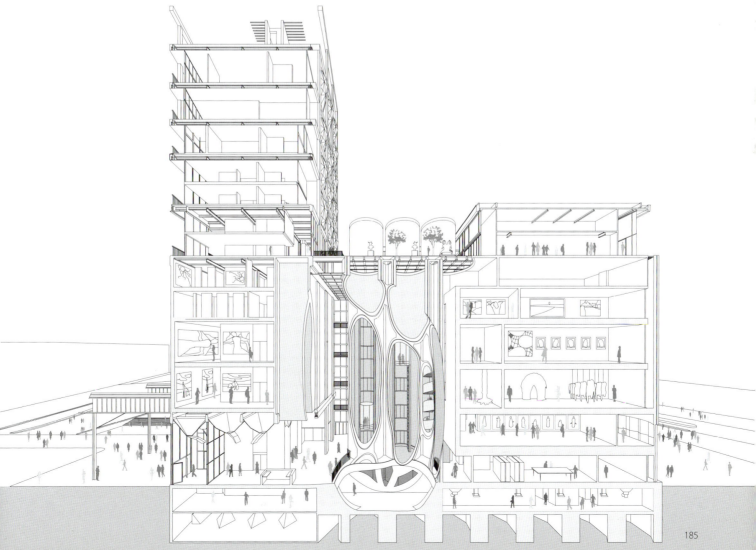

1 | Britam Tower
Nairobi, Kenya

Completion Date: November 2017
Height: 200 m (656 ft)
Stories: 31
Area: 74,074 sq m (797,326 sq ft)
Primary Function: Office
Owner/Developer: British American Insurance Company Limited
Architects: GAPP Architects & Urban Designers (design); Triad Architects (design)
Structural Engineer: Howard Humphreys (East Africa) Ltd. (design)
MEP Engineers: ChapmanBDSP (design); Maiteri & Associates (engineer of record)
Project Manager: Britam Properties Limited
Main Contractor: Laxmanbhai Construction
Other CTBUH Member Consultants: ChapmanBDSP (fire)
Other CTBUH Member Suppliers: David Engineers Ltd. (steel); Schindler (elevator)

2 | Iran Telecom Research Center
Tehran, Iran

Completion Date: January 2016
Height: 54 m (178 ft)
Stories: 10
Area: 21,000 sq m (226,042 sq ft)
Primary Function: Education
Owners: Ministry of Communications and Information Technology; Iran Telecommunication Research Center
Developer: Iran Telecommunication Research Center
Architect: Harmonic Trend [L] (design)
Structural Engineer: Tarho Mantagheh Consulting Engineers (design)
MEP Engineer: Tarho Mantagheh Consulting Engineers (design)
Main Contractor: Tehran Goruh Co.

3 | Landmark Group Headquarters
Dubai, United Arab Emirates

Completion Date: June 2016
Height: 132 m (431 ft)
Stories: 27
Area: 52,583 sq m (565,999 sq ft)
Primary Function: Office
Owner/Developer: Landmark Group
Architect: Archgroup Consultants (design)
Structural Engineer: Archgroup Consultants (design)
MEP Engineer: Ian Banham and Associates (design)
Project Manager: Archgroup Consultants
Main Contractor: Shapoorji Pallonji & Co. Ltd.

4 | The 118
Dubai, United Arab Emirates

Completion Date: 2016
Height: 208 m (682 ft)
Stories: 46
Area: 19,000 sq m (204,514 sq ft)
Primary Function: Residential
Owner/Developer: Signature Estates Limited
Architect: Archgroup Consultants (design)
Structural Engineer: Archgroup Consultants (design)
MEP Engineer: Archgroup Consultants (design)
Project Manager: SIDE International
Main Contractor: Al Basti & Muktha LLC

5 | The Shahar Tower
Givatayim, Israel

Completion Date: February 2017
Height: 202 m (661 ft)
Stories: 52
Area: 1,600 sq m (17,222 sq ft)
Primary Functions: Residential / Office
Developers: Sufrin Group; Tidhar Investments
Architects: AMAV A. Niv - A. Schwartz Architects (design); Barely Levitzky Kassif Architects (design)
Structural Engineer: David Engineers Ltd. (design)
MEP Engineers: Bar Akiva Engineers Ltd (engineer of record); M. Doron - I. Shahar & Co. Consulting Engineers Ltd. (engineer of record); Yosha Amnon Consulting Engineers Ltd (engineer of record)
Main Contractor: Tidhar Construction

3

4

5

URBAN HABITAT

The impact of a tall building is far wider than just the building itself. It is now recognized that the full potential of these buildings is not achieved unless they can make significant contributions to the urban realm. In this section, we see much evidence of those contributions, from green walls and occupiable green roofs, to inducements to pedestrians to enter and explore the site, to gracious engineering allowing the public realm to continue uninterrupted. Ultimately, the projects described here demonstrate a positive contribution to the surrounding environment, add to the social sustainability of both their immediate and wider settings, and represent design influenced by context, both environmentally and culturally.

Barangaroo South/ International Towers

Sydney, Australia

The International Towers Sydney are the driving force behind Barangaroo South, Sydney's largest urban regeneration project in decades. It unites the central business district with the western waterfront, providing a new financial services hub, transforming a contaminated former wharf into a new district of Sydney, reconnecting it to the harbor and giving people back a crucial part of the city. The city-defining development is creating thousands of jobs, and provides a vibrant new hub for work and play, injecting more than US$1.5 billion annually into the economy. When fully leased, more than 23,000 office workers and 2,000 residents will populate the district. They will be served by more than 80 cafés, bars, restaurants, and retail outlets.

Effectively, Barangaroo South is a 5.2-hectare western extension to the core CBD. International Towers is the epicenter of this "Six-Star Green Star Community," incorporating premium residential and commercial buildings; and a variety of shopping, hospitality and public realm experiences, including 14 kilometers of harborside walking tracks.

Extensive transport connections integrate the site to the city via an underground pedestrian link, a new ferry hub, overpass pedestrian bridges, an upcoming Sydney Metro station and more than 1,000 dedicated bike parking spaces incorporated into the towers. In fact, there are three times as many bike parking spaces as there are spaces for cars. There is a direct link to all major suburbs, in all directions, from one central point—making Barangaroo Australia's most accessible workplace. The award-winning Barangaroo Reserve, at the northernmost point of the site, was restored to echo Sydney Harbour's pre-1836 shoreline, with more than 75,000 native plants creating a beautiful lunchtime oasis for the community.

A centralized mechanical plant and district cooling system efficiently provide services to all towers, enabling the provision of roof-level terraces that extend the urban habitat

Completion Date: December 2016
Total Land Area: 78,400 sq m (843,890 sq ft)
Total Building Area: 37,000 sq m (398,264 sq ft)
Total Hardscape: 29,820 sq m (320,979 sq ft)
Total Softscape: 5,950 sq m (64,045 sq ft)
Owner/Developer: Lend Lease
Urban Planner: Ethos Urban
Architects: Rogers Stirk Harbour + Partners (design); Lendlease Design (architect of record)
Landscape Architects: Aspect Oculus; Gustafson, Guthrie, & Nichol
Project Manager: Lendlease Project Management
Main Contractor: Lendlease Building Pty Ltd

off the ground level. The air conditioning system routes all exhausts via dedicated heat recovery coils. A water treatment plant uses recycled water for toilets and irrigation—processing one megaliter a day. Six thousand square meters of solar photovoltaic panels provide electricity to offset the energy used by the recycling plant and public domain lighting. The construction of the project entailed 97 percent diversion of waste from landfills. Food service packaging is made from compostable materials, and is processed with food scraps into fertilizer or feed stock for energy production. More than 50,000 LED lamps are used throughout the public realm and buildings.

A large common basement with single vehicle access allows a continual active street front at ground level. The lobbies of the towers are transparent and inviting; open to visitors, they run through all the buildings as a continuation of the streets of Barangaroo South. This adds a new dimension to Sydney's outdoor culture and gives them human scale and impact at ground level. The buildings on the site address the waterfront, bringing a critical mass of activity and enabling the creation of a new public space, in an area where public space is at a premium.

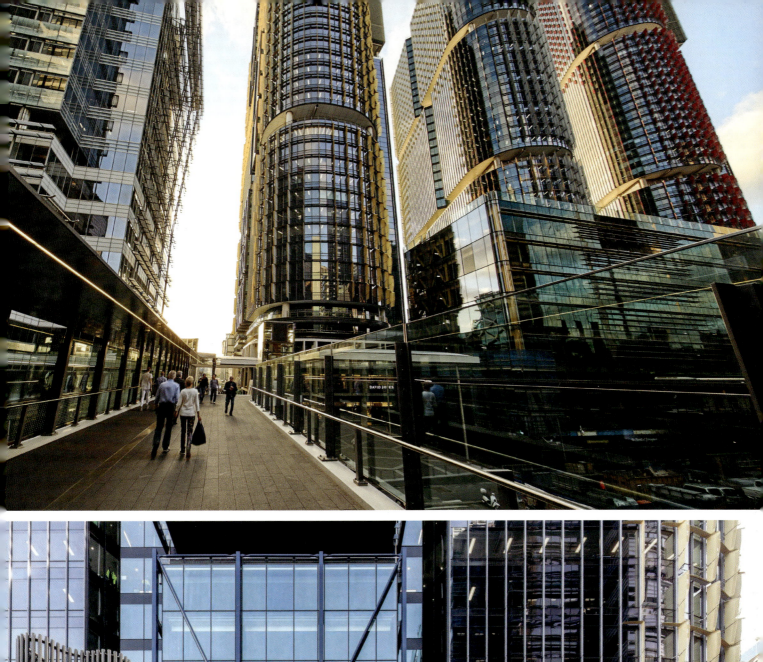

Left: The project aligns with, and provides access to, the walkway along Darling Harbour.

Below: The base of Tower 2 features al fresco dining, activating the street.

Opposite Top: Opportunities are taken to provide green covering wherever possible, including this "planted plant" facility.

Opposite Bottom: The three-tower development is skewed from the street grid to provide optimal view corridors, ventilation and sunlight. The podiums are topped with green roofs.

The community incorporates residential and commercial buildings and a variety of shopping, hospitality and public realm experiences, including 14 kilometers of harborside walking tracks.

City Tower Musashikosugi

Kawasaki, Japan

Completion Date: 2016
Total Land Area: 8,628 sq m (92,871 sq ft)
Total Building Area: 3,992 sq m (42,970 sq ft)
Total Open Area: 4,636 sq m (49,901 sq ft)
Total Hardscape: 1,936 sq m (20,839 sq ft)
Total Softscape: 1,350 sq m (14,531 sq ft)
Owner/Developer: Sumitomo Realty & Development Co., Ltd.
Urban Planner: Maeda Corporation
Architect: Maeda Corporation (design)
Landscape Architect: Maeda Corporation
Structural Engineer: Maeda Corporation (engineer of record)
MEP Engineer: Maeda Corporation (engineer of record)
Project Manager: Maeda Corporation
Main Contractor: Maeda Corporation

Located in a southern suburb of Tokyo near the intersection of multiple commuter train lines, the site is ideal from a connectivity standpoint. However, the area is highly congested and lacks common green space. The clearance of the site for an 800-unit residential tower provided a new opportunity to soften the cityscape and provide useful public right-of-way, combining this with greenery and amenities for the community's new and existing residents.

The site is an irregular shape of about 8,600 square meters in area, with major streets on two sides and a minor street on the third side. The most efficient tower footprint for the program was a rectilinear shape of about 4,000 square meters, leaving more than half the site open for green space. Auto entrances are kept to one side of the site, with two driveways for the porte-cochere/drop-off area and one for the parking garage. This allows for public pathways to follow pedestrian desire lines as they walk between several commercial areas and the train stations.

The pathways are lit by knee-height cylindrical lamps, and benches appear frequently along the route. Along the narrow back street at the site's south edge, pylons have been installed to separate pedestrians from cars that are also drawn to use the street as a shortcut. The shifting rectangles of the pedestrian walkway contrast with the firm colonnade of the building beyond and the soft greenery in between. Plantings are presented at a variety of scales, from pine trees several meters high to low and dense shrubs.

Opposite: The awkwardly-shaped site was played to advantage, as it opened opportunities for pedestrian passages and green space around the perimeter.

Top: There is plentiful open space and numerous pedestrian-scale elements at the base of the tower.

Left: The project entrance is well defined and inegrated into the landscape scheme.

Dua Menjalara

Kuala Lumpur, Malaysia

Completion Date: March 2016
Total Land Area: 3,845 sq m (41,387 sq ft)
Total Building Area: 2,527 sq m (27,200 sq ft)
Total Open Area: 2,763 sq m (29,740 sq ft)
Total Hardscape: 1,438 sq m (15,479 sq ft)
Total Softscape: 1,325 sq m (14,262 sq ft)
Owner/Developer: Radiant Symphony Sdn Bhd
Architect: Atelier Alan Teh Architect
Landscape Architect: Engky Design Sdn Bhd
Structural Engineer: KNK Consult Sdn Bhd
MEP Engineer: Juara Consult Sdn Bhd
Main Contractor: YWC Engineers & Constructors Sdn Bhd

The organization of communal facilities within a condominium project normally dictates the presence of a wide base podium. This project breaks from this notion, as well as the traditional restriction that only exclusive units enjoy the best views. It does so by providing an accessible communal hub for all the residents on a high floor, instead of on the typical podium, and through site orientation.

By concentrating the building footprint to the north side of the site, the southern sector's natural ground is preserved, with terraced greens surrounding an outdoor playground. The design has been executed in order to fit a point-block tower layout that takes the advantage of views and solar orientation onto the site. The 17th-floor communal sky lounge with a cantilevered swimming pool offers the best view for all residents. A vertical jigsaw of units in various configurations are intertwined with green communal spaces throughout.

Instead of a large podium car park, the project buries the parking within the slope of the landscape. Moving the amenities floor up and the car park down has allowed natural landscaping to dominate the ground plane of the small lot, where a community terrace and green deck including rain trees and lush shrubbery. These strategies increased the total green site coverage from a nominal 10 percent to about 35 percent of the site area. Other green features include hanging pocket gardens, and penthouse sky gardens, which push the green ratio of the project to nearly 50 percent of the site area.

Opposite: The tower is set to the rear of the property, affording plentiful green space on the site.
Top: The lift lobby is naturally ventilated, with additional cooling provided by the surrounding pond.
Bottom Left: A communal viewing deck is provided for residents.
Bottom Right: A terraced garden and playground are creatively incorporated within the site constraints.

Greatwall Complex

Wuhan, China

The Greatwall Complex comprises twin towers which are linked by four floors of podium located in the financial center of Wuhan, China. It provides a world-class workplace and retail facilities, a vibrant public realm, and a high-performance, sustainable building.

A main focus of the development and design team and the local government was to maximize the potential of the podium spaces and their relationship with the streetscape of Zhongbei Road. Through a series of open, terraced spaces, the pedestrian realm of the street was extended up and across the podium. The new public spaces offer diverse amenities, including restaurant terraces, art sculptures, a "water curtain wall," multimedia roof garden, and amphitheater.

The initial brief was for a standard retail mall podium; however, the clients' vision was for a "destination" public space. The optimum solution defined a new civic space right in front of the building, connected through a series of processional ramps to a roof garden on the podium. The processional ramp allowed all retail establishments to open up to a new raised ground level, thereby maximizing leasable value for the client. The ramp also presents a unique pedestrian experience in Wuhan, presenting the opportunity to partake of dining opportunities and public art while looking back across the city from a raised elevation. The sculpted form of the podium works in harmony with the two towers rising above. The relationship of the lower podium with the surrounding city context has been carefully considered, providing a positive addition to the streetscape, engagement with the existing urban realm, and the creation of new public space.

The concept of the accessible and active façade begins with a sunken plaza at Level B1, providing sheltered external café space and access to retail space, including a supermarket and food court. The start of the journey upwards along the façade from Level 1 is defined by an amphitheater space facing south, which provides

Completion Date: June 2016
Total Land Area: 22,000 sq m (236,806 sq ft)
Total Building Area: 8,505 sq m (91,547 sq ft)
Total Open Area: 13,495 sq m (145,259 sq ft)
Total Hardscape: 4,600 sq m (49,514 sq ft)
Owner/Developer: Greatwall Construction Holdings Group Co. Ltd.
Urban Planner: 10 DESIGN
Architects: 10 DESIGN (design); Citic Wuhan Architectural Design Institute (architect of record)
Landscape Architect: 10 DESIGN
Structural Engineer: Citic Wuhan Architectural Design Institute (engineer of record)
MEP Engineer: Citic Wuhan Architectural Design Institute (engineer of record)
Project Manager: DTZ Debenham Tie Leung
Main Contractor: China Construction Third Engineering Bureau Co., Ltd.

external seating space all year round for the public, and performance space during the weekends. The transition between each level is articulated by grand "stair spaces," animated by terraced garden spaces and art installations. The destination of the public route along the façade is a lush rooftop garden located at Level 4, activated by adjacent retail space. The garden, demarcated by a green wall set against the smooth backdrop of the building, is an interactive environment, providing space for art exhibitions and performances.

The principal aim of the urban design was to create a new dynamic and iconic working environment for Wuhan, which would attract high end tenants, facilitate the ongoing regeneration of the district, and raise the profile of the recently designated financial core of Wuhan.

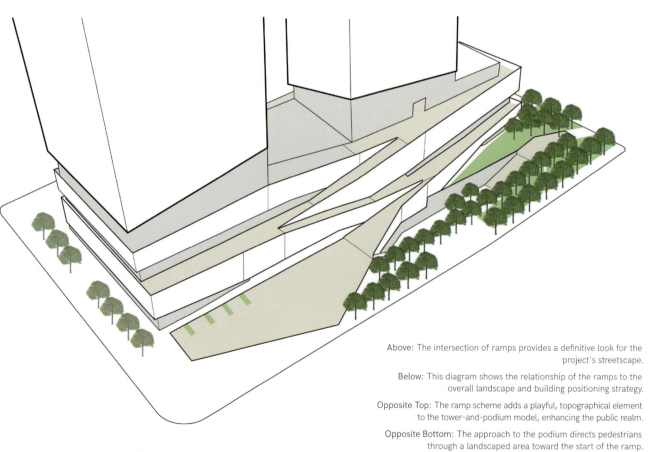

Above: The intersection of ramps provides a definitive look for the project's streetscape.

Below: This diagram shows the relationship of the ramps to the overall landscape and building positioning strategy.

Opposite Top: The ramp scheme adds a playful, topographical element to the tower-and-podium model, enhancing the public realm.

Opposite Bottom: The approach to the podium directs pedestrians through a landscaped area toward the start of the ramp.

The ramp system provides a new civic space right in front of the building, connecting to a roof garden on the podium.

National September 11 Memorial

New York City, United States

The National September 11 Memorial is a 3.2-hectare plaza set within the dense urban fabric of Lower Manhattan, where the former World Trade Center Twin Towers once stood. The Memorial Plaza is an integral part of the 6.5-hectare redeveloped World Trade Center Complex, and it reaches and connects the site to the city beyond. It is an open and welcoming design that is meant to foster the democratic values of public assembly that played such a pivotal role in the city's collective response to the attacks of September 11, 2001.

The Memorial Plaza forms a clearing in the middle of the city and is vaulted by a permeable canopy of close to 400 swamp white oak trees. As visitors to the memorial make their way towards the center of this space, they encounter the two reflecting pools that deeply puncture the vast flat expanse of the plaza, and form empty vessels. They are recessed n meters into the ground and are lined by waterfalls, delineating the location of the former towers. The voids are absence, made present and visible.

The National September 11 Memorial was designed to serve as a public gathering place, a memorial plaza, and to serve residents, commuters and tourists — the local and global public at large. It was designed with a deep conviction about the power of urban public space to catalyze social change and to inform public discourse. It is based on the fundamental belief that the best response to terror is the public affirmation of the virtues of democracy and freedom, virtues that are both embodied and further affirmed by the creation of an urban public realm. It was critical that the Memorial be an integrated part of the city, not a monument in isolation. Therefore, the design draws in the surrounding streets and sidewalks, knitting the site back into the urban fabric of Lower Manhattan. The plaza allows the site to be a living part of the city again.

The tree-filled plaza acts as a green roof for the Memorial Museum and the train station located 18 meters below it.

Completion Date: May 2014
Total Land Area: 33,221 sq m (357,588 sq ft)
Total Building Area: 1,945 sq m (20,936 sq ft)
Total Open Area: 31,276 sq m (336,652 sq ft)
Total Hardscape: 20,994 sq m (225,978 sq ft)
Total Softscape: 10,282 sq m (110,675 sq ft)
Owner: National September 11 Memorial and Museum
Urban Planners: Handel Architects LLP; PWP Landscape Architects
Architects: Handel Architects LLP (design); Davis Brody Bond (architect of record)
Landscape Architect: PWP Landscape Architects
Structural Engineer: WSP Cantor Seinuk (design)
MEP Engineer: Jaros, Baum & Bolles (design)
Project Manager: Lend Lease
Main Contractor: Lend Lease
Other CTBUH Member Consultants: Arup (security); Code Consultants, Inc.(code); Weidlinger Associates (foundation)

To support the trees, and isolate their roots from impact, a suspended paving system was used. The pavement sits atop troughs filled with nutrient-rich soil for the tree roots. Rainwater is harvested and used as irrigation for the trees. A majority of the daily and monthly irrigation requirements are met by the harvested water. As they grow, the trees provide shaded space to increase comfort for visitors and reduce heat absorption on the plaza. The transpiration of the many leaves cools the air throughout the district. An enormous volume of soil — 36,287 metric tons in total — makes up the foundation of the plaza and ensures that the oaks will grow and thrive to maturity.

The National September 11 Memorial is located in one of the densest urban areas in the world, and serves about five million visitors a year. The rebuilding of the WTC site as a public open space has become a valuable catalyst for the successful rebuilding of the mixed-use office towers that surround it, helping to regenerate the Lower Manhattan economy and real estate market.

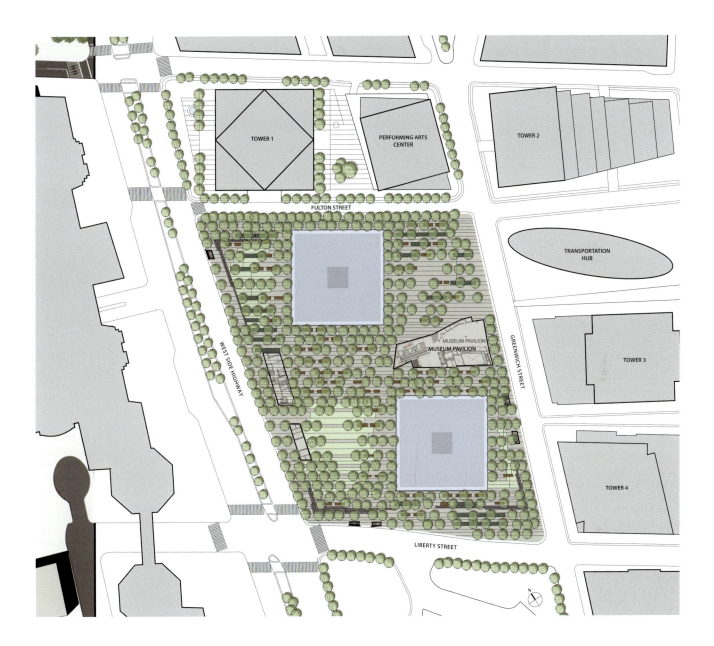

It was critical that the Memorial be an integrated part of the city, not a monument in isolation. The plaza allows the site to be a living part of the city again.

Opposite Top: The two main elements of the site, the voids containing the memorial fountains and the landscape strips with swamp white oak trees, converge throughout.

Opposite Bottom: The fountain voids provide both a somber memorial and a focal gathering point for downtown Manhattan.

Above: The Memorial provides a green bridge for pedestrians coming from the Hudson River path (upper left) and proceeding into the Financial District (lower right).

Oasia Hotel Downtown
Singapore

Envisaged as a "tropical tower" in the concrete jungle, the Oasia Hotel Downtown incorporates lush greenery on its façade and terraces, rejecting the notion that to build more densely means to retract into increasingly insular and sterile shells. The Oasia, by contrast, is like a giant tree — soft, layered, breathing, shading — providing respite and relief to its occupants, neighbors and city: a true vertical urban habitat. The tower stands out with its plant-covered façade of red and green and is a contrast to the sleek grey and blue high-rises, but it connects to the green of Singapore's cityscape.

Offices, hotel and club rooms are located on different strata, each with its own sky garden. These additional "ground" levels, open-sided for formal and visual transparency, create generous public areas for recreation and social interaction throughout the high-rise, despite the high-density location. Relocating the tower's core to four corner supports allows for a unique 360-degree view of the city, and opens the tall, yet sheltered gardens to allow breezes to pass through for cross-ventilation that doesn't require air conditioning, making them functional, comfortable tropical spaces. The hotel has swimming pools and sitting areas, as well as the main lobby in the sky gardens, while the office portion of the building also has its own dedicated sky garden and a swimming pool, where people can enjoy the green during a break from work. Passersby use the shaded walkways that the building provides to shelter from the sun and rain.

Landscaping is used extensively as an architectural surface treatment, and forms a major part of the development's material palette, both internally and externally, achieving an overall Green Plot Ratio of over 1,000%. The tower's red aluminum mesh cladding is designed as a backdrop and sun-shading "skin," revealing itself in a dynamic dance with the changing growth, attracting animals and insects. Instead of a flat roof, the tower is crowned with a tropical bower; living, diverse and floral.

Planting is one of the best ways to combat the urban heat island effect, as plants store solar energy as chemical bonds rather than converting it into heat. Twenty-one species of creepers sit in fiberglass planters that are easily accessible via walkways behind the aluminum mesh façade screen. Another 33 species of plants and trees were selected, providing a total of 54 species of plants and trees to improve biodiversity — both through plantings and by providing habitat for squirrels, small lizards and butterflies — in the downtown city center.

The site is located in Tanjong Pagar, which is home to iconic heritage sites, and borders the Central Business District on one side and Chinatown on the other. The contrast of the old and modern Singapore is reflected in the design of the building: the color red is very auspicious in Chinese culture and the permeable façade lets the interior light shine through at night, giving the tower the look of an illuminated abstraction of a Chinese lantern.

Completion Date: April 2016
Total Land Area: 2,311 sq m (24,875 sq ft)
Total Building Area: 19,416 sq m (63,701 sq ft), Gross Floor Area Only
Total Open Area: 6,130 sq m (20,112 sq ft), Terraces Only
Total Hardscape: 3,103 sq m (10,180 sq ft), Terraces Only
Total Softscape: 3,035 sq m (9,957 sq ft), Terraces Only, Excluding Planters on Façade
Owner: Far East SOHO Pte Ltd.
Developer: Far East Organization
Urban Planner: WOHA Architects
Architect: WOHA Architects
Landscape Architect: Sitetectonix Pte Ltd
Structural Engineer: KTP Consultants Pte Ltd (design)
MEP Engineer: Rankine & Hill Consulting Engineers (design)
Main Contractor: Woh Hup Pte Ltd
Other CTBUH Member Consultants: Rider Levett Bucknall (quantity surveyor); Windtech Consultants Pty Ltd (wind)

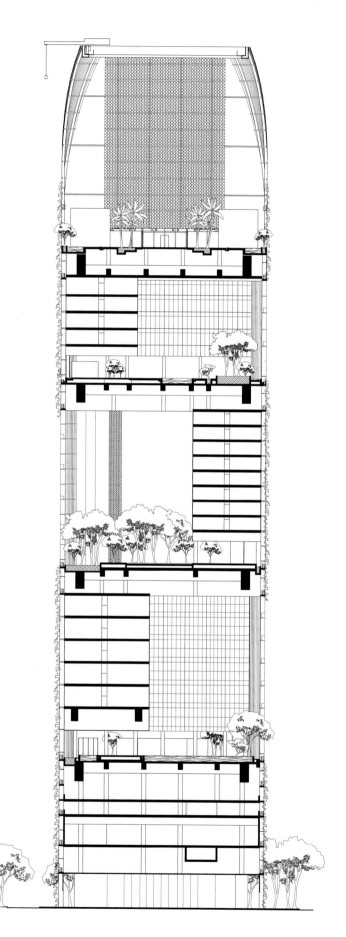

Landscaping is used extensively as an architectural surface treatment, and forms a major part of the development's material palette, achieving an overall Green Plot Ratio of over 1,000%.

Left: This section drawing shows the three distinct "Sky Terraces" that distribute public realm throughout the building.

Opposite Top: Despite its rooftop location, the Sky Terrace on the 27th floor is adequately protected by a large awning and encircling façade.

Opposite Bottom Left: An exterior view of the Sky Terrace demonstrates its porosity and integration with the building façade.

Opposite Bottom Right: The Sky Terraces bring greenery and common outdoor spaces to height in the building.

SKYPARK

Hong Kong, China

SKYPARK is a mixed-use development located at Mongkok, one of the densest urban districts in the city, including a shopping mall and residential units geared towards young singles and couples. Many tall buildings neglect the potential of their rooftops as usable space, but this project both emphatically embraces the potential of the rooftop and integrates it with habitat-enhancing design moves at the base of the tower.

The shopping mall — "the Forest" — enhances the streetscape by breaking down a large podium massing into smaller blocks, creating a more human-scaled "shopping village." The interaction of the open plaza, internal street, greenery, grand staircase, outdoor furniture, openable windows and skylights was designed to pull people in from the street and create an outdoor atmosphere throughout the mall, so that shoppers feel like they are "exploring." These features form buffer spaces for the overcrowded district and enhance the flow of air and people, and the quality of gathering spaces in the neighborhood. Planters and vertical green walls were strategically placed at different locations in the mall, so that they can be viewed from different parts of the interior, as well as from the surrounding streets.

The sense of exploration continues at the tower top, where a residential clubhouse connects to a landscaped garden on the roof via the broad "sky stair" — a large outdoor staircase bedecked with casual furnishings clustered in small, casual groups across several landings. This not only acts as a connection between clubhouse and garden, but also serves as an iconic architectural/landscape feature and a gathering space in its own right. At the clubhouse, an open, continuous and transformable communal space was created for residents to enjoy on the very top of the city; special social events and private parties can be facilitated by adjusted movable partitioning.

While the residents can enjoy a cosmopolitan life in this vibrant neighborhood, the roof also provides an escape from the urban hardscape with its openness, spectacular city views, greenery, fresh air and sunlight. Covered with vegetation, the roof reduces air pollution and carbon emissions, provides shade and removes heat from the surrounding air through evapotranspiration. A clipped lawn offers the novel experience of having a picnic in one of the world's densest places.

Other environmentally-friendly features include the solar water heating system, solar PV lighting, wind turbines, and a rainwater recycling system. At the Forest, materials such as textured tiles, stonework panels, wood-like textural glass-fiber reinforced concrete (GFRC) cladding and charcoal-grey aluminum panels were adopted for exterior durability. Planters and vertical green walls were also added at strategic locations on the façades to give a sense of lush greenery to the building. In order to create a sense of a "shopping village" with streets intervening among the shops, the mall interior was finished with similar finishes to those on the exterior. Internal and external spaces at clubhouse and the roof garden were also integrated and visually heightened by the interaction of hardscape and softscape. Paving materials are mainly natural aggregates, while seats and benches were designed as an extension of the paving, as if "peeled" from the floor.

Completion Date: October 2016
Total Land Area: 2,478 sq m (26,673 sq ft)
Total Building Area: 1,977 sq m (21,280 sq ft)
Total Open Area: 1,487 sq m (16,006 sq ft)
Total Hardscape: 2,024 sq m (21,786 sq ft)
Total Softscape: 833 sq m (8,966 sq ft)
Owner: Urban Renewal Authority
Developer: New World Development Company Limited
Architect: P&T Group (design)
Landscape Architect: Adrian L. Norman Ltd.
Structural Engineer: CM Wong & Associates Ltd (design)
MEP Engineers: WSP (design); WSP Hong Kong Ltd. (design, engineer of record)
Project Manager: New World Construction Company Limited
Main Contractor: New World Construction Company Limited

While many tall buildings neglect their rooftops, this project emphatically embraces the potential of the rooftop and integrates it with habitat-enhancing design moves at the base of the tower.

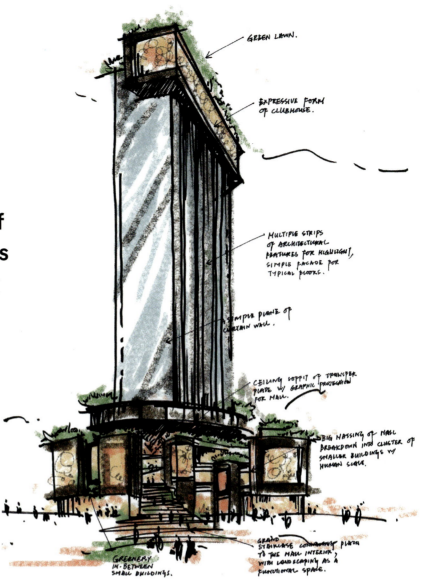

Opposite Top: The rooftop provides the unusual juxtaposition of green recreational space and an urban observatory.

Opposite Bottom Left: The Sky Stairs are lined with furniture, encouraging social gathering.

Opposite Bottom Right: The "Forest" shopping center occupies the first few floors of the project; it is both a vibrant extension of the street and a shaded urban oasis.

Top Left: A sketch drawing demonstrates how the project is anchored at top and bottom by greenery and a sense of accessibility.

Bottom Left: Every available space on the rooftop is used for planting or pedestrians, who can navigate around mechanical housings like explorers on a mountaintop.

SOHO Fuxing Plaza

Shanghai, China

The former French Concession in the heart of Shanghai is known for its typical rectilinear development — the *li long*. *Li* stands for "neighborhood," and *long* refers to the narrow rectilinear streets separating the buildings. This urban morphology creates narrow and intimate urban spaces. The SOHO Fuxing Plaza adopts the scale and orientation of its neighboring *li longs*. The ensemble consists of nine oblong building blocks with sloping roofs and an east-west orientation, and a high-rise building at the corner of the development, which provides a more general reference point to the urban landscape.

The development strives to continue the vibrant, human-scaled city environment of the French Concession quarter. The design, an urban quarter with restaurants, shops and offices primarily intended for young start-up companies, integrates existing historic buildings and, in this way, adds to the fabric of the inner city. The network of pedestrian pathways guides people inside the village-like block, where public plazas enrich the urban neighborhood with restaurants, shops and service functions embedded in an intimate, local atmosphere. Typical elements of the area, such as small balconies, bridges and roof terraces, generate public life at various levels.

Within the confines of this precinct, a network of pathways and small alleys converges at a central square with restaurants. A circular access portal provides entry to commercial facilities in the basement and to the Metro. The façades and roofs have been clad with light natural stone strips of different widths, and consist of a beige natural stone that is typical of Shanghai, especially near the Bund area. The dark grey mullions of the glass façades provide a contrast to these strips. The vertical filigreeing of the stone façades creates a semi-transparent screen that unites the street with the commercial façades beyond.

The office tower at the southwest corner of the site is the vertical landmark of the project integrating into the Shanghai skyline. The façade rhythm is structured by three-story-high, vertical stone strips, a scaled-up variation of the low-rise façades. In this way the office tower and the commercial buildings each are characterized by individual façade design, but still appear as parts of the same entity.

Completion Date: January 2015
Total Land Area: 20,084 sq m (216,182 sq ft)
Total Building Area: 10,654 sq m (114,679 sq ft)
Total Open Area: 6,879 sq m (74,045 sq ft)
Total Hardscape: 4,328 sq m (46,586 sq ft)
Total Softscape: 2,551 sq m (27,459 sq ft)
Owner/Developer: SOHO China Co. Ltd
Urban Planner: von Gerkan, Marg and Partners Architects
Architects: von Gerkan, Marg and Partners Architects (design); East China Architectural Design & Research Institute (architect of record)
Landscape Architects: AIM Architecture; iPD; von Gerkan, Marg and Partners Architects
Structural Engineer: East China Architectural Design & Research Institute (design)
MEP Engineers: East China Architectural Design & Research Institute (design); Parsons Brinckerhoff Consultants Private Limited (design)
Project Manager: SOHO China Co. Ltd
Main Contractor: Longyuan Construction Group Co., Ltd

The staggered, glazed gables, oriented towards the surrounding streets, generate a vivid and human-scale environment that reflects the traditional neighborhood. Green terraces interlace the street fronts with the surrounding pedestrian walkways. The high-rise tower has conditioned above- and below-ground links with the rest of the complex. A bridge and a sunken plaza provide convenient access to all commercial facilities for tower occupants without blocking the system of public pathways on the ground level.

The double-layer stone façade screens framing the warehouse-like podium houses control the visual impact of the commercial functions to the surrounding living area. The loft-style spatial organization of the low-rise buildings enables high functional flexibility, which has already been proven in the short life of the project. Currently, numerous retail floors have already been successfully repurposed as shared office spaces.

Set into context with an existing church, a kindergarten and a community center on the northwest corner of the block, SOHO Fuxing Plaza represents a functional mix that has more in common with the traditional *li long* way of life than a cold and sterile mega-development that this site could have otherwise become.

The design adopts the scale and orientation of the neighboring *li longs*, integrates existing historic buildings and, in this way, adds to the fabric of the inner city.

Top: The internal passages resemble the scale and character of the traditional Shanghai "li longs" (alleys).

Left: Care is taken to provide street-facing retail, to prevent the site from seeming closed-off.

Opposite Top: The vertical paneling integrates the high-rise and low-rise elements, maintaining the human scale of the development.

Opposite Bottom: The site plan maintains the narrow, rectilinear typology of early 20th-century Shanghai neighborhoods, while subtly and strategically providing access points for autos and patrons of the Metro system.

The Pavilia Hill

Hong Kong, China

Completion Date: April 2016
Total Land Area: 4,605 sq m (49,568 sq ft)
Total Building Area: 36,840 sq m (396,545 sq ft)
Total Open Area: 3,078 sq m (33,131 sq ft)
Total Hardscape: 3,780 sq m (40,688 sq ft)
Total Softscape: 989 sq m (10,646 sq ft)
Owner/Developers: New World Development Company Limited; Hip Shing Hong (Holdings) Company Limited
Architect: P&T Group (design)
Landscape Architect: Shunmyo Masuno + Japanese Landscape Consultants Ltd.
Structural Engineer: CM Wong & Associates Ltd (design)
MEP Engineer: Meinhardt (design)
Project Manager: NW Project Management Limited
Main Contractor: New World Construction Company Limited

The Pavilia Hill consists of five residential towers sitting on a podium with a clubhouse and a three-story car park. The residences are configured linearly among the five towers to capture the best spectrum of city and mountain views. A responsive master plan has been adopted to blend the new development with the community of Tin Hau, wedged between Victoria Harbour and the mountainside.

The podium and main entrance of the development are set back at the level of Tin Hau Temple Road to introduce an open space, which integrates the existing stone staircase on the site, so as to enhance the main pedestrian path used by the community to reach the MTR (metro) station. The improvement also encourages public use of the existing adjoining park. An upgraded 24-hour public pedestrian walkway with accessible lift provision at Dragon Road is integrated with the podium design as a means of barrier-free access to the adjoining buildings.

The landscaped garden at the podium level is designed to soften the visual impact to the community associated with the new structure. This podium, with a sophisticated and intimately-scaled façade treatment, achieves harmonious integration within the existing context at street level. Extensive use of natural granite stone along most of the external planes, including the driveway and landscape areas, addresses durability and maintenance concerns. Vertical greenery, water features, shrubs, trees, berms and sculptural stones are set throughout the podium levels.

Opposite: The tower footprints are set back and "stepped up" the hill to provide more open space in front of the complex.

Top Left: The tower entrance is a calming space, under shelter but well ventilated.

Top Right: The podium roof is landscaped and provides an oasis from the pulsing city beyond.

Bottom: The full height windows in the tower entrance lobby bring the serene outdoor garden inside.

Univ360 Place

Seri Kembangan, Malaysia

Completion Date: May 2015
Total Land Area: 16,390 sq m (176,420 sq ft)
Total Building Area: 16,414 sq m (176,679 sq ft)
Total Open Area: 10,520 sq m (113,236 sq ft)
Total Hardscape: 6,810 sq m (73,302 sq ft)
Total Softscape: 3,710 sq m (39,934 sq ft)
Owner/Developer: Zip Hill Development Sdn Bhd
Architect: Atelier Alan Teh Architect
Landscape Architect: Engky Design Sdn Bhd
Structural Engineer: ST Patners Sdn Bhd
MEP Engineer: Perunding Mektrik Sdn Bhd
Main Contractor: Pembenaan Leow Tuck Chui & Sons Sdn Bhd

The design intent of Univ360 emphasizes interaction among its inhabitants, emphasizing a communal spirit for its users and visitors over formal expression. On an urban scale, the project's roof garden with mature trees and green walls contrast sharply with the monolithic concrete towers of the urban skyline of southern Kuala Lumpur. The site orientation and a need to provide sufficient daylight and solar shading to unit interiors resulted in turning the units 45 degrees from the corridors serving them. This created interesting dynamics, such that intimate triangular "ante-spaces" were created outside each unit, offering a semi-private space that graduates the transition from unit to corridor.

A mid-level communal sky terrace garden, shaded by the building mass; pocket gardens on every third floor in common areas; and a sky deck/roof garden serve to complement the individual spaces, providing green, sociable spaces at a range of scales and exposure to the elements. The total amount of green space on site is 10,520 square meters — about 64 percent of the overall site area — with an additional 2,400 square meters provided by the hanging gardens/green walls.

Biophilic landscapes form an integral part of the architectural design, alongside references to Malaysian landscapes such as rice fields, the 1.5-meter-wide corridors alongside urban shophouses, and the tropical rainforest.

Opposite: The unit orientation and placement of open-air spaces give it a porous, "cracked open" appearance that breaks down its scale and makes it appear less monolithic.

Top: A substantial terrace provides evaporative cooling as well as extensive views.

Bottom Left: Trellises covered in greenery aid shading of the outdoor corridors.

Bottom Right: Pocket gardens appear on every third floor in common areas.

Wolf Point West

Chicago, United States

Completion Date: March 2016
Total Land Area: 4,586 sq m (49,363 sq ft)
Total Building Area: 979 sq m (10,538 sq ft)
Total Open Area: 3,606 sq m (38,815 sq ft)
Total Hardscape: 2,456 sq m (26,436 sq ft)
Total Softscape: 1,151 sq m (12,389 sq ft)
Owner: Wolf Point Owners LLC
Developers: Hines; Magellan Development Group
Urban Planner: Pelli Clarke Pelli Architects
Architect: bKL Architecture (design)
Landscape Architect: Wolff Landscape Architecture
Structural Engineer: Halvorson and Partners (engineer of record)
MEP Engineer: Alvine Engineering (engineer of record)
Main Contractors: Clark Construction Group, LLC; James McHugh Construction Co.

While Wolf Point West is a private residential tower set at the junction of two branches of the Chicago River, a garden and nine-meter landscaped setback upon the Riverwalk is available for public access, offering open space and views along the river for all to enjoy.

As part of Chicago's Planned Development requirements, the tower could not encroach upon the planned Riverwalk expansion, view corridors had to be maintained, and the chamfered property line following the river's edge had to be preserved. The architects met these challenges with creative solutions, such as raising the tower on pilotis to minimally impact the Riverwalk and create a unique interaction between the public open space and the tower. The decision to make the Riverwalk a cantilevered structure over the river allows for the natural plant and animal habitat to live and grow without being impeded by the building.

Outside the tower, residents and visitors are welcomed to the site's east garden, which is lined with benches, shrubbery, perennials, and birch trees. As one walks from the tower through the east garden, the Chicago River comes into view, as well as a grass amphitheater. A grand stair separates two distinct areas of plantings — a stepped terrace to the south and a more naturalistic hill to the north. Lined with native trees, these landscaped areas visually link the ground level of Wolf Point West with the Riverwalk.

Opposite: The thin aspect ratio of the tower leaves room for substantial landscaping and public realm at its feet.

Top: The public walkway, threaded under a lifted corner, and the amphitheater-like seating area make the most of the riverside location.

Bottom Left: The site plan shows the minimization of the building footprint in favor of open space.

Bottom Right: The public realm of the Riverwalk is sheltered by the building.

CONSTRUCTION

Little can be taken for granted when it comes to the art of constructing skyscrapers today — except that a "greenfield" pristine building site is probably out of the question. As the planet urbanizes, contractors are increasingly challenged to deliver ambitiously designed, time- and cost-sensitive projects on tight sites in crowded cities, often adjacent to or on top of major infrastructure, or even other buildings. Whether it's modular construction, innovative concrete-pouring techniques, or suspending floors so as to eliminate columns intruding on high-value spaces, the construction community is constantly innovating in order to deliver tall buildings that can meet the increasingly high expectations of their owners, occupiers and the communities of which they are part.

56 Leonard

New York City, United States

Completion Date: 2016
Height: 250 m (821 ft)
Stories: 57
Area: 46,452 sq m (500,005 sq ft)
Primary Function: Residential
Developer: Gerald D Hines Interests
Main Contractor: Lend Lease
Architects: Herzog & de Meuron Architekten (design); Costas Kondylis Design (architect of record)
Structural Engineer: WSP Cantor Seinuk (design)
MEP Engineer: Cosentini Associates (design)
Other CTBUH Member Consultants: Cosentini Associates (security); Enclos Corp. (façade); Langan Engineering (civil, environmental, geotechnical)
Other CTBUH Member Supplier: Schindler (elevator)

56 Leonard has been called the "Jenga" building due to its irregularly projecting floors, as well as the irregular spacing and location of the balconies throughout its 57 stories. Above the fifth floor, there is a 6-meter cantilever to the west and a 4.6-meter cantilever to the south, both of which were constructed over occupied New York Law School buildings.

To build the superstructure safely, emphasis was placed on designing a custom, stackable perimeter screen system that provided full, passive fall protection. From the 45th floor up, all concrete-shaping forms had to remain in place to provide the necessary structural support to form and cast the floors above. The system was engineered so that once the concrete on the roof was cured, removal of the formwork could proceed from the top down until it concluded on the 45th-floor platform.

The project was designed with architecturally exposed concrete on the edges of the floor slabs and the underside slabs of all balconies, in addition to the columns and walls of the interiors. The façade is a full-height window wall system that consists of 3.4-to-6.7-meter-tall panels, which were installed from each floor using a robotic arm. The amount of exposed concrete on the project required extensive mockups of the columns and slab edges, as well as for the patching, cleaning and grinding of the concrete. The project team also consulted with experts in the concrete field from around the United States and the world to discuss how to get the concrete mix as flawless as possible because the design intent was for the concrete to be untouched after being stripped.

The interpolation of the balconies along each façade presented an interesting potential. Normally, a perimeter protection system to guard against worker falls would have to be fitted loosely around both balcony projections and the superstructure. But in this case the 260 balconies from the 3rd floor to the 43rd floor do not stack over each other, allowing the team to install them separately in a second wave. This allowed a separate perimeter protection system to be installed, as tight to the slab edge as possible — thus adding an extra layer of safety — which progressed up this portion of the building for superstructure construction, before returning to install the cantilevered balconies below.

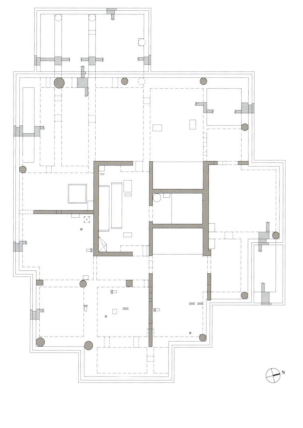

Opposite: View of the perimeter-screen system at work above level 45.

Top left: The irregular floor plates as seen in this structural plan required careful detailing.

Bottom left: The prevalence of exposed concrete on the interior as a high-end finish required a high-quality mix and careful detailing.

Bottom right: A view up at the finished project highlights the intricacy of the perimeter balconies.

111 Main

Salt Lake City, United States

Completion Date: October 2016
Height: 118 m (387 ft)
Stories: 25
Area: 501,455 sq m (5,397,617 sq ft)
Primary Function: Office
Developer: City Creek Reserve, Inc
Architects: Skidmore, Owings & Merrill LLP (architect of record)
Structural Engineer: Skidmore, Owings & Merrill LLP (engineer of record)
MEP Engineer: WSP (design)
Main Contractors: SME Steel Contractors; Okland Construction
Other CTBUH Member Consultants: Edgett Williams Consulting Group Inc. (vertical transportation); Jensen Hughes (code)

Located in the financial heart of Salt Lake City, 111 Main is a Class A office tower that anchors a larger urban redevelopment project in the area. The construction of the building followed a parallel timeline with the George S. and Dolores Doré Eccles Theater, designed by a separate architect, on a shared redevelopment site. The 111 Main architect and structural engineer developed an innovative solution to a complex site challenge: how to integrate the tower with the theater, which, for uncompromised functionality, required a significant part of the tower's site footprint.

The design solution suspends the southern portion of the office tower over a section of the four-story theater, avoiding perimeter tower columns puncturing its space. The tower hat truss, the basis of the integrated solution, is brought forward and expressed as a structural crown. 111 Main's structural engineering features a rare move — suspending the entire perimeter of a tower to achieve overhang at adjacent building.

Located in a region of high seismicity in close proximity to the active Salt Lake Segment of the Wasatch Fault Zone, 111 Main was designed to withstand maximum considered earthquake hazards using performance-based seismic design procedures. Six articulating spherical steel structural bearings are provided at the top of the reinforced concrete core wall to transfer compressive gravity and lateral loads from the penthouse-roof hat trusses.

The core wall loads are transferred to a deep foundation steel piling system extending to depths of 30.5 meters and greater below grade. Hanging perimeter steel columns create column-free office lease space and a completely column-free lobby with no perimeter columns meeting the ground level, allowing for unprecedented transparency between the lobby and the street.

The hat truss system was topped off in early 2016, with a sophisticated jacking process that transferred the compressive load from a temporary shoring system into the permanent structure during a single 12-hour period. To allow the construction of both the tower and theater to proceed uninterrupted, the design team developed a "saddle cable" temporary shoring system, anchored through the concrete core walls with temporary hydraulic jacks, allowing for conventional and efficient construction scheduling.

When the building and penthouse roof steel hat trusses were completed, gravity loads were transferred from perimeter hanging steel columns to the permanent truss system and temporary shores were removed.

TEMPORARY STRUCTURE

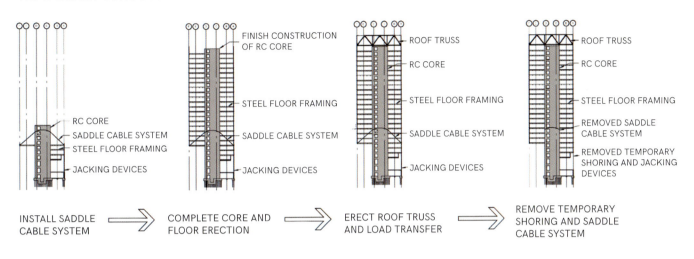

INSTALL SADDLE CABLE SYSTEM → COMPLETE CORE AND FLOOR ERECTION → ERECT ROOF TRUSS AND LOAD TRANSFER → REMOVE TEMPORARY SHORING AND SADDLE CABLE SYSTEM

Opposite: The "saddle cable" temporary support system for the cantilever at level 5.

Top: Construction sequence of the saddle cable system.

Bottom Left: Two overview axonometric drawings of the overall structure, including hat truss and cantilever over adjacent theater.

Bottom Right: The finished building, with the hat truss partially visible behind the frosted "crown" perimeter.

461 Dean Street

New York City, United States

Completion Date: November 2016
Height: 106 m (347 ft)
Stories: 32
Primary Function: Residential
Owner/Developer: Forest City Ratner Companies
Main Contractor: Turner Construction Company
Architect: SHoP Architects (design)
Structural Engineer: Arup (design)
MEP Engineer: Arup (design)
Project Manager: Skanska
Other CTBUH Member Consultant: Langan Engineering (geotechnical)

The first of several residential buildings in the 8.9-hectare Pacific Park Brooklyn development, 461 Dean Street, is constructed of volumetric modular units, large building elements that can be linked together to form complete buildings, without the need for additional superstructure. Constructors can create entire rooms in a factory setting, and then ship these out to be assembled on the site, saving time and labor costs, and reducing the potential for errors or accidents. The project contains 363 rental units, 50% of which are affordable to middle-income tenants. Amenities include a landscaped roof terrace, fitness center, dance studio, and street-level retail.

Its success hinged on careful pre-planning of construction activities, as well as the introduction of new construction means and methods. The use of modularization and prefabrication was critical to the success of the project. Modules were constructed off-site — and completely outfitted with structural, architectural and mechanical-electrical-plumbing (MEP) components — at the Brooklyn Navy Yard and transported to the site. In the corridor modules, MEP racks were pre-hung and transported inside the module. The stair modules included installed metal stairs and a fire-protection standpipe, an empty tube that can be pumped full of water from a fire truck or water main in the event of a fire.

To ensure the timely delivery of the modules to the site, a transportation plan was devised. Between the hours of 12:00 a.m. and 5:00 a.m., no more than four modules were escorted to the site using a series of "low-boy" trailers. Once on site, the modules were staged, inspected and subsequently hoisted into place, where they were bolted together.

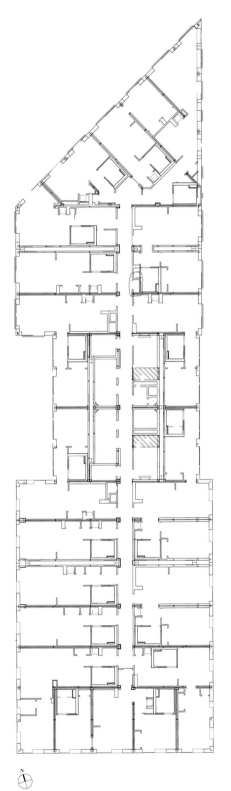

Opposite: The 461 Dean project nearing completion.

Left: A typical floor plan at 461 Dean, with 36 modules per floor. A total of 225 unique module types were created.

Top Right: During construction, modules were assembled off-site at the Brooklyn Navy Yards, then transported to the building site.

Bottom right: The façade pattern strikes a balance between variation and repetition, offering both aesthetic quality and efficiency of construction.

The EY Centre
Sydney, Australia

Completion Date: June 2016
Height: 155 m (509 ft)
Stories: 38
Area: 63,499 sq m (683,498 sq ft)
Primary Functions: Office / Retail
Owners: Mirvac George Street Pty Ltd; AMP Capital Investors Pty Ltd
Developer: Mirvac Projects Pty Ltd
Architect: Francis-Jones Morehen Thorp Pty Ltd (design)
Structural Engineers: BG&E (design); Enstruct Group Pty Ltd (peer review)
MEP Engineer: Arup (design)
Main Contractor: Mirvac Constructions Pty Ltd
Other CTBUH Member Consultants: Arup (fire, lighting, vertical transportation); BG&E (civil); Cermak Peterka Petersen (CPP), Inc. (wind); JBA (urban planner); Permasteelisa Group (façade)
Other CTBUH Member Supplier: Schindler (elevator); Permasteelisa Group (façade)

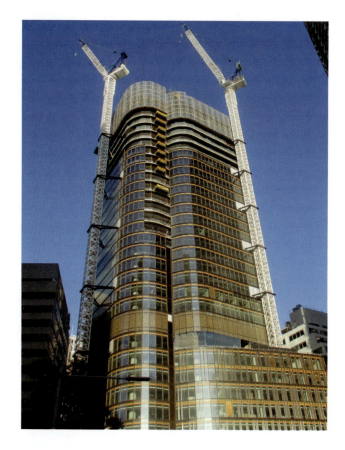

The distinctively sculptural, 38-story EY Centre building employs a world-first timber-and-glass closed-cavity façade (CCF) system, giving it a unique appearance — an instantly recognizable structure defined by its shimmering, organic, golden-hued curves, in striking contrast to the more conventional commercial towers surrounding it. Used before in a handful of low-rise buildings in Europe and Asia, the CCF had never been used in Australia or the southern hemisphere, or in a high-rise building anywhere in the world, and none had featured timber blinds within the cavity. The whole system is automated through a building management system. Smart-building technology monitors air quality, sunlight, power and water usage and adjusts the internal environment according to the needs of the building and its occupants, allowing for efficiency improvements to be made in real time. The CCF enables an energy savings of 30–40% compared to a typical façade.

The use of such a system was made possible as a result of significant prototyping and testing undertaken prior to the construction of the building's façade elements. This included accelerated UV and temperature testing, accelerated durability and wear testing, extensive visual prototyping, thermal testing, air leakage testing, off gassing testing, fogging and condensation testing / trial shipments, structural (SIROWET) testing, as well as degalzing and blind removal demonstrations.

Innovation in digital technologies across the project allowed for the delivery of a number of highly complex building elements to extremely high standards and tolerances. The construction of the triangulated timber soffit and awning were an example of this. The team used a 3D modeling platform to create an exact digital replica, which could be meshed with as-built survey information to allow for prefabrication and high quality pre-assembly directly from the 3D model. As a result, more than 10,000 panels and components were installed with significant safety, program and quality improvements.

Similar digital fabrication technology was used to construct other complex building elements, such as the striking 'Y' columns at the ground floor plane, which allows for the fabrication and installation of over 400 tons of heavy structural steel elements to form highly refined architectural building features, the curved and sweeping stair forms, lobby stone features and recycled timber kiosk.

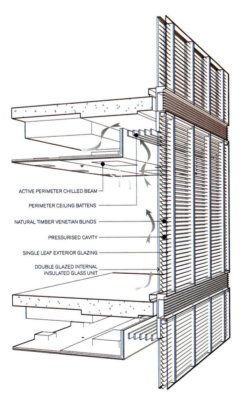

Opposite: The EY Centre under construction.

Top: Fabrication of the distinctive closed-cavity façade (CCF) system, with wooden blinds and vertical slats clearly visible.

Bottom Left: Detail drawing of the CCF system, demonstrating its environmental conditioning capabilities.

Bottom Right: The fully installed CCF system gives the tower its distinctive warm glow.

Warsaw Spire

Warsaw, Poland

Completion Date: May 2016
Height: 220 m (722 ft)
Stories: 49
Area: 82,918 sq m (892,522 sq ft)
Primary Function: Office
Owner/Developer: Ghelamco Poland
Architects: Jaspers-Eyers Architects (design); Polsko-BelgijskaPragownia Architektury Sp. z o.o. (architect of record)
Structural Engineers: Bakkala Consulting Engineers Limited (design); Bartels Polska Sp. z o.o. (engineer of record)
MEP Engineer: Pol-Con Consulting Sp z.o.o (design)
Project Manager: Ghelamco Poland
Main Contractor: Ghelamco Poland
Other CTBUH Member Consultants: Barker Mohandas, LLC (vertical transportation); Deerns (vertical transportation)
Other CTBUH Member Suppliers: Marioff Corporation Oy (fire suppression); Schindler (elevator)

Warsaw Spire comprises three slender office towers, with two 17-story towers framing a 49-story, 220-meter central tower. The tower is founded on the thick post-tensioned concrete composite raft on barrette piles. The project was accompanied by numerous construction challenges, and pioneering solutions. These included the construction of a five-story underground garage with an area of 43,610 square meters for approximately 1,300 cars, a 55-meter-deep diaphragm wall, and the design of a three-dimensional shell façade on the ellipsoidal projection of the main building.

The project uses high-ductility reinforcement steel, which together with appropriate configuration of post-tensioned slabs and other concrete elements protects the structure against disproportionate collapse. In the case of extreme unpredictable impacts, such as an explosion, the entire structure can withstand the removal of an external column.

The skyscraper at its base is based on V-shaped skewed columns of 12 to 26 meters' length. These are composite columns, where the cross section consists of steel pipes with a diameter of 900 millimeters, filled with reinforced concrete. Floor slabs above the ground floor are suspended from the structural elements above, using hangers.

A lateral force-resisting system, consisting of the central core walls and the perimeter columns, has been designed efficiently, with walls not thicker than 300 millimeters. The core is optimized, not only in terms of dimensions, but also to provide optimal space for vertical transportation, communication and installation shafts. Flat, thin post-tensioned slabs with no beams provide clear space for all services.

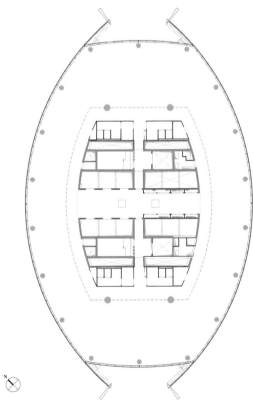

Opposite: Overall construction view of the complex.

Top: The interaction of the ellipsoidal shell of the central tower and the foundation and parking slabs is visible in this view.

Bottom Left: The tower's ellipsoidal shape in plan view, showing a typical office floor.

Bottom Right: The tower shortly after completion.

A LOOK FORWARD

In the quest to understand what cities of the future will look like, one must look no further than the cutting-edge technologies and practices that are beginning to be implemented in tall buildings today. Through this lens, it is clear that tall buildings are on the verge of a major evolution, with impacts on every stage of a project's lifecycle – from conception and design, to construction, operation, and beyond. Though some solutions may remain invisible to the untrained eye and others will quite visibly alter how we interact with tall buildings, there is immense value in exploring these innovations holistically.

3D-Printed Building

Innovation Design Team
R&D & Conceptual Design: Gensler
Detailed Architectural Design: Killa Design
Structural Design & Concept Development: Thornton Tomasetti
Structural Engineering & Detailed Design: eConstruct
Structural Preparation & Installation: Gulf Precast
Project Management, Site Supervision & Client Representation: PMK Consulting
Design, Concept Development & Project Management: IT-Serve IT & AV
Façade Research, Development & Application: Golden Elements
Façade Manufacture: NPPF
MEP & Air Conditioning: Daiken
MEP Concept Design & Sustainability Advisor: SYSKA Hennessy Group
MEP Detailed Design, Installation & Project Management: China State Construction Engineering Corporation (CSCEC)
Security, Access Control & Service Integration: Siemens
Infrastructure, Servers & Office Infrastructure: Huawei Data
Interior Fit Out, Detailed Design & Project Support: Projex
Furniture & Workplace Design: Bene Gmbh
Interiors & Furniture Design: Puckrin Design
Wall & Digital WhiteboardBASF Advanced Materials: Anoto/Weinspire Collaboration
Landscape Design: Cracknell Landscaping

The world's first fully functional and permanently occupied 3D printed building has been constructed in Dubai. The entire structure was printed in concrete using an additive manufacturing technique, the first fully occupied building in the world to be constructed using such techniques. Known as the Office of the Future, it is currently the temporary home for the Dubai Future Foundation, as well as an exhibition space and incubator for future emerging technologies in the region. Other projects have tested various elements of 3D printing before, but the Office of the Future is the first real building to be built at scale, with full services, that people can use daily.

The structure of the building was manufactured by using a 3D printer 6 meters high, 36.5 meters long and 12 meters wide. Printing took 17 days and the components were installed on-site over two days. Subsequent work on the building services, interiors, and landscape took approximately three months. The labor involved in the printing process included one technician to monitor the function of the printer, a team of seven people to install the building components on-site, as well as a team of 10 electricians and specialists to take care of the mechanical and electrical engineering. The cladding was fabricated using insulated panels, custom-cut to form the complex geometry of the façade and installed on-site. As a result, the labor cost was cut by more than 50 percent, compared to conventional buildings of similar size.

The project acted as a testing ground of the constraints and opportunities of 3D-printed concrete and continues to provide a great deal of sensing and performance data. The various sensors and probes on the building provide continuous feedback on structural performance, offering designers of future 3D-printed high-rise buildings valuable information that can feed into their basis of design.

There is still much work to be done. All modular and prefabricated design techniques yet devised require some kind of locking mechanism or supplementary bracing structure to maintain stability once a certain height threshold is passed. Buildings of up to five stories have been 3D-printed before, but their structural integrity and occupancy status is unknown. Nevertheless, this project represents an important step forward in the realization of mass multi-story 3D-printed structures.

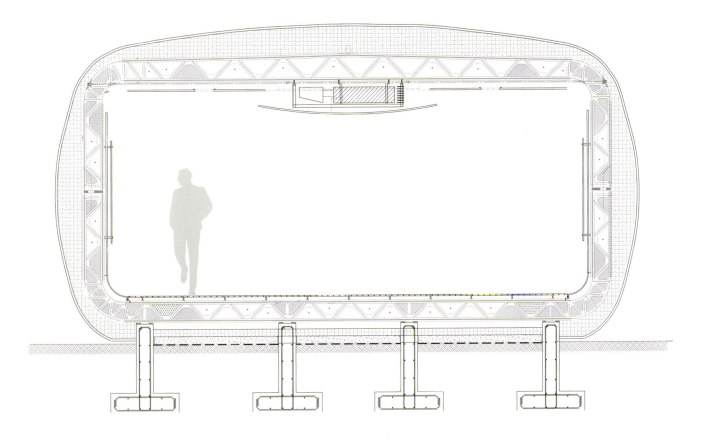

Opposite: Structural framing was "printed" off-site prior to installation.

Top: This is the first 3D-printed building to be fitted with services, as demonstrated in this section diagram.

Bottom: Exterior view of the Office of the Future, which serves as an example of the future potential of 3D printing.

CAST CONNEX High Integrity Blocks

Innovation Design Team
Structural Steel Products Supplier: CAST CONNEX
30 Hudson Yards – First High-Rise To Implement System
Design Architect: Kohn Pedersen Fox Associates
Developer: Related Companies
General Contractor: Tishman Construction
Structural Engineer: Thornton Tomasetti
Structural Steel Fabricator: Aceros Corey
Structural Steel Erector: W&W Steel

CAST CONNEX High Integrity Blocks are specially manufactured solid steel elements that simplify the design and fabrication of, and provide unparalleled strength, quality, and reliability in heavily-loaded steel connections. The result of intensive research and development, and paired with careful manufacturing control, it is now feasible to deliver ultra-heavy weldable steel sections as large as 1,200 by 1,200 millimeters and up to 15 meters in length, which exhibit remarkable strength in all three directions of loading, and through the full cross-section.

The blocks are the result of a new, hybrid manufacturing technique that marries the benefits of casting with those of forging. The product's creation was prompted by the need to facilitate heavily loaded and complex connections in the 30 Hudson Yards tower in New York City, which was built above an active rail yard. This required the development of a new, proprietary cast steel alloy and the establishment of a unique production methodology.

Conventional structural steel plate is manufactured via hot-rolling, a process that results in poor through-thickness mechanical performance in heavy sections. With increasing plate thickness, the achievable material strength diminishes and the potential for lamellar defects increases. These material limitations must be addressed in the design of structural connections.

Given the susceptibility of thick plates to layer defects and poor through-thickness properties, addressing pass-through forces in high-rise connection nodes requires designers to build up nodes using plates carefully aligned in the direction of loading. This often necessitates stacking and welding

plates together in complex arrangements and drives the need for large, multi-pass welds which are subject to quality issues, and which can cause distortion/tolerance problems. High Integrity Blocks are thus ideal for use within the center of multi-axis connections where the tearing of a plate may compromise the connection's quality and strength, or where the lamination of plates to build up a section is not advisable, due to the need to transmit forces through laminations.

The use of High Integrity Blocks in the fabrication of multi-axis nodal connections enables safer, higher-quality connections that are simultaneously less costly and more compact, thus maximizing occupiable space. This improves the overall resilience and economy of high-rise towers and will enable taller, safer structures.

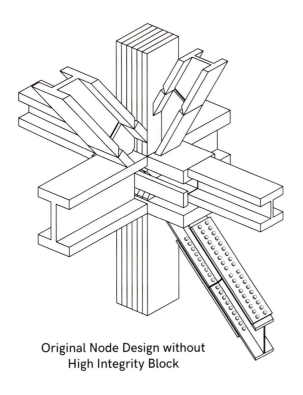

Original Node Design without High Integrity Block

High Integrity Blocks are ideal for use in the center of multi-axis connections, where the tearing of a plate may compromise the connection's quality and strength.

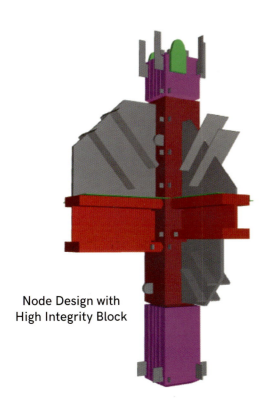

Node Design with High Integrity Block

Opposite: A detail view of the block in use in the field, supporting a multi-axis connection.

Above: Using High Integrity Blocks at a junction reduces the mass of steel, and the number of required welds.

Right: The 30 Hudson Yards tower, New York, uses High Integrity Blocks extensively.

Hickory Building Systems

Innovation Design Team
Builder: Hickory
Developer: Longriver Investments
Project Manager: Sinclair Brook
Architect: Rothelowman
Bathrooms: Sync Bathroom Pods (a division of Hickory)
Structural Engineer: Hickory Building Systems; Rincovitch Consultants Pty Ltd

A new prefabricated construction method, Hickory Building Systems (HBS), was used to construct the 137-meter, 44-level La Trobe Tower apartments, Australia's tallest prefabricated building. HBS is a structural system that integrates the core, shear walls, bathrooms and façade of a building into a unified structure that is built off-site and in parallel with on-site works. Delivered 30 percent faster (eight months earlier) than if a conventional approach were used, the methodology has proven to be a safer, less disruptive and more sustainable way to build.

The construction method used prefabricated building elements including modular bathroom pods, pre-cast concrete slabs and pre-attached windows. The basic structural architecture was designed to be scalable with occupancies that can span across multiple modules to generate generous floor spaces, and has the flexibility to provide limitless spatial layouts and the capability to build to indefinite heights. Utilizing HBS also means that a building can often be constructed with an extra floor without adding to the overall building height or reducing internal ceiling heights, giving developers millions of extra dollars in net saleable area.

The approach to building La Trobe Tower was to strategically integrate prefabricated HBS elements in order to overcome limited site access, a small site footprint and a slim tower design. To apply HBS structural construction, levels 3 to 43 were redesigned as pre-manufactured structural units. A transfer structure at level 2 was designed to receive HBS units from level 3, with matching loose steel columns installed at level 2 to receive the units above level 3. Full-scale testing was carried out for lifting of the largest modules.

In another first for Australian construction, much of the high-rise structure was erected during extended-hours construction shifts, trucking in the oversized prefabricated components at night to avoid disrupting tram and vehicle traffic on La Trobe Street. A quiet electric crane and strict noise control measures were put in place and monitored throughout the eight-month night work period to ensure neighboring residents were not disturbed by the activity.

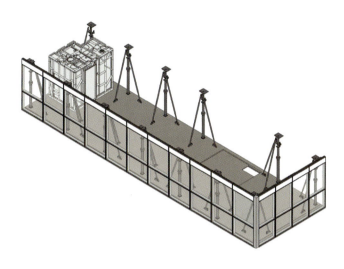

Opposite: An HBS module is lifted into place during night operations at La Trobe Tower, Melbourne.

Top Left: An axonometric view of the HBS module, showing locations of temporary shoring poles for the module above.

Top Right: The finished La Trobe Tower project.

Bottom Left: The light weight HBS modules are easily lifted into place.

High-Resolution CFD for Wind Loading Tall Buildings

Innovation Design Team
Wirth Research

Accurate analysis of the mean and resonant wind loads is vital for the structural design of tall buildings. Whereas physical Wind Tunnel Testing (WTT) to determine these loads is still accepted by the industry as the necessary default practice, the wind engineering community recognizes that a time will come when computational fluid dynamic CFD modelling is able to accurately model the interaction of wind and buildings. In the meantime, a combination of wind tunnel testing and CFD modelling is often undertaken.

High Resolution Computational Fluid Dynamics (HRCFD) is one of many experimental computational methodologies which could potentially move the industry forward. Ultimately, the objective would be where CFD can provide an accurate full pressure map on the building surfaces. However, we are not at that point yet. The technology has been adapted from motorsport racing, where aerodynamics is a fundamental factor in split-second timing differences between winning or losing a race. The process uses a full-scale digital model of a tall building, accurate to detailed features of 100 millimeters or smaller when necessary, placed within a surrounding area of up to 10 kilometers' radius. Wind conditions are simulated by using an atmospheric boundary layer profile and data from many decades of local historical wind data.

HRCFD takes advantage of recent advances in super-computing to model flow conditions, with correlations back to physical data when it exists. Novel methods of model generation, coupled with a rapid and flexible solving capability, lead to the potential to provide fast feedback into the design loop. The modeling environment is discretized into several hundred million cells, from which an initial solution can be obtained in a matter of hours to days, depending on the computing environment available. While HRCFD is still untested on real buildings, the advancement of computer aided engineering is occurring at a rapid pace. This method represents potential advancement in the field, and the importance of such technologies.

The technology has been adapted from motorsport racing, where aerodynamics is a fundamental factor in split-second timing differences between winning or losing a race.

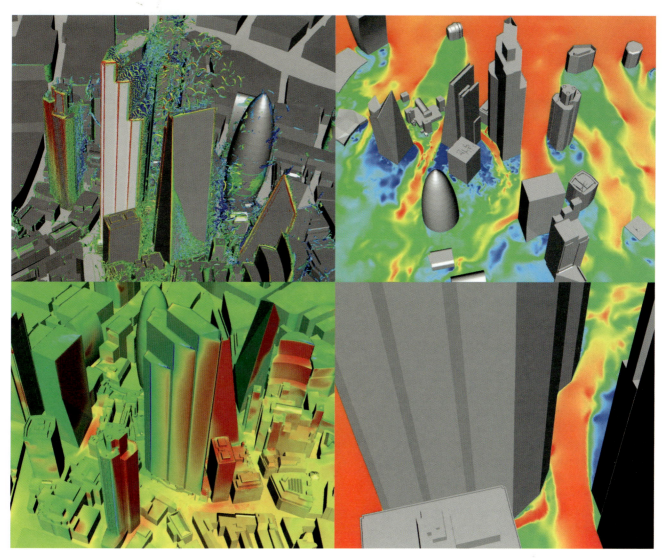

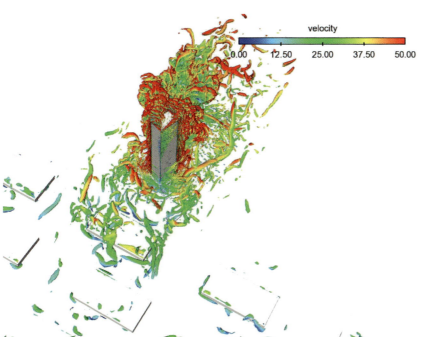

Above: Using Hi-Res CFD to measure loads and façade pressures can enhance understanding of underlying flow features.

Left: Accurate capture of vortex structures around an International High-Frequency Base Balance test case correlates highly with actual results.

Hummingbird Tuned Liquid Column Gas Damper

Innovation Design Team
Tuned Liquid Column Gas Damper Design: Hummingbird Kinetics LLC
Research and Development Engineering: Thornton Tomasetti
System Design and Engineering: RWDI

The Hummingbird is a tuned liquid column gas damper that uses a system of water pipes and independently tuned air springs to mitigate wind motion in tall buildings. Unlike traditional tuned liquid dampers, 100 percent of the water mass in the Hummingbird is active, which allows the device to provide equivalent damping with a lighter and smaller footprint. The Hummingbird is easily re-tuned in hours instead of weeks, and it is built from basic parts that can be sourced globally. These innovations allow for a lightweight, compact, flexible, easily maintained and cost-effective wind damping solution for the future of tall building design and development.

The first liquid-gas Hummingbird damper, whose development was influenced by NASA technology to mitigate similar vibrations in rockets, was modified for the unique characteristics of supertall structures. It was successfully installed in New York City at 461 Dean Street, where it performed exactly to engineered specifications. The design was then further improved by eliminating the upturned ends with the use of a proprietary membrane to retain the fluid against the air chamber, which made 100 percent of the water mass active and allows the damper to fit in a significantly shorter and/or smaller space. A full-scale prototype was built, and is being fatigue-tested over 20 million cycles, the equivalent of a 10-year life and counting. The combination of the pressurized air chambers and the proprietary membranes allows the damping mass to be distributed throughout a building and tuned to multiple frequencies, both of which represent significant technical advancements over current damping systems.

Current wind dampers are generally limited to human comfort applications because single mass damper systems are by nature limited to narrow frequency and/or response ranges. The Hummingbird's distributed multi-mass system greatly increases resiliency and system redundancy, which results in a safe solution that can maintain high performance across a range of wind scenarios. Additionally, because the device can be distributed into multiple smaller masses, it can be installed in floors, ceilings, walls, and in and around existing design constraints. This allows architects and engineers the flexibility to push the boundaries of design without being constrained by single massive envelope requirements of other damping solutions.

Because the device can be distributed into multiple smaller masses, it can be installed in floors, ceilings, walls, and in and around existing design constraints.

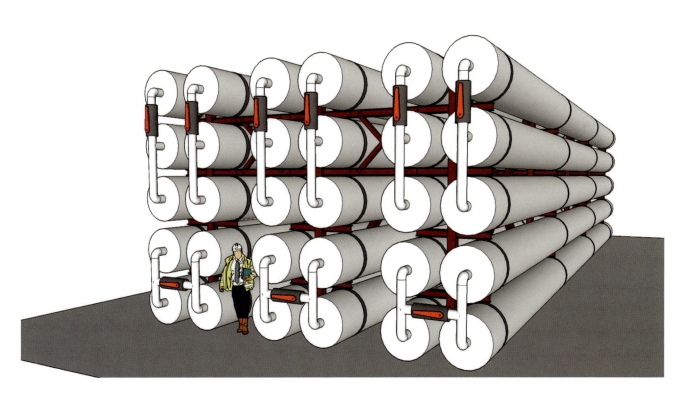

Top: Engineers inspect a live installation of Hummingbird on a rooftop in Brooklyn, New York.

Bottom: This example layout demonstrates the scale of the damper.

Lean Core + Prefab Blade Wall System

Innovation Design Team
Client: Mace/Realstar, Firstbase
Structural Engineer: AKTII
Contractor: Mace
Concept Architect: RSH+P
Delivery Architect: Axis
Services Engineer: AECOM

The development of the lean core + prefab blade wall system grew out of a brief to create a new high-rise living typology that was lean, flexible and driven by a standardized, prefabricated approach. The objective was to reduce reliance on the central core for stability, allowing the core design to be lean in terms of the size and thickness of walls. This drove the need to develop a supplementary stability system that could be integrated into the required residential brief.

To achieve this, the team researched using an outrigger system to mobilize the full stiffness of the tower footprint, but instead of dedicated outrigger floors, all the reinforced-concrete flat slabs act as outrigger arms, mobilizing the perimeter structure. The key to this unique system is that it relies on the concrete that is already required for vertical loads (i.e., there is no increase in slab depth). This makes the "typical frame" work harder and provide multiple functions.

An arrangement of four internal concrete blade walls provides buttressing to the central core, while every floor slab acts as an outrigger, engaging eight perimeter blade walls. The framing system works holistically, as all elements contribute to both lateral stability and vertical support. The structural framing of the floor plates follows the above principle, while pushing the majority of the vertical structure to the perimeter to maximize the outrigger effect. Between the internal core and the perimeter, further internal vertical structure is limited to just four elements that lock the two systems together. These are aligned with the 45-degree partition lines and thus promote the flexibility of the floor plates.

The lean core + prefab blade wall system was first deployed at the 80 Newington Butts residential tower, which is expected to complete construction in 2018. Acting as the flagship of the wider Elephant and Castle regeneration project in London, the tower block is octagonal in shape, providing most of its 470 units with corner balconies.

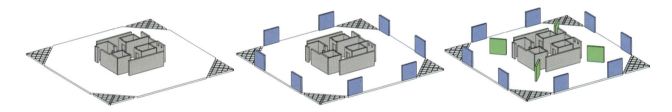

The framing system works holistically, as all elements contribute to both lateral stability and vertical support.

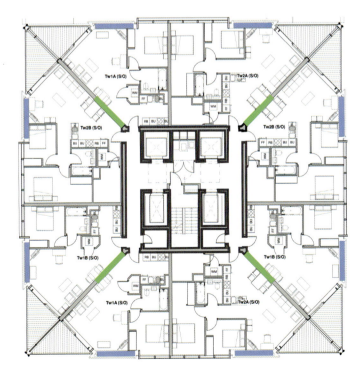

Opposite: The lean-core + blade-wall system was deployed successfully at 80 Newington Butts, a residential tower in London.

Top: Blade walls and the lean core are visible in this construction view. The limited number of repeatable components keeps floors stable and uncluttered.

Right: The placement of the "blade walls" are carefully integrated into the floor plan and eliminate the need for conventional outrigger floors.

MULTI

Innovation Design Team
thyssenkrupp

MULTI, the world's first rope-less, multi-directional elevator, ushers in the end of the exclusive 160-year reign of rope-dependent elevators, harnessing the power of linear motor technology to move multiple cars in a single shaft, vertically and horizontally. The system follows a powered track, and cars can change direction through an exchanger device, which shuttles the car from one shaft to another, or rotates to take the car in a new direction. The cars' motorized wheels follow the power rail independent of the passenger cabin. At intersections, the exchanger, laid flush with the track, rotates to match the new direction and locks in place, like a vertically oriented railway turntable. The car's motor assembly rotates in sync with the exchanger, while the cabin floor stays level.

The MULTI elevator system has been extensively tested at the 246-meter Aufzugtestturm in Rottweil, Germany. Three of the 12 elevator shafts at the test tower are devoted to testing MULTI.

The potential that can be realized from this innovation is extensive. In a typical high-rise building, more than 50 percent of the footprint needs to be reserved for transportation and service facilities. Because it does not need ropes, MULTI requires fewer and smaller shafts than conventional elevators, and can increase a building's usable area by up to 25 percent, adding rentable/leasable space. Instead of one cabin per shaft moving up and down, MULTI offers the potential to operate multiple cabins in a loop, much like a metro system inside a building. This results in a higher transport capacity – up to 5 percent – as well as reduced waiting times for passengers (an elevator cabin can now be available every 15 to 30 seconds). MULTI also requires up to 60 percent lower peak power levels when compared to conventional elevator systems, which allows for better management of a building's energy needs, and reduces investment costs in the power supply infrastructure.

Traditional elevators with one single cabin in a shaft not only restrict mobility and space; they also limit the height

of the building – with traditional wire suspension or ropes, the limit is around 600 meters. Considered solely as a factor of elevator capacity or capability, the potential heights and floor-plate sizes of tall buildings is now theoretically unlimited. Perhaps most exciting, the introduction of a multi-directional elevator opens up infinite combinations of vertical and horizontal building design opportunities. Because of its ability to move horizontally at any angle, the system can support traffic through and between buildings of previously unseen intricacy.

While further research is underway to fully unlock the potential of MULTI in future high-rise designs, the first installation has been announced. The new 140-meter East Side Tower in Berlin, expected to be completed by 2021, will utilize a MULTI elevator system.

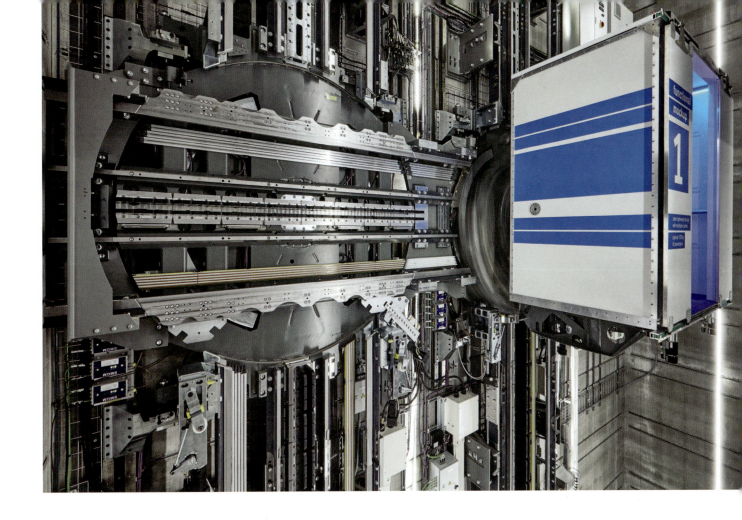

The introduction of a multi-directional elevator opens up infinite combinations of vertical and horizontal building design opportunities.

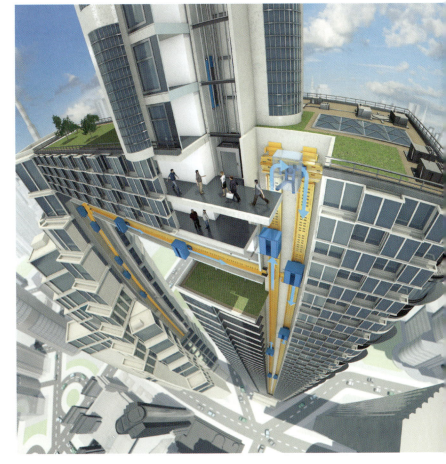

Opposite: The 246-meter Aufzugtestturm in Rottweil, Germany, where MULTI has been tested extensively.

Top: Detail view of the exchanger device that changes cabin direction.

Left: This conceptual drawing shows possible applications of MULTI moving through multiple horizontal and vertical shafts in a cluster of buildings.

Timber Construction at Tallwood House

Innovation Design Team
Architect: Acton Ostry Architects
Fire Science and Building Code: GHL Consultants Ltd.
Infrastructure and Development – Owner: UBC
Principal Contractor: Urban One Builders
Tall Wood Advisors: Architekten Hermann Kaufmann
Timber Supplier: Structurlam Products LP
Virtual Design Modelling: CadMakers Inc.
Wood Structure Erection: Seagate Structures

In recent years, substantial progress has been made in the design and construction of taller mass-timber buildings. One major component of this progress has been due to innovations in the field of cross-laminated timber (CLT) and glue-laminated timber (GLT).

The Tallwood House at Brock Commons is a 400-bed student residence at the University of British Columbia. Reaching 58 meters, it is currently the tallest mass-timber hybrid building in the world. The building is comprised of 18 stories of unique timber structure: five-ply CLT floor panels, point-supported by GLT columns, all resting on a concrete transfer slab at level two. Two full-height concrete cores provide lateral stability.

By utilizing the two-way spanning capabilities of CLT, the beam component of the classic "post-and-beam" system was eliminated, along with labor-intensive connections, which dramatically reduced fabrication and erection time and costs. This floor system also significantly reduced the structural depth and created a clean, flat, point-supported surface for unobstructed service distribution.

As there is minimal information available on two-way point-supported CLT, a significant amount of finite-element analysis was carried out to understand the force distributions within the laminations. To achieve the required performance, a custom layout was designed using machine-stress-rated spruce laminations. To verify the custom CLT panels' capacity and better understand the complex behavior of the system, the design team completed 18 full-scale load tests in a research laboratory at the University of British Columbia. The testing has provided invaluable information to the engineering community on the complex behavior of this system.

A further factor that was critical to the project's success was the involvement of a third-party digital modeler. This modeling team undertook a "digital build" process that facilitated coordination between all disciplines. For example, all CLT penetrations could be structurally assessed in the digital realm. The 3D model was also converted into fabrication files for computer numeric control (CNC) machining, allowing conflicts to be avoided during construction.

In an effort to better understand the behavior of the building, it was fitted with accelerometers, moisture meters, and vertical shortening string pots. A research team at the University of British Columbia are undertaking this work and will provide invaluable information back to the engineering community.

Opposite: A view of the finished Tallwood House project.

Top: The Tallwood House under construction. The timber system is stabilized by a concrete core through the height.

Bottom Left: Axonometric drawing shows the distribution of timber and concrete elements.

Bottom Right: The advantage of the two-way point-supported CLT system becomes obvious when observing the simple lines of structure that result.

A LOOK BACK

In seeming opposition to the forward-looking tendencies of the tall building industry, it is by reflecting on the past that we can develop an informed understanding of true "innovation." Buildings that have recently entered their decennial year provide a convenient time frame for such reflections — mature enough for their lasting influence to be apparent, but contemporary enough for their solutions to remain relevant today. There is also immense value in recognizing the people who have made large impacts on our urban environments, that we might glean and replicate the personal approaches leading to their success.

Ten Years On

Perhaps no other building typology has been as closely associated with "now-ness" — as a culmination of technological advances and the expression of contemporary values — as the skyscraper. However, it is also useful and worthwhile to reflect on those buildings that have continued to deliver on their original promises, and in some cases, revealed new attributes over time. In terms of social, functional, aesthetic and environmental performance, many tall buildings have withstood and passed a "test of time."

Looking back 10 years, some of the most memorable skyscrapers reflected the growing consciousness about sustainability, while still maintaining an iconic presence. **Bahrain World Trade Center (BWTC)**, Manama, integrates large-scale wind turbines into its design; and together with numerous energy-reducing and recovery systems, this development shows an unequivocal commitment to raising global awareness for sustainable design. Over the past 10 years, the BWTC has shown that commercial developments can be created with a strong environmental agenda and address the needs of future generations. The visual impact of the BWTC comes from placing the sustainability agenda — and the turbines — front and center.

The energy utility headquarters at **Manitoba Hydro Place**, Winnipeg, integrated time-tested environmental concepts with advanced technologies to achieve a "living building." The thin volume of its solar chimney at the center of the composition proclaims this commitment loud and clear to its public. The architectural solution relies on passive free energy without compromising on design quality and, most importantly, human comfort. Embraced and nicknamed the "Open Book" by citizens of Winnipeg, the towers converge at the north and splay open to the south, for maximum exposure to the abundant sunlight and consistently robust southerly winds unique to Winnipeg's climate, while radiant slabs act as an internal heat exchange with the geothermal field. Ultimately, Manitoba Hydro Place set a precedent for the seamless integration of architectural excellence and climate-responsive, energy-efficient and sustainable design, while enhancing and improving the quality and comfort of the human experience and the civility of urban life.

The **San Francisco Federal Building** set a precedent for high-performance, design-driven government buildings in the US and beyond, and its legacy holds governments accountable for developing and operating real estate that reflects their citizens' values of quality design and protecting the environment. The design of the 18-story tower of reinforced concrete, four-story steel braced-frame annex building, and a standalone restaurant pavilion is based largely on energy reduction through natural ventilation, taking advantage of the temperate Bay Area climate. This was achieved through exposed thermal mass, thinned slabs, and narrow floor

1 | Bahrain World Trade Center
Manama, Bahrain

Completion Date: 2008
Height: 240 m (787 ft)
Stories: 45
Primary Function: Office
Architect: Atkins (design)
Structural Engineer: Atkins (design)
Main Contractors: Murray & Roberts; Rambøll København
Other CTBUH Member Consultant: BMT Fluid Mechanics Ltd. (wind)

2 | Manitoba Hydro Place
Winnipeg, Canada

Completion Date: 2008
Height: 115 m (377 ft)
Stories: 22
Area: 64,567 sq m (694,993 sq ft)
Primary Function: Office
Architects: Kuwabara Payne McKenna Blumberg Architects (design); Smith Carter Architects and Engineers (architect of record)
Structural Engineers: Croslier Kilgour & Partners Ltd. (design); Halcrow Yolles (design)
MEP Engineer: AECOM (design)
Main Contractors: J.D. Strachan Construction Ltd.; PCL Constructions Eastern
Other CTBUH Member Consultants: RWDI (wind); Transsolar Energietechnik GmbH (environmental)

Opposite: Bahrain World Trade Center, Manama. The twin-tower complex put wind-driven energy generation at the center of its design and sparked conversations worldwide.

Top & Left: Manitoba Hydro Place, Winnipeg. The solar chimney at its center (left) and the social spaces resulting from its splayed floor plan (top) earned local and international recognition for integration of sustainability and usability.

plates. The project's tower building consumes 33 percent less energy than a conventional office building design under the same California energy code.

Tall buildings are often criticized for being aloof and closed-off, particularly at street level. But several buildings, public and private, broke the mold over the past decade. Despite being a corporate headquarters, the **Comcast Center** in Philadelphia includes a large outdoor public plaza at ground level, and a 33-meter-high, light-flooded public winter garden connects the concourse with its shops and food hall to the tower and plaza above. Three "sky atria" in the

Some of the most memorable skyscrapers completed a decade ago reflected the growing consciousness about sustainability, while still maintaining an iconic presence.

lower portion of the tower's south façade overlook the plaza and provide tenants with unique and identifiable homes, continuing the transition smoothly from fully public to private occupancy as the tower rises.

Numerous openings, atria, notches and several glass-enclosed and exposed staircases along the height of the **Hong Kong Polytechnic University Community College** tower provide glimpses into the pulsing student life within from the busy streets outside, as well as fresh views out for students as they move between classes. The building was among the first to signal different educational programs by way of varying volumes and porosities vertically, taking the place of buildings arrayed on a linear campus.

The **Mode Gakuen Cocoon Tower**, in addition to its novel approach to stacking an educational program inside an intensively patterned glass enclosure, crisscrossed by a steel diagrid, is also intensely connected at multiple levels to the Tokyo streets, subways, and underground pedestrian walkway systems. Here too, and especially at night, the

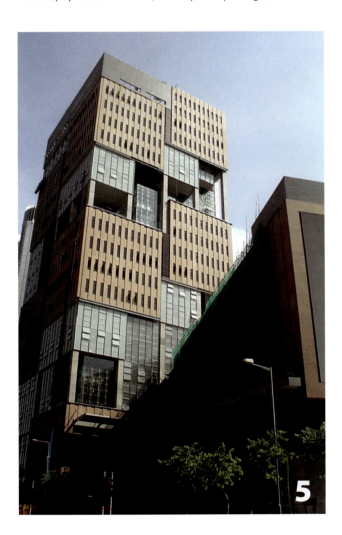

3 | San Francisco Federal Building
San Francisco, United States

Completion Date: 2007
Height: 71 m (234 ft)
Stories: 18
Area: 56,206 sq m (604,996 sq ft)
Primary Function: Office
Architects: Morphosis (design); SmithGroup (architect of record)
Structural Engineer: Arup (design)
MEP Engineer: Arup (design)
Main Contractor: Hunt Construction Group, Inc.
Other CTBUH Member Consultants: Kinemetrics Inc. (building monitoring); Permasteelisa Group (façade)

4 | Comcast Center
Philadelphia, United States

Completion Date: 2008
Height: 297 m (974 ft)
Stories: 57
Area: 130,064 sq m (1,399,997 sq ft)
Primary Function: Office
Owner: Comcast Corporation
Developer: Liberty Property Trust
Architects: Robert A.M. Stern Architects (design); Kendall / Heaton Associates (architect of record)
Structural Engineer: Thornton Tomasetti (design)
MEP Engineer: Paul H. Yeomans, Inc. (design)
Main Contractor: LF Driscoll
Other CTBUH Member Consultants: Alan G. Davenport Wind Engineering Group (wind); Enclos Corp. (façade); RWDI (wind); thyssenkrupp (vertical transportation)

5 | Hong Kong Polytechnic University Community College
Hong Kong, China

Completion Date: 2007
Height: 94 m (307 ft)
Stories: 19
Area: 26,300 sq m (283,091 sq ft)
Primary Function: Education
Architects: AD+RG Architecture Design and Research Group (design); AGC Design (design)
MEP Engineer: Parsons Brinckerhoff Consultants Private Limited
Main Contractor: Chevalier Construction Company Ltd

Opposite Top: San Francisco Federal Building, San Francisco. The thin profile (left) and exterior screen system (right) allowed the building to set precedents for low energy consumption.

Opposite Bottom: Comcast Center, Philadelphia. The building continues to be celebrated for its generous indoor and outdoor public spaces.

Left: Hong Kong Polytechnic University Community College, Hong Kong. The project was among the first "vertical campuses" to successfully fuse the benefits of high-rises and the traditional "college quad" of multiple single-function buildings.

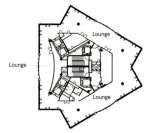
50th floor plan

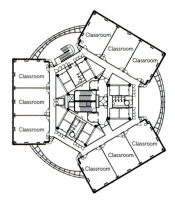
23rd floor plan

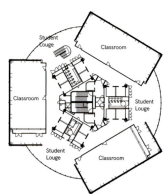
21st floor plan

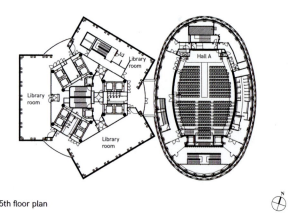
5th floor plan

6

7

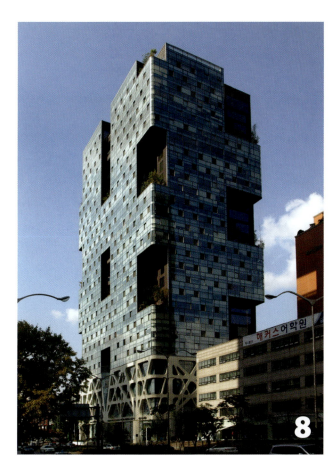

multistory atria along its height display the student "hive" to its bustling cityscape, while also communicating a protective, enveloping aesthetic that suggests a secure future for its young inhabitants.

Some of the strongest projects of this period are those which adopted a mixed-use program and gave each use a distinctive presence through manipulation of volumes and materials, but appear as an integrated whole. Sophisticated spatial integration is on display at Rotterdam's **The Red Apple**, a multi-building, mixed-use complex that uses variations in the scale of its paneling, floating cuboid volumes, and an activated ground-level façade to express the content within. Its overhanging cantilevered portion, defined by horizontal red bands, differentiates the office block from the apartment tower beyond, which, as it rises, is outlined by increasingly narrow vertical red aluminum strips. The unification is achieved through the strong use of color along bold orthogonal lines.

A high level of spatial integration on a tight site also took place at **Boutique Monaco** in Seoul, also with a mixed-use program. The tower's lower levels are composed of commercial, cultural, and community spaces and whose upper floors, from the 5th to 27th, are office-tels, which are residences that could also be used as offices during the day. Its extruded "C" shaped plan was carved away at points to achieve maximum floor area and optimal natural light conditions. As such, it proved a prime ground for

6 | Mode Gakuen Cocoon Tower
Tokyo, Japan

Completion Date: 2008
Height: 204 m (668 ft)
Stories: 50
Area: 80,865 sq m (870,424 sq ft)
Primary Function: Education
Owner/Developer: Mode Gakuen
Architect: Tange Associates (design)
Structural Engineer: Arup (design)
MEP Engineer: Kenchiku Setsubi Sekkei Kenkyusho (design)
Main Contractor: Shimizu Corporation

7 | The Red Apple
Rotterdam, Netherlands

Completion Date: 2008
Height: 124 m (405 ft)
Stories: 38
Primary Function: Residential
Owner/Developer: Winnervest Investment Pte Ltd
Architect: KCAP (design)
Structural Engineer: Corsmit Raadgevende Ingenieurs (design)
Main Contractor: Aannemersbedrijf v/h Boele & Van Eesteren
Other CTBUH Member Supplier: KONE (elevator)

8 | Boutique Monaco
Seoul, South Korea

Completion Date: 2008
Height: 117 m (384 ft)
Stories: 27
Area: 54,860 sq m (590,508 sq ft)
Primary Function: Office
Owner: Bumwoo Co., Ltd.
Developer: Leadway Co., Ltd.
Architect: MASS Studies (design)
Structural Engineer: TEO Structure (design)
MEP Engineer: Hana Consulting Engineers (design)
Main Contractor: GS E&C

Opposite Left & Top: Mode Gakuen Cocoon Tower, Tokyo. The tower's form (top), while eccentric, was not illogical. It was derived from strategically placed social and program areas in the plan (left), which find their expression on the exterior.

Opposite Bottom Right: The Red Apple, Rotterdam. The building modulates its height with strips of paneling of varying widths. Its office component is outlined in the same bright red, but the strip motif is rotated to the horizontal.

Top: Boutique Monaco, Seoul. The tower challenged its successors to "break the box" and express multi-functionalism in strong tectonic gestures.

experimentation with skybridges, unconventional unit configurations, protruding spiral staircases, and landscaping with trees that are visible from the inside and outside of the building — interventions that have been seen in many projects since, though rarely all in one place.

The eccentric mesh diagrid supporting Mode Gakuen's exterior and the pyramidal trusses supporting Boutique Monaco put these buildings in a small but vibrant category of tall buildings whose distinction continues to emanate from their expressive morphology, emphasized by structure.

Structural expression plays a strong role at **Poly Real Estate Headquarters Towers,** Guangzhou, with its distinctive X-braced frame structure that provides a bridge-like horizontal counterpoint to its vertically pronounced, off-set cores. Both of these strategies work together to afford unobstructed office floor space, social hubs, and a lightness and transparency throughout. These structural moves prefigured some of the prevalent trends in office design today, with emphasis on space supporting collaboration and flexibility.

A basket-woven diagrid also encloses and supports the **Tornado Tower**, in Doha. With its simple form and gentle curves, the tower offers a memorable, elegant silhouette that is recognizable from all vanishing points. Sitting strongly on a pristine plaza, Tornado Tower tapers gently inwards towards its slender mid-height point, then outwards again towards its summit. This form, along with the tower's kinetic lighting sculpture, has been seen in similar projects around the world since.

Torre Cepsa, Madrid, a corporate headquarters, makes a sparing and intricate use of structure, placing cores off-center and containing services within a giant arch that encloses discrete volumes of upper office floors. The arch peaks above the top volume with a dramatic "air gap" that supports stability under wind conditions.

Beyond structure, the other equally vital element for existential protection as well as aesthetic distinction on tall buildings is of course, the façade. While the vast majority of tall office buildings constructed since the 1950s, when International Style became a default standard, have adopted a floor-to-ceiling "glass box" approach, more recently, the

9 | Poly Real Estate Headquarters Towers
Guangzhou, China

Completion Date: 2007
Height: 161 m (527 ft)
Stories: 34
Area: 122,000 sq m (1,313,197 sq ft)
Primary Function: Office
Developer: Poly Real Estate Group Co. Ltd.
Architects: Skidmore, Owings & Merrill LLP (design); Guangzhou Design Institute (architect of record)
Structural Engineer: Skidmore, Owings & Merrill LLP (design)
MEP Engineer: WSP Flack + Kurtz
Project Manager: Skidmore, Owings & Merrill LLP

10 | Tornado Tower
Doha, Qatar

Completion Date: 2008
Height: 195 m (640 ft)
Stories: 51
Area: 80,000 sq m (861,113 sq ft)
Primary Function: Office
Architects: CICO Consulting Architects & Engineers (design); SIAT (design)
Structural Engineer: Stroh + Ernst AG
Other CTBUH Member Consultants: Prof. Quick und Kollegen - Ingenieure und Geologen GmbH (geotechnical); Wacker Ingenieure (wind)

11 | Torre Cepsa
Madrid, Spain

Completion Date: 2008
Height: 248 m (815 ft)
Stories: 49
Area: 107,966 sq m (1,162,136 sq ft)
Primary Function: Office
Owner: Pontegadea Inmobiliaria
Developer: Repsol YPF
Architects: Foster + Partners (design); Gonzalo Martínez-Pita Copello (design)
Structural Engineer: Halvorson and Partners (design)
MEP Engineer: Aguilera Ingenieros S.A (design)
Other CTBUH Member Consultant: Lerch Bates Europe (vertical transportation)
Other CTBUH Member Suppliers: AkzoNobel (paint/coating); Alimak Hek (construction hoists); ArcelorMittal (steel); CoxGomyl (façade maintenance equipment); Otis Elevator Company (elevator)

Opposite: Poly Real Estate Headquarters Towers, Guangzhou. With its off-set core (top) and supporting exterior diagrid (bottom), this building bridged the gap between mid-century International Style and the Parametric Age, offering clean floor plans and expressive exteriors.

Top: Tornado Tower, Doha. The building's structural expression is seen in the elegant simplicity of its "cinched-waist" shaped.

Left: Torre Cepsa, Madrid. The dramatic arch that crowns the building continues the visual expression of the offset cores holding office floors between.

same growing concern with environmental performance that led to investments in new energy systems and materials, also called the all-glass façade into question, as evidenced by strong alternatives deployed in several key projects.

Among these, the **New York Times Tower** stands out, with its distinctive grille of white ceramic brises-rods wrapping around the structure, achieving a high level of transparency while reducing the heat load to a point where the building is energy-efficient and yet has the great luxury of floor-to-ceiling, water-white glass. The façade includes a first-of-its-kind shading system that automatically adjusts to block glare, and the lights dynamically adjust to dim or turn off if the natural light is sufficiently bright.

Also a standout project that carefully off-sets the requirements for transparency and solar protection, the **Hegau Tower**, Singen, Germany, exploits a simplicity of form and selective

12 | New York Times Tower
New York City, United States

Completion Date: 2007
Height: 319 m (1,046 ft)
Stories: 52
Area: 143,601 sq m (1,545,708 sq ft)
Primary Function: Office
Owner: New York Times Company
Developer: Forest City Ratner Companies
Architects: FXFOWLE (design); Renzo Piano Building Workshop (design)
Structural Engineer: Thornton Tomasetti (design)
MEP Engineer: WSP Flack + Kurtz (design)
Main Contractor: American Landmark Properties, Ltd.
Other CTBUH Member Consultants: Gensler (interiors); RWDI (wind); Vidaris, Inc. (energy concept)
Other CTBUH Member Suppliers: AkzoNobel (paint/coating); ArcelorMittal (steel); Dow Corning Corporation (sealants); Grace Construction Products (fire proofing)

13 | Hegau Tower
Singen, Germany

Completion Date: 2008
Height: 68 m (221 ft)
Stories: 18
Area: 17,056 sq m (183,589 sq ft)
Primary Function: Office
Owner/Developer: GVV Singen
Architects: Murphy/Jahn Architects (design); Riede Architekten (architect of record)
Structural Engineer: Werner Sobek Group (design)
MEP Engineers: IB Schwarz (design); Schreiber Ingenieure
Main Contractor: Züblin
Other CTBUH Member Consultants: Transsolar Energietechnik GmbH (energy concept); Wacker Ingenieure (wind)
Other CTBUH Member Consultants: RWDI (wind); Transsolar Energietechnik GmbH (environmental)

Opposite: New York Times Tower, New York City. In a first-of-its-kind application, the tower's sheathing in ceramic tubes (top) allowed for floor-to-ceiling glass and controlled light to the interior (bottom).

Top & Left: Hegau Tower, Singen. This building also uses a novel shading system, which provides an elegant appearance and substantial interior comfort whether mostly closed (top) or open (left).

use of materials. It was the first large-scale application of a novel shading screen. The façade module of 2.7 meters provides a generous ambiance of space. A windproof, exterior automatic operable sunshade on the southwest façade allows for reduction of solar loads along with automatic interior perforated louvers on the other three façades. The exterior sunshade is a retractable curtain of stainless steel bars. Either by sensors or the user's command, the sunshade covers the entire façade, reducing the solar load to a minimum while still providing a visual connection to the outside.

In temperate climates, opportunities abound for creating permeable tall buildings — but with the "sealed box" as the default approach, it was never a given that this would happen. Projects such as **Lumiere Residences**, Sydney, showed the way. Ten years on, the tower's numerous green features and common-sense amenities have been replicated by many other residential towers throughout the country, validating its impact as a model for the future. The dual emphasis on comfort and sustainability manifests is several key ways. Winter gardens in every unit offer an alternative to balconies. The internal-external spaces can be opened via an operable façade at any time of year, while maintaining a clean external appearance. Due to its structural composition, each of the tower's tenants also

14 | Lumiere Residences
Sydney, Australia

Completion Date: 2007
Height: 152 m (499 ft)
Stories: 47
Primary Function: Residential
Owner/Developer: Greencliff (CPL) Developments Pty Ltd
Architects: Foster + Partners (design); Peddle Thorp & Walker (design)
Structural Engineers: Robert Bird Group (design); Taylor Thomson Whitting (design)
MEP Engineers: Connell Mott MacDonald (design); Warren Smith and Partners (design)
Main Contractor: Multiplex Constructions
Other CTBUH Member Consultants: Connell Mott MacDonald (façade); Foster + Partners (interiors); JBA Urban Planning Consultants Pty Ltd (urban planner)
Other CTBUH Member Supplier: Permasteelisa Group (cladding)

15 | Newton Suites
Singapore, Singapore

Completion Date: 2007
Height: 120 m (394 ft)
Stories: 36
Area: 11,835 sq m (127,391 sq ft)
Primary Function: Residential
Owner/Developer: UOL Group Ltd
Architect: WOHA Architects (design)
Structural Engineer: LBW Consultants (design)
MEP Engineer: WSP Lincolne Scott (design)
Main Contractor: Kajima Corporation

enjoys a heightened sense of privacy, as the apartments are arranged in eight slender volumes circling a central core, with deep recessions separating what would have been shared walls. Meanwhile, a kit of sustainable elements allowed the tower to achieve a NABERS 3.5 Star rating, including water-efficient plumbing fixtures, double glazing, and operable window coverings.

Perhaps the most literal representation of the dawning environmental consciousness can be found in the tide of green walls rising up the façades of tall buildings, particularly in the equatorial regions. **Newton Suites**, Singapore is a study in environmental solutions to tropical high-rise living. The exterior of the tower uses sun shading elements, patterned planes of textured panels and protruding balconies to create a façade that is functional

Opposite: Lumiere Residences, Sydney. Deep recessions between what would have been shared walls (top) and the substitution of winter gardens for balconies in each unit (bottom) showed the way forward for permeable tall buildings in temperate climates.

Above: Newton Suites, Singapore. Here, landscape is used as a façade material, a move that has been repeated successfully on buildings throughout equatorial Asia and beyond.

16

yet expressive. The horizontal, metal expanded mesh sun shading screens the strong tropical sunlight. The angled mesh reduces solar radiation while permitting visual connection to the ground. Landscape is used as a façade material — rooftop planting, sky gardens and green walls are incorporated into the design. Creeper screens are applied to otherwise blank walls to create visual delight, absorb sunlight and carbon and create oxygen in the dense urban environment. Most available horizontal and vertical surfaces are landscaped, creating an area of landscaping that is 130 percent (110 percent planted) of the total site. Most strikingly, the residential building features a 104-meter-high, vertically-continuous green wall on the south of the building, utilizing a simple structural support system, along with an automatic irrigation system.

Skyscrapers are associated in the popular imagination with skyline iconicity and defining the brand of the cities in which they are built. For example, the **Shanghai World Financial Center**, is a symbol of commerce and culture that speaks to the city's emergence as a global capital. Shaped by the intersection of two sweeping arcs and a square prism — shapes representing ancient Chinese symbols of heaven and earth, respectively — the tower's tapering form supports programmatic efficiencies, from large floor plates at its base for offices to rectilinear floors near the top for hotel rooms. Its boldest feature, the 43-meter-wide portal carved through its upper levels, is dramatic, but also serves a distinct structural function — it relieves the enormous wind pressures on the building. This design boldness has allowed the SWFC to endure as an indelible feature of the city's skyline, even as it has been eclipsed in height by its neighbor, Shanghai Tower.

The most innovative tall buildings of the past decade ultimately all have something to say about the future that has been borne out by time. A more humanistic, aesthetically varied, and environmentally sound skyline was on the horizon, and these buildings helped sketch the outline that is now filling in.

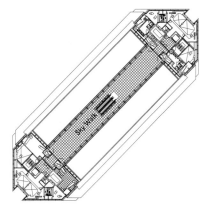

97th floor

83th floor

77th floor

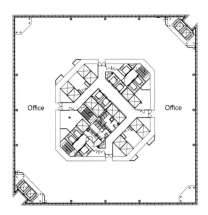

7th floor

16 | Shanghai World Financial Center
Shanghai, China

Completion Date: 2008
Height: 492 m (1,614 ft)
Stories: 101
Area: 381,600 sq m (4,107,508 sq ft)
Primary Functions: Hotel / Office
Owner: Shanghai World Financial Center Co., Ltd.
Developer: Mori Building
Architects: Kohn Pedersen Fox Associates (design); Mori Building (design); Irie Miyake Architects and Engineers (design); East China Architectural Design & Research Institute (architect of record); Shanghai Modern Architectural Design Company (architect of record)
Structural Engineer: Leslie E. Robertson Associates (design)
MEP Engineer: Kenchiku Setsubi Sekkei Kenkyusho (design)
Main Contractors: China State Construction Engineering Corporation; Shanghai Construction Group
Other CTBUH Member Consultants: Alan G. Davenport Wind Engineering Group (wind); ALT Limited (façade); CBRE (marketing); Langdon & Seah (quantity surveyor); Permasteelisa Group (façade); Rolf Jensen & Associates (fire)
Other CTBUH Member Suppliers: AkzoNobel (paint/coating); ArcelorMittal (steel); CoxGomyl (façade maintenance equipment); Dow Corning Corporation (sealants); HALFEN (cladding); Hitachi, Ltd. (elevator); Otis Elevator Company (elevator); thyssenkrupp (elevator)

Opposite & Left: Shanghai World Financial Center, Shanghai. The transition in plan (left) from four-sided office plate, through to six-sided hotel, with a dramatic termination in a glass-floored observation deck, gave the tower a distinctive shape (opposite), and thus an indelible status on the Shanghai skyline, seen here shortly after its completion.

Larry Silverstein
Lynn S. Beedle Lifetime Achievement Award

Larry A. Silverstein is the Chairman of Silverstein Properties, Inc., a New York-based real estate development and investment firm that has developed, owned and managed 3.7 million square meters of office, residential, hotel and retail space. The firm currently has $10 billion worth of development activity in the pipeline.

Silverstein is probably best-known for his tenacity and steady hand on New York real estate during tumultuous times. In July 2001, Silverstein completed the largest real estate transaction in New York history when he signed a 99-year lease on the World Trade Center for $3.25 billion, only to see it destroyed in terrorist attacks six weeks later on September 11, 2001. Since then, he has worked diligently to rebuild the office components of the World Trade Center site, a $30 billion undertaking. In May 2006, Silverstein Properties opened 7 World Trade Center, the first office tower to be rebuilt at the site, and the first LEED-certified office building in New York City. The 52-story, 156,181 square-meter building is fully leased to an eclectic group of tenants. In November 2013, the company opened 4 World Trade Center, a 72-story, 232,258 square-meter building designed by Fumihiko Maki, having secured online music company, Spotify, as its anchor tenant. Nearby, the company opened the Four Seasons Hotel and Private Residences New York Downtown at 30 Park Place in 2016. The company continues developing two other office towers on the WTC site — 3 World Trade Center, expected to open in 2018, and 2 World Trade Center still in development. The renaissance of Lower Manhattan would not have taken its current form without Silverstein's intensive involvement.

Outside the World Trade Center, Silverstein owns and manages many successful and high-profile commercial and residential properties in New York City, including 120 Broadway, 120 Wall Street, 529 Fifth Avenue and 1177 Avenue of the Americas. Mr. Silverstein recently opened Silver Towers, two 60-story residential towers at 600 West 42nd Street, the companion to 1 River Place, a 40-story, 921-unit tower which opened in 2000. The square block development houses over 2,200 families. Outside of New York, the firm opened a Four Seasons Resort at Walt Disney World in Orlando, and is exploring opportunities in China and the Middle East.

A 1952 graduate of New York University, Mr. Silverstein served as Vice Chairman of the NYU Board of Trustees, where he continues to serve as a member of the Board of Trustees for the New York University Langone Medical Center. He is the Founder and Chairman Emeritus of the advisory board of the NYU Real Estate Institute. As a Professor of Real Estate at NYU, his "Silverstein Workshop" became one of the most attended and informative educational sources for learning real estate development and investment analysis.

Through enterprises such as these, Silverstein has demonstrated his commitment to the continuous improvement of the tall building industry and to education of the inheritors of his legacy.

Opposite: Larry Silverstein has worked diligently to rebuild the office components of the World Trade Center Site since September 2001. The rendered skyline view (top) shows the impact the completed development will have on the skyline. The first building to open was 7 World Trade Center in May 2006 (bottom left), while work continues on-site today, with the latest tower, 3 World Trade Center nearing completion (bottom right).

Aine Brazil

Fazlur R. Khan Lifetime Achievement Medal

Throughout her nearly 40-year career, Aine Brazil has been responsible for the design and construction of some of the most significant high-rise buildings in the world. Brazil holds a bachelor's degree in civil engineering from the National University of Ireland in Galway, which in 2015 presented her with an honorary doctorate in engineering. She also holds a master's degree in engineering from Imperial College of Science and Technology in London. She joined Thornton Tomasetti in 1982 and was named vice chairman in 2011.

Brazil has been instrumental in shaping skylines around the world. Her work includes the 169-meter-tall Kristal Kule Finansbank Headquarters (formerly Soyak Tower) in Istanbul, Turkey; 280-meter-tall Torre KOI in Monterrey, Mexico; and Palazzo Lombardia, the 43-story home of the Lombardy Regional Government in Milan, Italy (named Best Tall Building Europe by CTBUH in 2012).

In Philadelphia, her work includes the 58-story, 300-meter-tall Comcast Center and adjacent 60-story Comcast Technology Center, which, at 342 meters, is the city's tallest building. In Oklahoma City, Brazil engineered the 50-story, 260-meter-tall Devon Energy Center (a CTBUH Best Tall Building Award Finalist in 2013).

She has led structural engineering teams for the design of more than 275,000 square meters of high-rise office development in New York City's Times Square neighborhood, including Five, Seven and Eleven Times Square. The latter is the city's first core-first office tower. This project utilized PERI jump forms to construct the concrete core ahead of the steel floor framing, allowing for a well-organized structural design and faster construction. The tower's clean and efficient design and construction opened the door for the use of concrete cores in many other projects in New York.

Brazil has been actively involved in the development of 30 and 10 Hudson Yards, two tall towers that are part of the massive Hudson Yards development constructed over an active rail yard. 10 Hudson Yards features a unique composite structural system utilizing a concrete core lateral system with a filigree slab system spanning to steel-formed wide/shallow beam framing in the floors. This created a clean and beautiful concrete ceiling finish that can be exposed in a loft-type office environment. The 270-meter-tall tower is the one of the tallest concrete office buildings, and one of the first of its type, in New York, challenging the status quo in the city's real estate market that office buildings should be framed in structural steel alone.

Brazil has always been, and continues to be, passionate about encouraging women to join the engineering profession. She established a mentoring/discussion program at Thornton Tomasetti, Women @ TT, to help the firm's female employees grow in their careers and to encourage greater gender diversity in the architecture, engineering and construction fields. She also started a scholarship at her alma mater, the National University of Ireland, to provide financial support to young women pursuing engineering degrees.

Opposite: Aine Brazil's work includes the Kristal Kule Finansbank Headquarters in Istanbul, 2014 (top left), Torre KOI in San Pedro Garza García, 2016 (bottom left), Comcast Technology Center in Philadelphia, scheduled for completion in 2018 (top right), and Palazzo Lombardia in Milan, 2011 (bottom right).

273

About the CTBUH & its Tall Building Awards Program

The Council on Tall Buildings and Urban Habitat (CTBUH) is the world's leading resource for professionals focused on the inception, design, construction, and operation of tall buildings and future cities. Founded in 1969 and headquartered at Chicago's historic Monroe Building, the CTBUH is a not-for-profit organization with an Asia Headquarters office at Tongji University, Shanghai; a Research Office at Iuav University, Venice, Italy; and an Academic Office at the Illinois Institute of Technology, Chicago. CTBUH facilitates the exchange of the latest knowledge available on tall buildings around the world through publications, research, events, working groups, web resources, and its extensive network of international representatives. The Council's research department is spearheading the investigation of the next generation of tall buildings by aiding original research on sustainability and key development issues. The Council's free database on tall buildings, The Skyscraper Center, is updated daily with detailed information, images, data, and news. The CTBUH also developed the international standards for measuring tall building height and is recognized as the arbiter for bestowing such designations as "The World's Tallest Building."

The content of this publication was driven by the submissions to the CTBUH's 2018 Awards program which recognizes projects and individuals that have made extraordinary contributions to the advancement of tall buildings and the urban environment, and that achieve sustainability at the highest and broadest level. The objective of this awards program is to deliver a comprehensive and sophisticated view of these important buildings, while advocating for improvements in every aspect of their performance, especially those that have the greatest effect on the people who use these buildings each day. This often means that the buildings highlighted are not the tallest in a given year, but represent the best qualities and innovations in the typology.

The Council initiated this program in 2001, with the creation of the Lynn S. Beedle Lifetime Achievement Award, later adding the Fazlur R. Khan Medal in 2004. It began recognizing the team achievement in tall building projects by issuing Best Tall Building awards in 2007. CTBUH issues four regional awards each year (Americas, Asia & Australasia, Europe, and Middle East & Africa), and from these regional awards, one project is awarded the honor of overall Best Tall Building Worldwide. The awards program has continued to expand over the years to address specific industry developments and recognize those buildings/innovations that are pushing the typology forward: Innovation Award (2012), 10 Year Award (2013), Urban Habitat Award (2014), and Construction Award (2017).

Celebration of the award winning projects is recognized through the annual Tall + Urban Innovation Conference, where Finalists in each award category present their projects to an international audience and live juries. Winners are selected during the event and awards are conferred at the Ceremony & Dinner held at the close of the event. The four regional Best Tall Building Winners also compete for the title of overall Best Tall Building Worldwide, which is announced at the close of the Ceremony & Dinner.

Projects are judged by four esteemed juries:

Main Jury:
The Main Jury is responsible for selecting the four regional Best Tall Building Winners, and from those, the Best Tall Building Worldwide. The five-member jury is multidisciplinary (architect, urban planner, building developer/occupier, socio-economist, etc.) and represents a diverse geographic spread. The CTBUH Board of Trustees selects the Jury Chairs.

2018 Jurors:
Chair: **Karl Fender,** *Director, Fender Katsalidis Architects,* Melbourne, Australia
Mohammad Ali Alabbar, *Founder & Chairman, Emaar,* Dubai, UAE
Kamil Merican, *Founding Partner, GDP Architects,* Kuala Lumpur, Malaysia
Steve Watts, *Chairman, CTBUH / Partner, alinea Consulting,* London, UK
Antony Wood, *Executive Director, CTBUH,* Chicago, USA

Technical Jury
The Technical Jury is responsible for selecting the Innovation Award and the Construction Award. Jurors also provide technical insight on regional Best Tall Building Award candidates, to assist the Main Jury in choosing the Regional

Finalists. The engineering disciplines are broadly represented in the Technical Jury and may include: construction/contracting, structural engineering, MEP engineering, environmental engineering, façade engineering, etc.

2018 Jurors:
Chair: **Abrar Sheriff,** *President & CEO, Turner International LLC,* New York City, USA
Jerry Jackson, *Vice President – Architecture, Engineering, Construction, Dassault Systemes,* Waltham, USA
Rene Lagos, *Founder & Chairman, Rene Lagos Engineers,* Santiago, Chile
Lester Partridge, *Director, LCI Australia Pty,* Sydney, Australia
Dario Trabucco, *Research Manager, CTBUH,* Venice, Italy

Urban Habitat Jury:
The Urban Habitat Jury is responsible for selecting the Urban Habitat Award winner. This jury also provides urban-design insights on regional Best Tall Building Award candidates, to assist the Main Jury in choosing the Regional Finalists. The jury is typically made up of urban planners, city planners, landscape architects, academics, and architects with a strong urbanistic viewpoint.

2018 Jurors:
Chair: **James Parakh,** *Urban Design Manager, City of Toronto Planning Department,* Toronto, Canada
James Burnett, *Founder, OJB Landscape Architecture,* Solana Beach, USA
Ron Henderson, *Founding Principal, L+A Landscape Architecture,* Newport, USA
Shaun Killa, *Founder, Killa Design,* Dubai, UAE
Helen Lochhead, *Dean, Faculty of Built Environment, University of New South Wales,* Sydney, Australia

CTBUH Board of Trustees:
The CTBUH Board of Trustees is responsible for selecting both Lifetime Achievement winners, the 10 Year Award winner, and any CTBUH Fellows for that year. The Trustees are also responsible for possibly designating a "Global Icon" winner, which may or may not be at the Main Jury's suggestion (Global Icon winners are rare — only one has been issued to date: the Burj Khalifa in 2010).

2018 Trustees:
Chair: **Steve Watts,** *Partner, alinea Consulting,* London, UK
David Malott, *Founder & CEO, AI. / SpaceFactory,* New York City, USA
Antony Wood, *Executive Director, CTBUH,* Chicago, USA
Tim Neal, *President & CEO, CallisonRTKL,* London, UK
Mounib Hammoud, *CEO, Jeddah Economic Company,* Jeddah, Saudi Arabia
Timothy Johnson, *Design Partner, NBBJ,* New York City, USA
Dennis Poon, *Vice Chairman, Thornton Tomasetti,* New York City, USA
Abrar Sheriff, *President & CEO, Turner International,* New York City, USA
Charu Thapar, *Managing Director – Property & Asset Management Services, Jones Lang LaSalle,* Mumbai, India
Kam-Chuen (Vincent) Tse, *Managing Director, Building MEP, China Region, WSP,* Hong Kong, China

CTBUH Fellows:
CTBUH Fellows are recognized for their contribution to the Council over an extended period of time, and in recognition of their work and the sharing of their knowledge in the design and construction of tall buildings and the urban habitat.

2018 Fellows:
Mark Garland, *President, LCL Builds Corporation,* Toronto, Canada
Craig Gibbons, *Principal, Arup,* Brisbane, Australia
Jianping Gu, *General Manager, Shanghai Tower Construction and Development Co., Ltd.,* Shanghai, China
Elena Shuvalova, *CEO, Lobby Agency,* Moscow, Russia
Junjie Zhang, *Chairman, ECADI,* Shanghai, China

To read the specific awards criteria, view past winners, and learn more about the awards program generally visit: http://awards.ctbuh.org

Index of Buildings

1 Parramatta Square, *Parramatta* 128
1 William Street, *Brisbane* 72
30 Park Place, *New York City* 62
35 Spring Street, *Melbourne* 74
35XV, *New York City* 16
56 Leonard, *New York City* 226
88 Scott, *Toronto* 62
111 Main, *Salt Lake City* 11, 228
150 North Riverside, *Chicago* 9, 20
161 Sussex Street, *Sydney* 76
177 Pacific Highway, *Sydney* 128
461 Dean Street, *New York City* 10, 230
609 Main at Texas, *Houston* 62
615 South College, *Charlotte* 62

A'DAM Toren, *Amsterdam* 8, 138
American Copper Buildings, *New York City* 9, 24
Angel Court, *London* 11, 140
AQWA Corporate, *Rio de Janeiro* 62
Aquaria Grande Tower B, *Mumbai* 128
Arena Tower, *London* 166
Axis, *Frankfurt* 144
Azrieli Sarona, *Tel Aviv* 170

Bahrain World Trade Center, *Manama* 256
Beirut Terraces, *Beirut* 174
Boutique Monaco 261
Biscayne Beach, *Miami* 64
BRIC Phase 1, *San Diego* 64
Britam Tower, *Nairobi* 186

Canaletto, *London* 11, 146
CF Calgary City Centre Phase I, *Calgary* 64
Chaoyang Park Plaza, *Beijing* 6, 78
Chinachem Central, *Hong Kong* 128
Cielo, *Seattle* 64
City Center Tower, *Taguig City* 82
City Hyde Park, *Chicago* 28
City Tower Musashikosugi, *Kawasaki* 194
Comcast Center, *Philadelphia* 258

De Verkenner, *Utrecht* 166
Dollar Bay, *London* 150
Dua Menjalara, *Kuala Lumpur* 196

Enbridge Centre, *Edmonton* 30
Eq. Tower, *Melbourne* 84
Equus 333, *San Pedro Garza García* 64

Federation Tower, *Moscow* 166
FV, *Brisbane* 86

Gaia Building, *Quito* 32
Golden Eagle International Shopping Center, *Nanjing* 128
Gravity Tower, *Melbourne* 130
Greatwall Complex, *Wuhan* 198
Green Residences, *Hangzhou* 130
Grove at Grand Bay, *Miami* 36
Guangzhou CTF Finance Centre, *Guangzhou* 12, 88

Hegau Tower, *Singen* 264
Hong Kong Polytechnic University Community College, *Hong Kong* 259
Hotel EMC2, *Chicago* 38
Hotel Las Americas Golden Tower, *Panama City* 66
Hangzhou Gateway, *Hangzhou* 90
Huangshan Mountain Village, *Huangshan* 6, 92

IM Tower, *Tokyo* 130
INDX Condominiums, *Toronto* 66
International Towers, *Sydney* 9, 190
Iran Telecom Research Center, *Tehran* 186

Jade Signature, *Sunny Isles Beach* 66
Jersey City Urby, *Jersey City* 40

Kyobashi EDOGRAND, *Tokyo* 130

L'Avenue, *Montreal* 66
Landmark Group Headquarters, *Dubai* 186
Level BK, *New York City* 66
Light House, *Melbourne* 96
Lotte World Tower, *Seoul* 98
Lumiere Residences, *Sydney* 266

Madison Square Park Tower, *New York City* 42
Manitoba Hydro Place, *Winnipeg* 256
Marina One, *Singapore* 6, 102
Metropolitan, *Quito* 44
Millennium Center 1, *Sofia* 166
Mode Gakuen Cocoon Tower, *Tokyo* 259

Nakanoshima Festival Tower West, *Osaka* 130
Namdaemun Office Building, *Seoul* 106
National September 11 Memorial, *New York City* 10, 202
New'R, *Nantes* 152
Newton Suites, *Singapore* 267
New York Times Tower, *New York City* 264
Ningbo Bank of China, *Ningbo* 132
Northwestern Mutual Tower and Commons, *Milwaukee* 68

Oasia Hotel Downtown, *Singapore* 6, 206
One Avighna Park, *Mumbai* 132
Optima Signature, *Chicago* 68

Park Avenue West, *Portland* 68
Parnas Tower, *Seoul* 132
Ping An Finance Center, *Shenzhen* 12, 108
Poly International Plaza, *Beijing* 11, 112
Poly Real Estate Headquarters Towers, *Guangzhou* 262
Porsche Design Tower, *Sunny Isles Beach* 46

Q22 Tower, *Warsaw* 166

Raffles City Hangzhou, *Hangzhou* 116
River Point, *Chicago* 48
Rosewood Sanya and Sanya Forum, *Sanya* 132
Rothschild Tower, *Tel Aviv* 178

San Francisco Federal Building, *San Francisco* 256
Shanghai World Financial Center, *Shanghai* 268
Shirley Ryan AbilityLab, *Chicago* 9, 50
Shenyang K11, *Shenyang* 132
SKYPARK, *Hong Kong* 6, 210
SOHO Fuxing Plaza, *Shanghai* 214

Talan Towers, *Astana* 134
Telkom Landmark Tower 2, *Jakarta* 134
Ten Thousand, *Los Angeles* 68
Tencent Seafront Towers, *Shenzhen* 9, 118
The 118, *Dubai* 186
The Collection, Tower, *Honolulu* 68
The Encore, *New York City* 70
The EY Centre, *Sydney* 232
The Globe and Mail Centre, *Toronto* 52
The Hub, *New York City* 70
The Pavilia Hill, *Hong Kong* 218
The Red Apple, *Rotterdam* 261
The Shahar Tower, *Givatayim* 186
The Silo, *Copenhagen* 8, 154
The Summit - Plot 554, *Suzhou* 134
The Suzhou Modern Media Plaza, *Suzhou* 134
The Tembusu, *Singapore* 122
Three Alliance Center, *Atlanta* 54
Tornado Tower, *Doha* 262
Torre Cepsa, *Madrid* 262
Torre KOI, *San Pedro Garza García* 56
Tribunal de Paris, *Paris* 158
Tsinghua Ocean Center, *Shenzhen* 124

Univ360 Place, *Seri Kembangan* 220
University of Chicago Campus North Residential Commons, *Chicago* 58
Upper West, *Berlin* 162
Upper West Side, *Melbourne* 136
Urbana Tower 2, *Kolkata* 136

Warsaw Spire, *Warsaw* 234
White Collar Factory, *London* 12, 164
Wilshire Grand Center, *Los Angeles* 60
Wolf Point West, *Chicago* 9, 222

Zeitz MOCAA, *Cape Town* 8, 182
Zhengzhou Greenland Central Plaza, *Zhengzhou* 126
Zhongzhou E-ClASS, *Shenzhen* 136

Index of Companies

10 DESIGN 198
35XV Condominiums 16

A

Aannemersbedrijf v/h Boele & Van Eesteren 261
Aanneming Maatschappij J.P. van Eesteren 138
Able Engineering Inc. 66
Access Advisors Ltd. 116, 132
Aceros Corey 240
AC Martin 60
aCTa asia private limited 136
Acton Ostry Architects 252
A'DAM Toren 138
ADP Consulting 86
AD+RG Architecture Design and Research Group 259
Adrian L. Norman 210
AECOM 54, 76, 96, 118, 128, 132, 164, 248, 257
AGC Design 259
Aguilera Ingenieros S.A 263
AHA Consulting Engineers 54
AIM Architecture 214
AJD Construction 40
AKFA 134
AKTII 164, 248
AkzoNobel 263, 265, 269
Alan G. Davenport Wind Engineering Group 259, 269
Al Basti & Muktha LLC 186
ALBDO 152
Alchemy Properties 16
Alimak Hek 263
All Area Plumbing 68
Allford Hall Monaghan Morris 164
Altitude Façade Access Consulting Pty Ltd 72, 84
ALT Limited 88, 98, 108, 269
Aluvisa 56
Alvine Engineering 48, 68, 222
AMA Consulting Engineers, P.C. 40
AMAV A. Niv - A. Schwartz Architects 186
American Landmark Properties, Ltd. 265
Amfion 166
AMP Capital Investors Pty Ltd 232
AMSYSCO 50, 68
Angelo, Gordon & Co. 16
Anoto/Weinspire Collaboration 238
Antheus Capital, LLC 28
Aon Fire Protection Engineering 48, 98
Arcadis 128
ArcelorMittal 20, 48, 166, 263, 265, 269
Archgroup Consultants 186
Architects 61 102
Architectus 128
Architekten Hermann Kaufmann 252
ARC Studio Architecture & Urbanism 122
Ardmore Ltd 146
Arélia 158
Armstrong World Industries 118, 126
ARTS Group Co, Ltd. 134
Arup 38, 62, 68, 88, 102, 108, 116, 118, 140, 164, 174, 182, 202, 230, 232, 259, 261
Aspect Oculus 190
Aspect Studios 72, 128
Astana Property Management LLC 134
Atelier Alan Teh Architect 196, 220
Atkins 118, 257
Aurecon 76, 134
Axis Architects 146, 248
Azrieli Group 170

B

Bakkala Consulting Engineers Limited 234
Balslev and Wessberg 154
Bar Akiva Engineers Ltd 170, 186
Barely Levitzky Kassif Architects 178, 186
Barker Mohandas, LLC 234
Barrett Woodyard & Associates 62
Bartels Polska Sp. z o.o. 234
Bates Smart 74, 76, 128
BAUM Architects 98
BC Architects 64
Beca Carter Hollings & Ferner (SE Asia) Pte. Ltd. 102
Beijing Fortune Lighting System Engineering Co., Ltd. 108
Beijing Institute of Architectural Design 112
Beijing Jingfa Properties Co., Ltd. 78
Beique Legault Thuot Architectes 66
Beltec Estrutura Metalica 62
Benchmark 174
Bene Gmbh 238
Bengal NRI Pvt Ltd 136
Berggruen Residential Ltd. 178
Berim 158
BETAP 152
BG&E 84, 136, 232
Bird Construction 62
Bjarke Ingels Group 36
bKL Architecture 222
Blue Earth Group 130
BMT Fluid Mechanics Ltd. 88, 132, 257
Bollinger + Grohmann 144
Bouygues Batiment International 158
Brandow & Johnston Inc 60
Britam Properties Limited 186
British American Insurance Company Limited 186
Broadway Malyan 134
Broccolini Construction 66
Bumwoo Co., Ltd. 261
Bureau of Public Works of Shenzhen Municipality 124
BuroHappold Engineering 24, 68, 132, 146, 166

C

Cadillac Fairview Corporation Ltd 64
CadMakers Inc. 252
CallisonRTKL 134
CapitaLand China 116
Cardno 84, 96
Cardno Haynes Whaley, Inc. 62
Carlos Ott Architect 66
CAST CONNEX 68, 240
CAZA 82
C & B Consulting Engineers 68
CBRE 20, 269
Cbus Property 72, 74
CCDI Group 78, 108
CentreCourt Developments 66
Cerami & Associates 16, 24, 48, 62, 68
Cermak Peterka Petersen (CPP) 232
CG Schmidt 68
Chang-Jo Architects 132
Chang Minwoo Structural Consultants 98
ChapmanBDSP 186
Charter Hall 128
Chevalier Construction Company Ltd 259
China Academy of Building Research 108
Chinachem Group 128
China Construction Eighth Engineering Division 78, 92
China Construction First Group Construction & Development Co., Ltd. 108
China Construction Second Engineering Bureau Ltd. 118
China Construction Third Engineering Bureau Co., Ltd. 112, 198
China CUC 90
China Nulcear Industry Huaxing Construction Co., Ltd 128
China Overseas 128
China State Construction Engineering Corporation 88, 132, 166, 238, 269
China United Engineering Corporation 116
CHM Structural Engineers, LLC. 46
Chow Tai Fook Enterprises 88
Christian Wiese Architects 44
CICO Consulting Architects & Engineers 263
Citic Wuhan Architectural Design Institute 198
City Creek Reserve, Inc 228
C J O'Shea Group Ltd 166
Clark Construction Group 20, 48, 222
CM Wong & Associates Ltd 210, 218
Coastal Construction 46
COBE 154
Code Consultants, Inc. 202
Coheco 44
Comcast Corporation 259
Concert Properties Ltd. 62
Concrete 40
Connell Mott MacDonald 267
Constructa Ingenieros Panama S.A. 66
Constructora DOCSA 56
Constructura Naranjo Vela SA 32
Continuum Company, LLC 42
Corsmit Raadgevende Ingenieurs 261
Cosentini Associates 20, 68, 70, 226
Costas Kondylis Design 226
Cottee Parker Architects 136
Cox Architecture 76
CoxGomyl 88, 134, 166, 263, 269
CPB Contractors 128
Cracknell Landscaping 238
Crescent Heights 68
Critchfield Mechanical Inc. 68
Croslier Kilgour & Partners Ltd. 257
CS Associates, Inc. 68
Cupertino Electric Inc. 68
Curtain Wall Design and Consulting, Inc. 62, 64

D

Dagher Engineering, PLLC 16
Daiken 238
David C. Hovey, FAIA 68
David Engineers Ltd. 170, 178, 186
Davis Brody Bond 202
Davis Langdon 116, 174
Davis Langdon & Seah 116
dbHMS 58
DBT Ingenieursozietät 144
DCI Engineers 64
Deerns 138, 234
Dennis Lau & Ng Chun Man Architects & Engineers (HK) Ltd. 128, 132
Derwent London 164
Design Partners, Inc. 68
DeSimone Consulting Engineers 36, 40, 42, 70
Dezer Development 46
D. Hahn Consulting Engineers LTD 178
DIALOG 30
Diamond Schmitt Architects 52
DIB Tower Sal 174
Dizayn Group 134
Donglim Co Ltd 106

Donglim Construction Co Ltd 106
Dong Yang Structural Engineers 132
Douglaston Development 66
Dow Corning Corporation 88, 108, 265, 269
DS-Plan GmbH 162
DTZ Debenham Tie Leung 198
Duda | Paine Architects 64
Duncan Stutterheim 138
Dupras Ledoux 66

E

East China Architectural Design & Research Institute 214, 269
Ebert-Ingenieure 166
EC Harris 146
Echo Investment 166
eConstruct 238
Edgett Williams Consulting Group Inc. 68, 112, 228
Eduardo A. Delgado Acosta 66
Edwards & Zuck Engineers 66
Ed. Züblin AG 162
EGS2 Corp. 46
Eichner Properties, Inc. 42
Elemec UAE 132
Elenberg Fraser 84, 86, 96
Elhar Engineering Construction Ltd. 170
EMF Griffiths 72
Enclos Corp 226, 259
Energoprojekt 134
Engky Design Sdn Bhd 196, 220
Enstruct Group Pty Ltd 232
Entuitive 68
enuTEC Energietechnik und Umweltmanagement GmbH 162
Environmental Systems Design, Inc. 50
Epexyl 158
ERA Bouw 166
Esa Consultoria e Ingenieria 56
Esteban Y. Tan and Gavino L. Tan Partners 82
Ethos Urban 190

F

Fairis 44
Faithful+Gould 134
Far East Consortium International Limited 136
Far East Organization 206
Far East SOHO Pte Ltd. 206
Felix Claus en Dick Van Wageningen Architecten 138
FE Moran 38, 68
Fideicomiso Mercantil Metropolitan 44
Firstbase 248
First Gulf 52
Fisher Marantz Stone 62
Fletcher Priest Architects 140
Forest City Ratner Companies 230, 265
Fortin, Leavy, Skiles, Inc. 46
Fortune International Group 66
Fortune International Reality 66
Fortune Shepler Consulting 60, 98, 108
Fortune Shepler Saling Inc. 62, 64
Foster + Partners 62, 263, 267
Francis-Jones Morehen Thorp Pty Ltd 232
Frogmore 166
Fusion Project Management 130
FXCollaborative 16
FXFOWLE 16, 265

G

Gallagher Jeffs 96
Galliard Homes 166
GAPP Architects & Urban Designers 186
GCI Consultants 64
GEI Consultants 38, 50
Gensler 50, 118, 238, 265
Gerald D Hines Interests 226
GERB Vibration Control Systems, Inc 42

Gesellschaft für Städtebau und Projektentwicklung 162
Ghelamco Poland 234
GHL Consultants Ltd. 252
Gibson Electric 38
Gilbane Building Company 68
Gilsanz Murray Steficek 16, 66
Glenwood Management 70
Glumac 60
Goettsch Partners 20, 132, 134
Golden Elements 238
Gonzalo Martínez-Pita Copello 263
Grace Construction Products 108, 265
Gradient Wind Engineering Inc. 40
Graduate School at Shenzhen, Tsinghua University 124
Greatwall Construction Holdings Group Co. Ltd. 198
Greencliff (CPL) Developments Pty Ltd 267
Greenland Group 92, 126
Grontmij GmbH 144
Groveworld 146
Grupo Inversiones Talarame 66
GS E&C 102, 132, 261
GS Retail 132
GTIS Partners 64
Guangzhou Design Institute 88, 132, 263
Gulf Precast 238
GURNER TM 86
Gustafson, Guthrie, & Nichol 190
GVV Singen 265

H

Hakim Information Technology Co Ltd 90
Halcrow Yolles 257
HALFEN 269
Halvorson and Partners 222, 263
Hamilton Marino 130
Hamonic + Masson & Associés 152
Hana Consulting Engineers 261
Hanbury 58
Handel Architects LLP 68, 202
Hangzhou Jiahe Real Estate GmbH 130
Hangzhou Xintiandi Group LTD 90
Hanjin International Corporation 60
Hans Brouwer 138
Harmonic Trend [L] 186
Harmon, Inc. 54, 62
Harvey Builders 62
Hawaiian Dredging & Construction Company 68
HDR Architecture Inc. 50
Heatherwick Studio 182
Hengyi Pacific Pty Ltd 96
Hensel Phelps Construction Co. 64
Herzog & de Meuron Architekten 66, 174, 226
Heungkuk Life Insurance Co., Ltd. 106
Hickory 242
Hickory Building Systems 242
Hidi Rae Consulting Engineers Inc. 52
Hill International 174
Hill West Architects 42, 70
Hilti AG 108, 116, 134, 140
Hines 48, 62, 68, 222
Hip Hing Construction (China) Co. Ltd. 132
Hip Shing Hong (Holdings) Company Limited 218
Hitachi, Ltd. 88, 269
HLW International 40
HNGS Engineers 36
Hoare Lea 146
Hochtief do Brasil 62
Hoffman Construction Company 68
Holder Construction Company 62
Howard Humphreys (East Africa) Ltd. 186
HSArchitects 92
Huawei Data 238
Hummingbird Kinetics LLC 246
Hunt Construction Group, Inc. 259
Huygen Installatie Adviseurs 138
Hyder Consulting 72
Hydrautech 136

Hyopan Land Phils., Inc. 82
Hyundai Engineering & Construction 102

I

Ian Banham and Associates 186
IBI Group Architects 62, 66
IB Schwarz 265
ICD Property 84
IM Property 130
I. M. Robbins P.C. 70
ingenhoven architects 102
Ingeniero Patricio Ramos 32, 44
Inhabit Group 118, 128, 134
Instalaciones Sanitarias Hidraulicas y Soldaduras 56
Insynergy Engineering, Inc. 68
Integrated Design Engineers 64
Interface Engineering 68
Interium Srl. 134
Internacional de Inversiones 56
Invesco Real Estate 166
iPD 214
IP PROYECTOS 64
Iran Telecommunication Research Center 186
Irie Miyake Architects and Engineers 269
Ironstate Development 40
Isagani M. Martinez Consulting Engineers 82
ISPT Core Fund 72
ITG Consult Atlas AG 144
IT-Serve IT & AV 238
Ivanhoé Cambridge 48

J

Jablonsky, Ast and Partners 62, 66
Jackson Coles 164
Jacobs Parker Architects 182
James Law Cybertecture International 128
James McHugh Construction Co. 28, 50, 222
Jaros, Baum & Bolles 202
Jaspers-Eyers Architects 234
JBA 232
JBA Urban Planning Consultants Pty Ltd 76, 128, 267
JDS Architects 90
JDS Construction Group 24
JDS Development Group 24
J.D. Strachan Construction Ltd. 257
Jensen Hughes 50, 58, 64, 228
Jiangsu Province Huajian Construction Co., Ltd. 136
Jiangsu Provincial Architectural D&R Institute Ltd 128
JKMF 62
JLL 72, 134
John Day Developments 30
John Holland Group Pty Ltd 128
John Portman & Associates 62, 64
Jones Lang LaSalle, Inc. 108, 134
JORDAHL 132
J. Roger Preston Limited 108
Juara Consult Sdn Bhd 196
J. van Toorenburg BV 166

K

Kajima Corporation 267
Kaufman & Broad 152
KCAP 261
Kenchiku Setsubi Sekkei Kenkyusho 261, 269
Kendall / Heaton Associates 48, 62, 68, 259
Khatib & Alami 174
Killa Design 238
Kinemetrics Inc. 259
Kinetica 64
KJWW Engineering Consultants 68
KK Lim & Associates Pte Ltd 102
Klaus Kastbjerg 154
KMD Architects 132
KNK Consult Sdn Bhd 196
Kohn Pedersen Fox Associates 42, 88, 98, 108, 240, 269

KONE 66, 84, 96, 108, 126, 134, 138, 158, 178, 261
KOO 38
Korean Air 60
KPFF Consulting Engineers 68
KSP Jurgen Engel Architekten 162
KTP Consultants Pte Ltd 206
KUKBO 134
Kuryowicz & Associates 166
Kuwabara Payne McKenna Blumberg Architects 257
Kwan Henmi Architecture Planning 64
Kyobashi 2-chome West District Redevelopment Associates 130

L

Lab Architecture Studio 128
Laconia Development 64
Landmark Group 186
Langan Engineering 16, 36, 62, 64, 226, 230
Langdon & Seah 269
Langhof 162
Larsen & Toubro 136
Laxmanbhai Construction 186
LBS Properties 166
LBW Consultants 267
Leadway Co., Ltd. 261
Ledcor Construction Limited 30
Legado Corporativo Inmobiliaria, S.A. DE C.V. 64
Leigh & Orange 88
Leighton Properties 128
Lend Lease 48, 190, 202, 226
Lendlease Building Pty Ltd 190
Lendlease Design 190
Lendlease Project Management 190
Leppanen + Anker Arquitectos 32
Lerch Bates 36, 60, 64, 98
Lerch Bates Europe 263
Leslie E. Robertson Associates 88, 98, 269
Levine Builders 66
LF Driscoll 259
Liberty Property Trust 259
Lifetime Developments 66
Lighting Planners Associates 88, 108
Lingotto 138
Longriver Investments 242
Longyuan Construction Group Co., Ltd 214
LOTTE Engineering & Construction 98
Lotte Property & Development 98
LPP Lane Field, LLC 64
Lucid Consulting Australia 130

M

Mace Limited 140, 182, 248
Mace/Realstar 248
Mack-Cali Realty Corporation 40
Mack Scogin Merrill Elam Architects 54
MAD Architects 78, 92
Maeda Corporation 130, 194
M.A. Engineering 38
Magellan Development Group 222
Magnusson Klemencic Associates 20, 28, 48, 58, 68, 102
Mahimtura Consultants Pvt. Ltd. 128, 132
Maiteri & Associates 186
MAN Enterprise 174
Man Lick Engineering and Trading Co. Ltd. 128
Manny SY Associates 82
Mapletree Project Management Pte Ltd 102
Marioff Corporation Oy 234
Martin Project Management 60
MASS Studies 261
McNAMARA & SALVIA 66
McParlane & Associates, Inc. 64
MCW Consultants Ltd. 30
M. Doron - I. Shahar & Co. Consulting Engineers Ltd. 170, 186
Mecanoo Architecten 106
ME Engineers 62

Mei architects and planners 166
Meinhardt 116, 136, 218
Meinhardt Facade Technology (S) Pte. Ltd. 132, 134
Meixner Schlüter Wendt Architekten 144
MEP Consulting Engineers 128
Metal Yapi 134
MG Engineering DPC 42
MHA Engenharia Ltda. 62
Michael Wall Engineering 64
Ministry of Communications and Information Technology 186
Mirvac Constructions Pty Ltd 232
Mirvac George Street Pty Ltd 232
Mirvac Projects Pty Ltd 232
Mitros 166
Mitsui Fudosan Co. Ltd. 140
M&L Hospitality 76
Modzelewski & Rodek 166
Mode Gakuen 261
Mordue Engineering 130
Mori Building 269
Morphosis 259
Mortenson Development Company Inc. 58
Moshe Tzur Architects and Town Planners 170
Moss & Associates LLC 64
Mount Anvil 150
MovvéO Ltd. 158
M+S Pte Ltd 102
Mudi 90
Multiplex 72, 74, 76, 84, 86, 136, 164
Multiplex Constructions 96, 267
Mulvey & Banani 64
Murchie Consulting 84, 96
Murphy/Jahn Architects 265
Murray & Roberts 257
MV Shore Associates 62

N

Nanjing Golden Eagle International Group Co., Ltd. 128
National September 11 Memorial and Museum 202
NBBJ 118
NCK Inc. 66
Neo Modern Architects Pvt. Ltd 132
NES Structures 136
New Line Structures 70
New World China Land Co. Ltd. 88
New World Construction Company Limited 210, 218
New World Development Company Limited 132, 210, 218
New York Times Company 265
Nichols, Brosch, Wurst, Wolfe & Associates 36
NIKKEN SEKKEI LTD 130, 134
NIKMI JSC 166
Ningbo Eastern New City Development Investment Ltd. 132
NIPPON TOCHI-TATEMONO Co., Ltd. 130
Nish Developers Pvt Ltd 132
NOHO Construction LLC 16
Norman Disney & Young 96
Northwestern Mutual 68
Nova Fire Protection 68
NPPF 238
nps tchoban voss 166
NRE Denmark 154
NW Project Management Limited 218

O

OJB Landscape Architecture 48, 62, 68
Okland Construction 228
Olsson Fire & Risk (fire) 130
One Housing Group 150
OPEN Architecture 124
Optima Center Chicago II, LLC. 68
Optima, Inc. 68
Orion City Road Trustee Limited 146
O'Sullivan Plumbing Inc. 38

Otis Elevator Company 98, 108, 263, 269
Outokumpu 108
OZ 138

P

Pangman Development Corporation 30
Pappageorge Haymes Partners 68
Parnas Hotel 132
Parsons Brinckerhoff Consultants Private Limited 78, 126, 132, 214, 259
Paul H. Yeomans, Inc. 259
PCL Construction Management Inc. 64
PCL Constructions Eastern 257
PCL Construction Services, Inc. 64
PDW Architects 134
Peddle Thorp & Walker 267
Pelli Clarke Pelli Architects 222
Pembenaan Leow Tuck Chui & Sons Sdn Bhd 220
Pepper Construction Company 38
Perkins+Will 134
Permasteelisa Group 20, 42, 48, 50, 116, 134, 158, 232, 259, 267, 269
Perunding Mektrik Sdn Bhd 220
Peter Ruge Architekten 130
Pickard Chilton 48, 62, 68
Pierre-Yves Rochon, Inc. 66
Pieters Bouwtechniek 166
Ping An Financial Center Construction & Development 108
Pladis Arquitectura + Inteligencia 64
Planungsgruppe für technische Gebäudeausrüstung GmbH & Co 144
Plaza Construction Corporation 42, 64
Plus Architecture 130
PMK Consulting 238
PMP Consultores 56
Pol-Con Consulting Sp z.o.o 234
Polsko-BelgijskaPragownia Architektury Sp. z o.o. 234
Poly Real Estate Group Co. Ltd. 112, 132, 263
Polytec 152
Pontegadea Inmobiliaria 263
Portman Holdings 62
Postensa 64
Power Construction Company 50
Prof. Quick und Kollegen - Ingenieure und Geologen GmbH 263
Projex 238
Promotora Las Americas Golden Tower SA 66
PT Adhi Karya 134
PT Architecture Design (Shenzhen) Co., Ltd. 136
PT Arnan Pratama Consultants 134
P & T Consultants Pte Ltd 122
P&T Group 210, 218
PT. Haerte 134
Puckrin Design 238
PWP Landscape Architects 202

R

Radiant Symphony Sdn Bhd 196
RAF Arquitetura 62
Rambøll København 257
Rankine & Hill Consulting Engineers 206
RBS Architectural Engineering Design Associates 132
R. Cohen & Associates 178
RCP 74
Read Jones Christoffersen Ltd 64
Related Companies 240
Renaissance Construction Company 134, 166
Renzo Piano Building Workshop 158, 265
Repsol YPF 263
RFR Realty LLC 162
RGJ Electrosystem Consultants Inc. 82
Richard Dattner & Associates 70
Richard Meier & Partners Architects 178
Rick Brown Associates 182
Rider Levett Bucknall 88, 98, 108, 122, 136, 206
Riede Architekten 265

Rimax Design 166
Rincovitch Consultants Pty Ltd 242
River Point Holdings LLC 48
Riverside Investment & Development 20
RJC Engineers 52
Robert A.M. Stern Architects 62, 259
Robert Bird Group 74, 84, 267
Rogers Stirk Harbour + Partners 190
Rolf Jensen & Associates 269
Roseland Residential Trust 40
Rosenwasser/Grossman Consulting Engineers P.C. 70
Rothelowman 242
Royal Haskoning DHV 138
RSH+P 248
R.S. Ison & Associates 82
RWDI 48, 60, 62, 64, 68, 88, 98, 108, 146, 246, 257, 259, 265

S

Sander Groet 138
Sandu Environmental Signage 108
Sato & Associates, Inc. 68
Savills 76
Schindler 20, 102, 108, 112, 118, 132, 166, 186, 226, 232, 234
Schlaich Bergermann und Partner 126
Schreiber Ingenieure 265
Schüco 132
Seagate Structures 252
SENSA 64
Setec Bâtiment 158
Setec TPI 158
Severud Associates Consulting Engineers 16
Shanghai Construction Group 269
Shanghai Construction No.2 Group Co., Ltd. 126
Shanghai Construction No.4 (Group) Co., Ltd. 116
Shanghai Modern Architectural Design Company 269
Shanghai SAIYO Construction Engineering Co.,Ltd 116
Shanghai World Financial Center Co., Ltd. 269
Shapoorji Pallonji & Co. Ltd. 186
Shenyang Yuanda Aluminium Industry Engineering Co.,Ltd. 108, 116, 134, 166
Shenzhen Institute of Building Research Co., Ltd 124
Shenzhen Tongji Architects 118
Shimizu Corporation 122, 130, 261
Shirley Ryan AbilityLab
SHoP Architects 24, 230
Shunmyo Masuno + Japanese Landscape Consultants Ltd. 218
SIAT 263
Sichuan Huashi Group Co., LTD 124
SIDE International 186
Siemens 238
SIGNA Prime Selection AG 162
Signature Estates Limited 186
Silliman Group 28
Silverstein Properties 62, 270
Simplex Infrastructures Ltd. 132
SimpsonHaugh & Partners 150
Sinclair Brook 84, 242
Sino-Ocean Land 84
Sitetectonix Pte Ltd 206
Skanska 230
Skidmore, Owings & Merrill LLP 112, 132, 134, 166, 228, 263
Skyforce Engineering Limited 128
SLCE Architects 62
Smallwood, Reynolds, Stewart, Stewart 54
Smart-hero (HK) Investment Development Ltd. 78
SMASHotels Chicago LLC 38
SME Steel Contractors 228
Smith + Andersen 64
Smith Carter Architects and Engineers 257
SmithGroup 259
Socsa 64
SOHO China Co. Ltd 214
Solution Station 182
Sowlat Structural Engineers 68
SPEECH 166

Stanhope 140
Stanley D. Lindsey & Associates, Ltd. 54
Stantec Ltd. 66, 70
Stark + Ortiz 56
State Mechanical 38
Steiner NYC 70
Stephen B. Jacobs Group P.C. Architects and Planners 66, 70
Steven Feller P.E. 46
Stolitsa 166
ST Patners Sdn Bhd 220
Strabag Real Estate GmbH 162
Stroh + Ernst AG 263
Structurlam Products LP 252
Studco Australia Pty Ltd 96
Studio Gang 28, 58
Suffolk Construction Company, Inc. 66
Sufrin Group 186
Sumitomo Realty & Development Co., Ltd. 194
Suntec Real Estate Investment Trust 128
Surtidora Electrica del noreste 56
Sutherland 182
Suzhou Broadcasting System 134
Suzhou Institute of Architectural Design Co., Ltd. 134
SWA Group 112
Swinerton Builders 68
Sync Bathroom Pods 242
SYSKA Hennessy Group 98, 238

T

Takenaka Corporation 130
Tange Associates 261
Tarho Mantagheh Consulting Engineers 186
Taylor Thomson Whitting 76, 267
Tehran Goruh Co. 186
Teknika 62
Telkom Group 134
Tencent Technology Company Limited 118
TEO Structure 261
Terra Group 36
The Asahi Shimbun Company 130
The Collection LLC 68
The Levy Organization 48
The Sieger Suarez Architectural Partnership 46
The Wadhwa Group 128
Thornton Tomasetti 50, 56, 60, 98, 108, 118, 166, 238, 240, 246, 259, 265, 272
Three Alliance Buckhead, L.P. 54
thyssenkrupp 16, 50, 54, 70, 166, 250, 259, 269
Ticino Holdings Inc. 82
Tidhar Construction 186
Tidhar Investments 186
Tishman Construction 62, 240
Tishman Speyer Properties 54, 62, 134
tk1sc 64
TMT Development 68
Tokyo Tatemono Co., Ltd. 130
TOMMY SCHWARZKOPF 44
Tongji Architectural Design (Group) Co., Ltd. 118, 126
TOWN Tower Sal 174
Transsolar Energietechnik GmbH 58, 257, 265
Triad Architects 186
Turner Construction Company 54, 60, 230
Turner International LLC 134, 166
TVA Architects 68
Two Roads Development 64

U

UBC 252
UEM Sunrise Berhad 102
UltraTech Cement Lanka (Pvt.) Ltd. 132
Umow Lai 74
United Projects Consultants Pte Ltd 122
University of Chicago 58
UNStudio 116, 146
UOL Group Ltd 267
Urban One Builders 252
Urban Renewal Authority 210
Uribe & Schwarzkopf 32, 44

URS 146
URS Corporation 54

V

Van Der Merwe Miszewski Architects 182
Van Deusen & Associates 16, 54, 134
Verny Capital 134
VFO Arquitectos 56
Victoria and Alfred Waterfront 182
Vidaris, Inc. 42, 62, 265
Vipac Engineers & Scientists 84, 86
Vizafire 56
von Gerkan, Marg and Partners Architects 126, 214

W

Wacker Ingenieure 134, 144, 263, 265
Walter P. Moore 62
Wang Weixian 92
Warren Smith and Partners 267
Waterman Building Services Ltd 140
Waterman Group 140
Waxman Govrin Geva Engineering LTD. 170, 178
Webber Design 86
Weidlinger Associates 202
Werner Sobek Group 265
West 60th Development LLC 70
West 60th Street LLC 70
W Group 82
Whitecode Design Associates 166
WHLC Architecture 64
Wilma Wohnen Süd GmbH 144
Windtech Consultants Pty Ltd 72, 102, 134, 206
Wing Tai Holdings Limited Singapore 122
Winnervest Investment Pte Ltd 261
Winward Structures 96
Wirth Research 244
WMA Consulting Engineers 28
WOHA Architects 206, 267
Woh Hup Pte Ltd 206
Wolff Landscape Architecture 222
Wolf Point Owners LLC 222
Wood and Grieve Engineers 136
Woods Bagot 72, 134
Wordsearch 88
WSP 24, 38, 64, 118, 128, 134, 136, 166, 210, 228
WSP Built Ecology 112
WSP Cantor Seinuk 62, 202, 226
WSP Flack + Kurtz 62, 112, 263, 265
WSP Group 66, 72, 96, 118, 150
WSP Hong Kong Ltd. 210
WSP Lincolne Scott 267
WSP | Parsons Brinckerhoff 88, 98, 132
WSP Structures 136
WT Partnership 72, 76, 118
W&W Steel 240

X

Xavier High School 16

Y

Yosha Amnon Consulting Engineers Ltd 170, 186
Yrys Batys LLP 134
Yuanda 72, 128
YWC Engineers & Constructors Sdn Bhd 196

Z

ZAO Bashnya Federatsiya 166
Zeidler Partnership Architects 64
Zhejiang Kun hung Construction Co., Ltd. 130
Zhejiang Zhongshe Engineering Design Co. Ltd. 130
Zhongtian Construction Group Co., Ltd. 126
Zhongyifeng Construction Group Co., Ltd. 134
Zhongzhou Baocheng Real Estate Co., Ltd. 136
Zhubo Design 136
Zip Hill Development Sdn Bhd 220
Züblin 265

Image Credits

Pg 7:	Top © H.G. Esch/ ingenhoven architects; bottom left © Patrick Bingham-Hall; bottom right © New World Development Company Limited
Pg 8:	Top © Rasmus Hjortshøj - COAST; bottom © Mark Williams
Pg 9:	© James Florio
Pg 10:	Top © Handel Architects LLP; bottom © Touhey Photography
Pg 11:	Left © Skidmore, Owings & Merrill LLP; right © Hufton + Crow
Pg 12:	© Ping An Financial Center Construction & Development
Pg 13:	Left © thyssenkrupp Elevator; right © Killa Design
Pg 17:	© David Sundberg/Esto
Pg 18:	Drawings @ FXCollaborative; photo © David Sundberg/Esto
Pg 19:	Top © David Sundberg/Esto; bottom © Chris Cooper
Pg 21:	© Tom Rossiter
Pg 22:	All © Goettsch Partners
Pg 23:	All © Tom Rossiter
Pg 25:	© JDS Development Group by Jonathan Morefield
Pg 26:	Photo © JDS Development Group by Max Touhey; drawing © SHoP Architects
Pg 27:	All © JDS Development Group by Max Touhey
Pg 28:	© Steve Hall (c) Hedrich Blessing
Pg 29:	Top © Steve Hall (c) Hedrich Blessing; bottom right © Tom Harris Photography; bottom left © Studio Gang
Pg 30-31:	All © Stark Imagery
Pg 33-34:	© Sebastian Crespo
Pg 35:	Drawing © Leppanen + Anker Arquitectos; photo © Sebastian Crespo
Pg 36-37:	Photos © Rasmus Hjortshoj; drawing © DeSimone Consulting Engineers
Pg 38:	© Tom Rossiter Photography
Pg 39:	Photos © Michael Kleinberg Photography; drawing © KOO LLC
Pg 40:	© John W. Cahill
Pg 41:	Photos © Ewout Huibers; drawing © HLW International.
Pg 42:	© Michael Moran_OTTO
Pg 43:	Drawings © KPF; top © Michael Moran_OTTO; middle © Raimund Koch; bottom © 45 East 22nd Street
Pg 44-45:	All © Christian Wiese Arquitectos
Pg 46-47:	All © Kreps DeMaria
Pg 48-49:	Photos © David Sundberg/Esto; drawing © Pickard Chilton
Pg 50:	© 2016 Dave Burk	Design by HDR	Gensler, in association with Clive Wilkinson Architects and EGG Office
Pg 51:	Drawing © HDR	Gensler, in association with Clive Wilkinson Architects and EGG Office; top © Michael Moran	Design by HDR	Gensler, in association with Clive Wilkinson Architects and EGG Office; bottom © Tom Harris 2017	Design by HDR	Gensler, in association with Clive Wilkinson Architects and EGG Office
Pg 52:	© Tom Arban Photography
Pg 53:	Drwaings © Diamond Schmitt Architects; top © Garrison McArthur Photographers; bottom © Lisa Logan Photography
Pg 54:	© Timothy Hursley
Pg 55:	Top & bottom right © Timothy Hursley; top right © Galina Coada; drawing © Mack Scogin Merrill Elam Architects
Pg 56-57:	Photos © Rodrigo Ramos - TIF Digital; drawings © Internacional de Inversiones
Pg 58:	Top © Tom Harris Photography; bottom © Steve Hall (c) Hedrich Blessing
Pg 59:	Top © Tom Harris Photography; bottom © Studio Gang
Pg 60:	© Ewing/AC Martin
Pg 61:	Top left © Laignel/AC Martin; top right © Ewing/AC Martin; drawing © AC Martin
Pg 62-63:	30 Park Place © © Peter Aaron/OTTO for Robert A.M. Stern Architects; 609 Main at Texas © Alan Karchmer; 615 South College © John Portman & Associates; 88 Scott © IBI Group Architects (Canada) Inc.; AQWA Corporate © Mario Grisolli
Pg 64-65:	Biscayne Beach © Schwartz Media Strategies; BRIC Phase 1 © John Portman & Associates; CF Calgary City Centre Phase I © Zeidler Architecture; Cielo © PCL Construction; Equus 333 © Paúl Rivera, Inc. Architectural Photography
Pg 66-67:	Hotel Las Americas Golden Tower © Carlos Ott Architect; INDX Condominiums © IBI Group Architects (Canada) Inc.; Jade Signature © McNAMARA • SALVIA; L'Avenue © Anthony Broccollini; Level BK © Stephen B. Jacobs Group P.C. Architects and Planners
Pg 68-69:	Northwestern Mutual Tower and Commons © Tom Rossiter; Optima Signature © Optima, Inc.; Park Avenue West © Lawrence Anderson; Ten Thousand © Crescent Heights; The Collection Tower © DPeebles
Pg 70:	The Encore © Stephen B. Jacobs Group P.C. Architects and Planners; The Hub © Dattner Architects
Pg 72:	© Luke Mahoney
Pg 73:	Top © Christopher Frederick Jones; bottom © Trevor Mein; drawing © CBus Property & ISPT
Pg 74-75:	All © Cbus Property
Pg 76-77:	All © John Gollings Photography
Pg 79:	© Hufton + Crow
Pg 80:	Photo © Hufton + Crow; drawing © MAD Architects
Pg 81:	Top right © Hufton + Crow; bottom right © Iwan Baan; drawing © MAD Architects
Pg 82-83:	All © CAZA
Pg 84-85:	All © Red Agency
Pg 86-87:	All © Gurner TM
Pg 88-89:	All © New World China Land Co. Ltd.
Pg 90-91:	All © Julien Lanoo
Pg 93:	All © Hufton + Crow
Pg 94:	Drawing © MAD Architects; photo © Laurian Ghinitoiu
Pg 95:	Top © Shu He; bottom © Tian FangFang
Pg 96:	© Hengyi
Pg 97:	Top © Hengyi; bottom © Elenberg Fraser; drawing © Elenberg Fraser
Pg 99:	© Tim Griffith
Pg 100:	Photo © Tim Griffith; drawings © Lotte Property & Development
Pg 101:	Top © Lotte Property & Development; bottom © Tim Griffith
Pg 103:	© ingenhoven architects / HG Esch
Pg 104:	All © ingenhoven architects / HG Esch
Pg 105:	Photos © ingenhoven architects / HG Esch; drawing © ingenhoven architects
Pg 106-107:	All © Kyungsub Shin
Pg 109:	© Tim Griffith
Pg 110:	All © Ping An Financial Center Construction & Development
Pg 111:	Top © Ping An Financial Center Construction & Development; bottom © Tim Griffith
Pg 113-115:	All photos © Bruce Damonte; drawing © Skidmore, Owings & Merrill LLP
Pg 116:	© Seth Powers
Pg 117:	Drawings © UNStudio; top © Seth Powers; bottom © Jin Xing
Pg 119-121:	All © Tongji Architectural Design (Group) Co., Ltd.
Pg 122-123:	All © Darren Soh for Arc Studio Architecture + Urbanism Pte Ltd
Pg 124:	© Zhang Chao

Pg 125: Top © OPEN Architecture; bottom © Iwan Baan; drawing © OPEN Architecture

Pg 126-127: All photos © Zeng Jianghe; drawing © von Gerkan, Marg and Partners Architects

Pg 128-129: 1 Parramatta Square © Architectus; 177 Pacific Highway © Brett Boardman; Aquaria Grande Tower © James Law Cybertecture International Holdings Ltd.; Chinachem Central © Dennis Lau & Ng Chun Man Architects & Engineers (HK) Ltd. (DLN); Golden Eagle International Shopping Center © Lab Architecture Studio

Pg 130-131: Gravity Tower © Plus Architecture; Green Residences © Yan Binfeng; IM tower © Maeda corporation; Kyobashi EDOGRAND © SS.inc; Nakanoshima Festival West Tower © Higashide Photo Studio

Pg 132-133: Ningbo Bank of China © Archexist; One Avighna Park © Avighna India Ltd.; Parnas Tower © KMD Architects/Chang-Jo Architects; Rosewood Sanya and Sanya Forum © Shen Zhonghai, 1st Image; Shenyang K11 © Dennis Lau & Ng Chun Man Architects & Engineers (HK) Ltd. (DLN)

Pg 134-135: Talan Towers © Astana Property Management LLC; Telkom Landmark Tower 2 © Woods Bagot; The Summit - Plot 554 © Shen Zhonghai, 1st Image; The Suzhou Modern Media Plaza © Hu Wenkit; Upper West Side © Cottee Parker Architects

Pg 136: Urbana Tower 2 © ACTA asia pte ltd; Zhongzhou E-ClASS © PT Design

Pg 138: All © Lingotto

Pg 139: Top © Lingotto, photographer Theo Krijgsman; bottom right © Lingotto, photographer Martijn Kort; drawing © Lingotto

Pg 141: © Edmund Sumner

Pg 142: Top left © Edmund Sumner; top right © Edmund Sumner; bottom © Fletcher Priest Architects

Pg 143: Photo © Edmund Sumner; drawing © Fletcher Priest Architects

Pg 144: © Meixner Schlüter Wendt Architekten

Pg 145: Top © Christoph Kraneburg; bottom & drawing © Meixner Schlüter Wendt Architekten

Pg 147-148: All © Hufton + Crow

Pg 149: Photo © Eva Bloem; drawing © UNStudio

Pg 150: © Hufton+Crow

Pg 151: Top © Ben Anders; bottom © Hufton+Crow; drawing © SimpsonHaugh

Pg 152-153: All photos © Takuji Shimmura; drawing © Hamonic + Masson & Associés

Pg 155-157: All photos © Rasmus Hjortshøj - COAST; drawing © COBE

Pg 159: © RPBW, ph. Sergio Grazia

Pg 160: Top left © RPBW, ph. Sergio Grazia; top right © Michel Denancé; drawing © RPBW

Pg 161: All © RPBW, ph. Sergio Grazia

Pg 162-163: All © KSP Jurgen Engel Architekten

Pg 164: © Tim Soar

Pg 165: Top & bottom right © Tim Soar; bottom left © Christian Pohl GmbH

Pg 166-167: Arena Tower © WSP; De Verkenner © Mei architects and planners; Federation Tower © CJSC Federation Tower; Millennium Center 1 © Amfion Ltd; Q22 Tower © Kurylowicz & Associates

Pg 171-173: All © Moshe Tzur Architects and Town Planners

Pg 175-177: All © Benchmark Development

Pg 179-181: All photos © Roland Halbe; drawing © Richard Meier & Partners Architects

Pg 183: © Mark Williams Photography

Pg 184: Top left & bottom © Mark Williams Photography; top right © Hilton Teper

Pg 185: Photo © Mark Williams Photography; drawing © Heatherwick Studio

Pg 186-187: Britam Tower © GAPP Architects & Urban Designers; Iran Telecom Research Center © Harmonic Trend [L]; Landmark Group Headquarters © Archgroup Consultants; The 118 © Archgroup Consultants; The Shahar Tower © Sufrin Group Asaf Pinchuk photographer

Pg 191: Top © LendLease; bottom © Brett Boardman, courtesy of Rogers Stirk Harbour + Partners

Pg 192-193: All photos © Brett Boardman Photography; drawing © Rogers Stirk Harbour + Partners

Pg 194-195: All © Maeda corporation

Pg 196-197: All © Atelier Alan Teh Architect

Pg 199-200: All photos © 10 DESIGN and GREATWALL CONSTRUCTION HOLDINGS GROUP CO. LTD.; drawing © 10 DESIGN

Pg 201: Top © 10 DESIGN; bottom © 10 DESIGN and GREATWALL CONSTRUCTION HOLDINGS GROUP CO. LTD.

Pg 203-204: All © Handel Architects LLP

Pg 205: © CTBUH based on drawings from PWP Landscape Architecture

Pg 207: All © Patrick Bingham-Hall

Pg 208: © WOHA

Pg 209: Top & bottom left © K. Kopter; bottom right © Patrick Bingham-Hall

Pg 211-213: All © New World Development Company Limited

Pg 215-217: All photos © Zeng Jianghe; drawing © von Gerkan, Marg and Partners Architects

Pg 218-219: All © New World Development Company Limited

Pg 220-221: All © Atelier Alan Teh Architect

Pg 222-223: All photos © Jon Miller (c) Hedrich Blessing; drawing © bKL Architecture LLC

Pg 226: © John Cahill (CTBUH)

Pg 227: Drawing & bottom left © Alexico Group; bottom right © John Cahill (CTBUH)

Pg 228: © Skidmore, Owings & Merrill LLP

Pg 229: Drawings © Skidmore, Owings & Merrill LLP; photo © Paul Richer

Pg 230: © Miralem Dervisevic (CTBUH)

Pg 231: Drawing © Turner Construction Company; top right © Elena Generalova; bottom right © Touhey Photography

Pg 232: © Mirvac Construction

Pg 233: Top & bottom right © Mirvac Construction; drawing © FJMT

Pg 234-235: All © Ghelamco Poland

Pg 238-239: All © Killa Design

Pg 240: © Tishman Construction

Pg 241: Drawings © CAST CONNEX; photo © Marshall Gerometta (CTBUH)

Pg 242-243: All © Hickory Group

Pg 245: All © Wirth Research

Pg 247: Top © Thornton Tomasetti (photo by Bess Adler); bottom © Thornton Tomasetti (Image by Pierre Ghisbain, PhD)

Pg 248-489: All © AKT II

Pg 250-251: All © thyssenkrupp

Pg 252: © Acton Ostry Architects Inc. Michael Elkan Photography

Pg 253: Top © University of British Columbia; bottom left © Acton Ostry Architects Inc.; bottom right © Seagate Structures

Pg 256: © cc by-sa ITU slash I.Wood

Pg 257: Top © Tom Arban Photography Inc.; bottom © Smith Carter Architects

Pg 258: Top left © Griffith; top right © NicLehoux; bottom © John Cahill

Pg 260: Drawings © Tange Associates; top right © Kouji Horiuchi; bottom right © Marshall Gerometta

Pg 261: © Marshall Gerometta

Pg 262: All © Skidmore, Owings & Merrill LLP

Pg 263: All © Terri Meyer Boake

Pg 264: Top © Marshall Gerometta; bottom © NicLehoux

Pg 265: All © Rainer Viertlbock

Pg 266: All © Photograph by Tom Evangelidis, courtesy of Frasers Property Australia

Pg 267: © Patrick Bingham-Hall

Pg 268-269: All © Kohn Pedersen Fox

Pg 271: Top © DBOX; bottom left & right © Marshall Gerometta

Pg 273: Top left © Igor Butyrskii; bottom left © Rodrigo Ramos - TIF Digital; top right © John W. Cahill; bottom right © Dario Trabucco/CTBUH

CTBUH Structure & Members

Board of Trustees
Chairman: Steve Watts, *alinea Consulting*, London
Vice-Chairman: David Malott, *AI. / SpaceFactory*, New York City
Executive Director: Antony Wood, *CTBUH / Illinois Institute of Technology*, Chicago / *Tongji University*, Shanghai
Secretary: Tim Neal, *CallisonRTKL*, London
Trustee: Mounib Hammoud, *Jeddah Economic Company*, Jeddah
Trustee: Timothy Johnson, *NBBJ*, New York City
Trustee: Dennis Poon, *Thornton Tomasetti*, New York City
Trustee: Abrar Sheriff, *Turner International*, New York City
Trustee: Charu Thapar, *Jones Lang LaSalle*, Mumbai
Trustee: Kam-Chuen (Vincent) Tse, *WSP*, Hong Kong

China Office Board
Jianping Gu, *Shanghai Tower Construction & Development*, Shanghai
Eric Lee, *JLL*, Hong Kong
Ellen Sun, *UTRC*, Shanghai
Antony Wood, *CTBUH / Illinois Institute of Technology, USA / Tongji University*, China
Changfu Wu, *Tongji University*, Shanghai
Junjie Zhang, *ECADI*, Shanghai
Qihui Zhang, *Ping An Real Estate*, Shenzhen
Kui Zhuang, *CCDI*, Shanghai

Staff / Contributors
Executive Director: Antony Wood
Associate Director: Steven Henry
China Office Director & Academic Coordinator: Peng Du
Research Manager: Dario Trabucco
Operations Manager: Patti Thurmond
Events Manager: Jessica Rinkel-Miller
Communications Manager: Jason Gabel
Editor: Daniel Safarik
Membership Coordinator: Stephanie Bowman
Publications & Design Coordinator: Annan Shehadi
Public Relations Coordinator: Matt Watson
Website Editor: Aric Austermann
Web Developer: Paul Tuskevicius
Skyscraper Database Editor: Marshall Gerometta
Skyscraper Database Editor: Shawn Ursini
Global Initiatives Assistant: Nicole McLellan
Events Assistant: Natalie Schoetz
Events Assistant: Nicole Durkin
Publications Associate: Tansri Muliani
Production Assistant: Liwen Kang
Staff Accountant: Yanming Zhu
Research Assistant: Martina Belmonte
Research Assistant: William Miranda
Research Assistant: Angela Mejorin
General Counsel: Matt Rossetti
Special Media Correspondent: Chris Bentley

Advisory Group
Adrian Betanzos, *Apple*, San Francisco
Jim Bilger, *CBRE*, Los Angeles
Albert Chan, *Shui On*, Shanghai
Joseph Chou, *Taipei Financial Center Corporation*, Taipei
Christopher Colasanti, *JBB*, New York City
Donald Davies, *Magnusson Klemencic*, Seattle
Scott Duncan, *SOM*, Chicago
Karl Fender, *Fender Katsalidis Architects*, Melbourne
John Gaskin, *Brookfield Multiplex*, Brisbane
Jean-Claude Gerardy, *ArcelorMittal*, Esch-sur-Alzette
Jerry Jackson, *Dassault Systèmes*, Boston
René Lagos, *René Lagos Engineers*, Santiago
Stephen Lai, *Rider Levett Bucknall*, Hong Kong
William Murray, *Wordsearch*, London
James Parakh, *City of Toronto*, Toronto
Jon Van Benthem, *Autodesk*, Denver
Peter Weismantle, *Adrian Smith + Gordon Gill Architecture*, Chicago
Derry Yu, *New World China Land Limited*, Hong Kong

Committee Chairs
Urban Habitat / Urban Design: James Parakh, *City of Toronto Planning Department*, Toronto
Expert Peer Review Committee: Antony Wood, *CTBUH / Illinois Institute of Technology*, Chicago / *Tongji University*, Shanghai
Height & Data: Peter Weismantle, *Adrian Smith + Gordon Gill Architecture*, Chicago
2016-18 Awards: Karl Fender, *Fender Katsalidis Architects*, Melbourne
Expert Chinese Translation Committee: Nengjun Luo, *CITIC HEYE Investment CO., LTD.*, Beijing
Skyscraper Center Editorial Board: Marshall Gerometta, *CTBUH*, Chicago
Young Professionals, New York: Ilkay Can-Standard, *GenX Design & Technology*, New York City & Larry Giannechini, *Lendlease*, New York City
Young Professionals, Seattle: Joey Piotrowski, *Magnusson Klemencic Associates*, Seattle & Jeremy Hasselbauer, *Magnusson Klemencic Associates*, Seattle
Young Professionals, Shanghai: Yong Ding, *Kohn Pedersen Fox*, Shanghai; Zhou Fan, *Gensler*, Shanghai & Zhizhe Yu, *AI.*, New York City
Young Professionals, United Kingdom: Marc Easton, *Arup*, London

Working Group Co-Chairs
Building Damping Technologies: Marc Blondeau, Paris; Fabienne Foucault, Paris; André Ly, Paris
Demolition: Dario Trabucco, Venice
Façade Access: Lance McMasters, Chicago; Kevin Thompson, New York City; Peter Weismantle, Chicago
Fire Performance of Façades: David Scott, London
Passivhaus for High-Rise: Philip Oldfield, Sydney
Program & Construction Management: Derek Roy, Jeddah; Ro Schroff, Seattle
Security: Sean Ahrens, Chicago; Caroline Field, London
Sustainable Design: Antony Wood, Chicago
Tall Timber: Rob Foster, Brisbane; Carsten Hein, Berlin; Volker Schmid, Berlin
Vertical Transportation: Robin Cheeseright, London

Regional Representatives
Australia: Brian Wooldridge, *Opus International Consultants*
Belgium: Georges Binder, *Buildings & Data S.A.*
Brazil: Antonio Macedo Filho, *Universidade Cidade de São Paulo*
Bulgaria: Manuela Belova, *Vertical Alignment Architects*
Cambodia: Michel Cassagnes, *Archetype Group*
Canada: Richard Witt, *Quadrangle Architects*
China: Peng Du, *CTBUH*
Costa Rica: Victor Montero, *Victor Montero Architects & Associates*
Finland: Santeri Suoranta, *KONE Industrial, Ltd.*
France: Marc Blondeau, *Bouygues Construction*
Germany: Roland Bechmann, *Werner Sobek Stuttgart GmbH & Co.*
Greece: Alexios Vandoros, *Vandoros & Partners*
India: Girish Dravid, *Sterling Engineering*
Indonesia: Prasetyo Adi, *PDW Architects*
Iran: Matin Alaghmandan, *University of Tehran*
Israel: Israel David, *David Engineers*
Italy: Dario Trabucco, *Iuav University of Venice*
Mongolia: Marine Ros, *Archetype Group*
Myanmar: Mark Petrovic, *Archetype Group*
Nigeria: Shola Sanni, *Sanni, Ojo & Partners Consulting*
Philippines: Felino A. Palafox Jr., *Palafox Associates*
Poland: Ryszard M. Kowalczyk, *University of Beira Interior*
Russia: Elena A. Shuvalova, *Lobby Agency*
Saudi Arabia: Bassam Al-Bassam, *Rayadah Investment Company*, KSA
Scandinavia: Julian Chen, *Henning Larsen Architects*
South Korea: Dr. Kwang Ryang Chung, *Dongyang Structural Engineers Co., Ltd*
Spain: Iñigo Ortiz Diez de Tortosa, *Ortiz Leon Arquitectos*
Sri Lanka: Shiromal Fernando, *Civil and Structural Engineering Consultants (Pvt.) Ltd*
Taiwan: Richard Lee, *C.Y. Lee & Partners Architects/Planners*
Turkey: Mehmet Kilic, *Turner International*
UAE: Christian Vasquez, *National Engineering Bureau*
United Kingdom: Javier Quintana de Uña, *IDOM*
Vietnam: Phan Quang Minh, *National University of Civil Engineering*

CTBUH Organizational Members
(as of April 2018) http://membership.ctbuh.org

Supporting Contributors
AECOM
AI.
alinea consulting LLP
ARCADIS
Autodesk Inc
Brookfield Property Group
BuroHappold Engineering
CCDI Group
CITIC Heye Investment Co., Ltd.
Dassault Systèmes
Dow Chemical Company
Emaar Properties, PJSC
Hanking Group
Illinois Institute of Technology
IUAV - Università Iuav di Venezia
Jeddah Economic Company
Kingdom Real Estate Development Co.
Kohn Pedersen Fox Associates, PC
KONE Industrial, Ltd.
Lotte Property & Development
National Engineering Bureau
Otis Elevator Company
Samsung C&T Corporation
Schindler Top Range Division
Shanghai Tower Construction & Development Co., Ltd.
Shenzhen Parkland Real Estate Development Co., Ltd.
Shenzhen Ping An Financial Centre Construction and Development Co. Ltd.
Siemens Building Technologies
Skidmore, Owings & Merrill LLP
Sun Hung Kai Properties Limited
Taipei Financial Center Corp. (TAIPEI 101)
Tongji University
Turner Construction Company
Underwriters Laboratories (UL) LLC
Wentworth House Partnership Limited
WSP
Yuanda Group (CNYD)

Patrons
BG&E Pty., Ltd.
BMT Fluid Mechanics, Ltd.
Dar Al-Handasah (Shair & Partners)
DeSimone Consulting Engineers
Durst Organization
East China Architectural Design & Research Institute (ECADI)
Gensler
HOK, Inc.
Hongkong Land, Ltd.
ISA Architecture
KLCC Property Holdings Berhad
Kuraray America, Inc. (Trosifol)
Langan
Meinhardt Group International
NBBJ
OJB Landscape Architecture
PACE Development Corporation PLC
Pelli Clarke Pelli Architects
POHL Group
Rene Lagos Engineers
Rider Levett Bucknall
Rowan Williams Davies & Irwin, Inc.
SL Green Management
Studio Libeskind
Thornton Tomasetti, Inc.
thyssenkrupp Elevator
Tishman Speyer Properties
Windtech Consultants Pty., Ltd.

Donors
A&H Tuned Mass Dampers
Adrian Smith + Gordon Gill Architecture, LLP
Altair Engineering
Arcadis Australia Pacific
Architectural Design & Research Institute of South China University of Technology
Arquitectonica International

Arup
Aurecon
BALA Engineers
Beijing Fortune Lighting System Engineering Co., Ltd.
Bjarke Ingels Group
Bosa Properties Inc.
Broad Sustainable Building Co., Ltd.
CBRE Group, Inc.
China Construction Eighth Engineering Division
China State Construction Engineering Corporation
EID Architecture
Enclos Corp.
Fender Katsalidis Architects
FINE DNC
Fly Service Engineering S.r.l.
Halfen USA
Hill International
Investa Office Management Pty Ltd
Jensen Hughes
JLL
JORDAHL
Jotun Group
JT + Partners
Larsen & Toubro, Ltd.
Leslie E. Robertson Associates, RLLP
Magnusson Klemencic Associates, Inc.
Make
McNamara • Salvia
Mirvac Group
Multiplex Construction Europe Ltd.
New World Development Company Limited
Nishkian Menninger Consulting and Structural Engineers
Outokumpu
PDW Architects
Peckar & Abramson, P.C.
Pei Cobb Freed & Partners
Permasteelisa Group
Pickard Chilton Architects, Inc.
PLP Architecture
PNB Merdeka Ventures SDN Berhad
PT Gistama Intisemesta
Quadrangle Architects Ltd.
SAMOO Architects and Engineers
Saudi Binladin Group / ABC Division
Schuco
Severud Associates Consulting Engineers, PC
Shanghai Construction (Group) General Co. Ltd.
Shenzhen AUBE Architectural Engineering Design Co., Ltd
Shenzhen Capol International & Associates Co. Ltd
Sika Services AG
Studio Gang Architects
Syska Hennessy Group, Inc.
TAV Construction
Tongji Architectural Design (Group) Co., Ltd.
UEM Sunrise (Developments) Pty Ltd
Ultra-tech Cement Sri Lanka
V&A Waterfront Holdings (Pty) Ltd
Walter P. Moore and Associates, Inc.
WATG URBAN
Werner Voss + Partner
Woods Bagot
Wordsearch
Zaha Hadid Limited

Contributors
Aedas, Ltd.
Akzo Nobel
Aliaxis
Alimak Hek AB
Allford Hall Monaghan Morris Ltd.
Altitude Façade Access Consulting
Alvine Engineering
AM Project Srl, Joseph di Pasquale Architects
AMSYSCO
Andrew Lee King Fun & Associates Architects Ltd.
ArcelorMittal
architectsAlliance
Architectural Design & Research Institute of Tsinghua University
Architectus
Armstrong Ceiling Solutions
Armstrong World Industries (China) Co., Ltd.
AvLaw Pty Ltd
Azrieli Group Ltd.
Barker Mohandas, LLC
Bates Smart
Benoy
bKL Architecture LLC
Bonacci Group
Boundary Layer Wind Tunnel Laboratory

Bouygues Batiment International
Broadway Malyan
Brunkeberg Systems
Cadillac Fairview
Canary Wharf Group, PLC
Canderel Management, Inc.
Careys Civil Engineering
CB Engineers
CCL
Cerami & Associates, Inc.
China Architecture Design & Research Group (CADI)
China State Construction Overseas Development Co., Ltd.
CITYGROUP DESIGN CO., LTD
Civil & Structural Engineering Consultants (Pvt) Ltd.
Code Consultants, Inc.
Conrad Gargett
Cosentini Associates
Cottee Parker Architects
Cotter Consulting Inc.
Cox Architecture Pty. Ltd.
CoxGomyl
CPP Inc.
Craft Holdings Limited
CRICURSA (CRISTALES CURVADOS S.A.)
CS Group Construction Specialties Company
CS Structural Engineering, Inc.
Cubic Architects
Daewoo Engineering & Construction
Davy Sukamta & Partners Structural Engineers
DB Realty Ltd.
DCA Architects
DCI Engineers
DDG
Deerns
DIALOG
Dong Yang Structural Engineers Co., Ltd.
dwp|suters
EG
Elenberg Fraser Pty Ltd
Elevating Studio
Eric Parry Architects
Eversendai Engineering Qatar WLL
FM Global
Foster + Partners
FXCollaborative Architects
GEI Consultants
GERB Vibration Control Systems (Germany/USA)
GGLO, LLC
Global Wind Technology Services (GWTS)
Glumac
gmp • Architekten von Gerkan, Marg und Partner GbR
Goettsch Partners
Gradient Wind Engineering Inc.
Graziani + Corazza Architects Inc.
Grimshaw Architects
Guangzhou Design Institute
Guangzhou Yuexiu City Construction Jones Lang La Salle Property Management Co., Ltd.
Hariri Pontarini Architects
Harman Group
HASSELL
Hathaway Dinwiddie Construction Company
Heller Manus Architects
Henning Larsen Architects
Hera Engineering Pty Ltd
Hilti AG
Hitachi, Ltd.
HKA Elevator Consulting
HOK Architects Corporation
Housing and Development Board
Humphreys & Partners Architects, L.P.
Hutchinson Builders
ICD Property
IDOM UK Ltd.
Inhabit Group
Irwinconsult Pty., Ltd.
Israeli Association of Construction and Infrastructure Engineers (IACIE)
ITT Corporation
JAHN
Jaros, Baum & Bolles
John Portman & Associates, Inc.
Kajima Design
Kawneer Company
KEO International Consultants
KHP Konig und Heunisch Planungsgesellschaft
Killa Architectural Design
Kinemetrics Inc.
Koltay Facades
Larson Engineering, Inc.

LCI Australia Pty Ltd
LCL Builds Limited
LeMessurier
Lendlease Corporation
Liberty OneSteel
Longman Lindsey
Lusail Real Estate Development Company
M Moser Associates Ltd.
M.S. Aluminum
Mace Limited
Maeda Corporation
Maurer SE
Mori Building Co., Ltd.
Nabih Youssef & Associates
National Fire Protection Association
Nikken Sekkei, Ltd.
Norman Disney & Young
NORR Group Consultants International Limited
O'Donnell & Naccarato
OMA
Omnium International
Omrania
Ornamental Metal Institute of New York
Pakubuwono Development
Palafox Associates
Pavarini McGovern
Pepper Construction
Perkins + Will
Plus Architecture
Profica
R.G. Vanderweil Engineers LLP
Radius Developers
Raftery CRE, LLC
Ramboll
RAW Design Inc.
Related Midwest
Rhode Partners
RJC Engineers
Robert A.M. Stern Architects
Rogers Stirk Harbour + Partners
Ronald Lu & Partners
Ronesans Holding
Royal HaskoningDHV
Sanni, Ojo & Partners
Savills Property Services (Guangzhou) Co. Ltd.
SECURISTYLE
SETEC TPI
Shimizu Corporation
Shui On Management Limited
SilverEdge Systems Software, Inc.
Silverstein Properties
SimpsonHaugh
Spiritos Properties LLC
Stanley D. Lindsey & Associates, Ltd.
Steel Institute of New York
Stein Ltd.
Studco Australia Pty Ltd
SuperTEC
Surface Design
SVA International Pty Ltd
SWA Group
Taisei Corporation
Takenaka Corporation
Terracon
Trimble Solutions Corporation
Uniestate
Vetrocare SRL
Vidaris, Inc.
Werner Sobek Group GmbH
Weston Williamson + Partners
wh-p GmbH Beratende Ingenieure
WilkinsonEyre
WME Engineering Consultants
WOHA Architects Pte., Ltd.
WTM Engineers International GmbH
WZMH Architects
Y. A. Yashar Architects

Participants/Academic & Media Institutes
There are an additional 318 members of the Council at the Participant/Academic Institute/Media Institute level. Please see online for the full member list. **http://members.ctbuh.org**